REA

FRIENDS
OF ACPL

D0855760

2-15-77

2-15-77

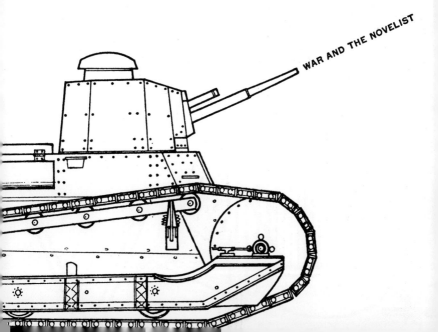

WAR AND THE NOVELIST

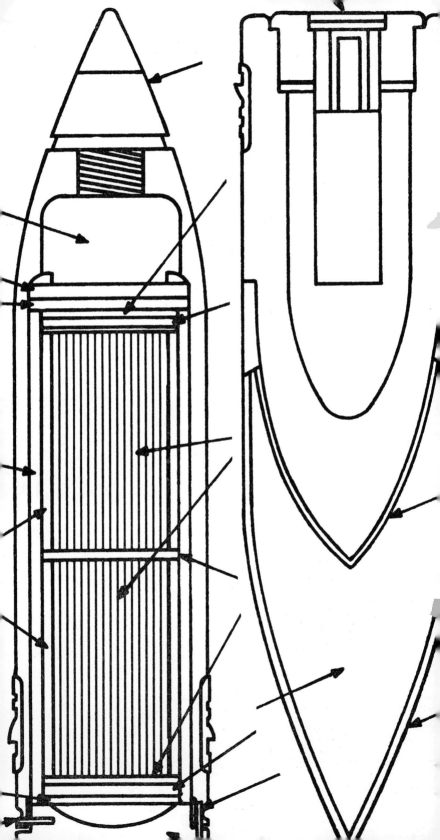

WAR AND THE NOVELIST

APPRAISING THE AMERICAN WAR NOVEL

Peter G. Jones

With a Foreword by M. L. Rosenthal

University of Missouri Press
Columbia & London
1976

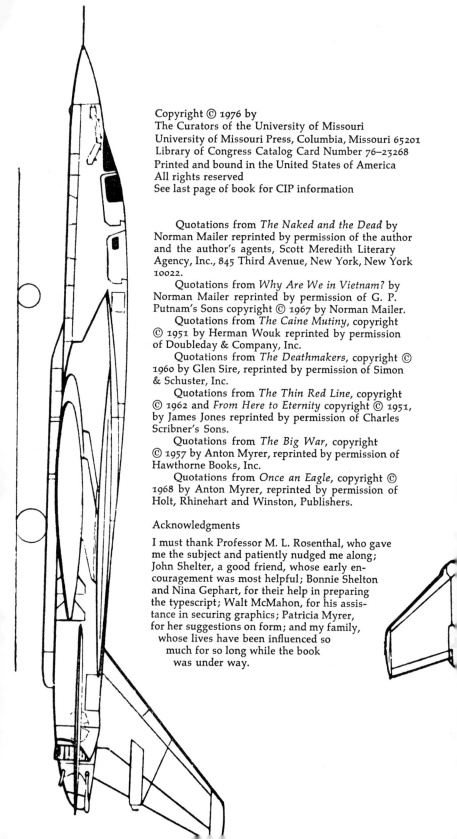

Copyright © 1976 by
The Curators of the University of Missouri
University of Missouri Press, Columbia, Missouri 65201
Library of Congress Catalog Card Number 76–23268
Printed and bound in the United States of America
All rights reserved
See last page of book for CIP information

Quotations from *The Naked and the Dead* by
Norman Mailer reprinted by permission of the author
and the author's agents, Scott Meredith Literary
Agency, Inc., 845 Third Avenue, New York, New York
10022.

Quotations from *Why Are We in Vietnam?* by
Norman Mailer reprinted by permission of G. P.
Putnam's Sons copyright © 1967 by Norman Mailer.

Quotations from *The Caine Mutiny*, copyright
© 1951 by Herman Wouk reprinted by permission
of Doubleday & Company, Inc.

Quotations from *The Deathmakers*, copyright ©
1960 by Glen Sire, reprinted by permission of Simon
& Schuster, Inc.

Quotations from *The Thin Red Line*, copyright
© 1962 and *From Here to Eternity* copyright © 1951,
by James Jones reprinted by permission of Charles
Scribner's Sons.

Quotations from *The Big War*, copyright
© 1957 by Anton Myrer, reprinted by permission of
Hawthorne Books, Inc.

Quotations from *Once an Eagle*, copyright ©
1968 by Anton Myrer, reprinted by permission of
Holt, Rhinehart and Winston, Publishers.

Acknowledgments

I must thank Professor M. L. Rosenthal, who gave
me the subject and patiently nudged me along;
John Shelter, a good friend, whose early encouragement was most helpful; Bonnie Shelton
and Nina Gephart, for their help in preparing
the typescript; Walt McMahon, for his assis-
tance in securing graphics; Patricia Myrer,
for her suggestions on form; and my family,
whose lives have been influenced so
much for so long while the book
was under way.

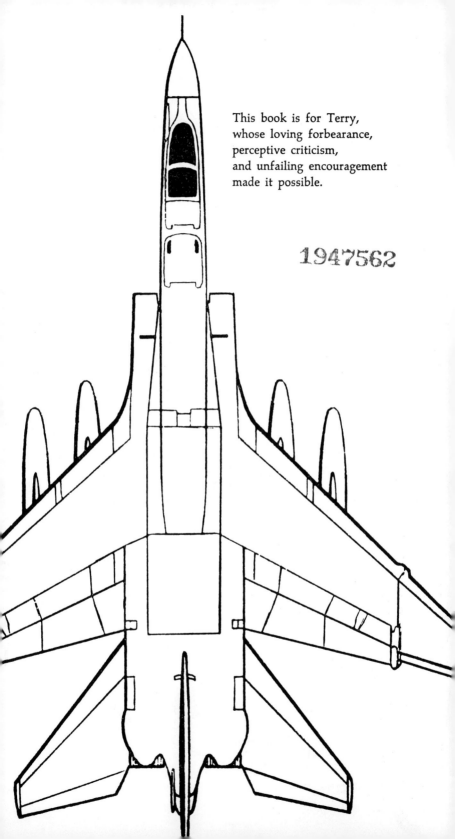

This book is for Terry,
whose loving forbearance,
perceptive criticism,
and unfailing encouragement
made it possible.

1947562

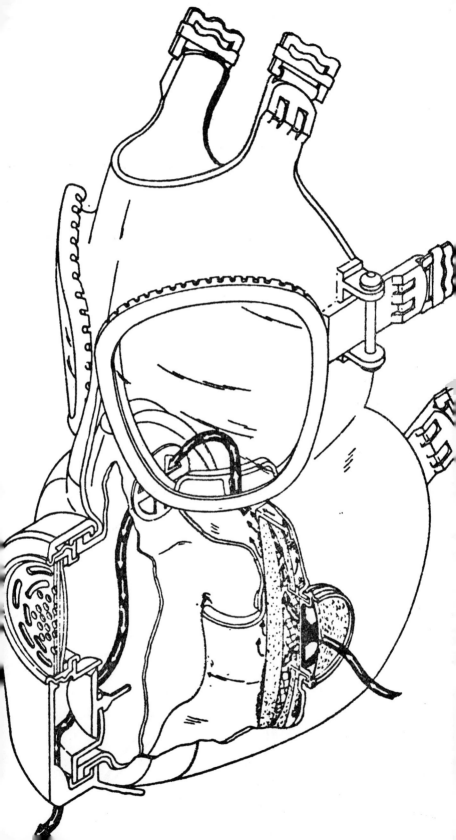

FOREWORD by M. L. Rosenthal

"The real war will never get in the books." So wrote
Walt Whitman, at the end of the Civil War. He was thinking
of the unspeakable side of the war, no longer so considered by
the modern mind. *Our* vocabulary adapts itself to the grossest
reality, a reality that leaps into books with a vengeance.
It has lost most of its ability to shock, for it is gentility now
that is virtually taboo. It is true that war's horrors, and their
obvious counterparts in "normal" civilian life, can still dismay
us profoundly for a moment of clarifying awareness. But
then they are quickly taken for granted, as though each
separate instance were not a cry to us to set all other concerns
aside and put things right.

In our century, more than the horror of war gets into the
books. Compassion does so as well, for all the victims: the
killed and maimed and shattered, but the psychically destroyed and the incredibly humiliated too. And compassion,
like shocked dismay, flames up and then is muffled by the
sheer number of demands on it and the usual distance of most
of us from what is happening. Lieutenant Colonel Jones's very
thorough study recognizes the subjective, emotional realiza-
tions saturating our war fiction. His preoccupation, though, is
with putting the massive body of such fiction in clear intellectual perspective. He focuses on literary form: "the war novel
as *Bildungsroman*"; on the internal politics of war organization: "the developing attitudes toward military commanders"
the war novel reveals; and on the psychological processes: "relationships of sexuality and violence" and the "psychology of
combat"—matters that have obsessed many novelists' artistic
attention.

His somewhat detached stance does not betoken insensitivity, although the fact that Jones is a professional Army
man puts him at considerable remove from people who find it
impossible to imagine using a gun or a bayonet. A literary
scholar with an eye for philosophical and psychological resonances, he nevertheless knows at first hand the worlds of experience his authors deal with. For *Dr.* Jones has also been an
artillery officer in Vietnam and been through both the violence
and what Wilfred Owen called "the Pity." (I first became
aware of him in a graduate seminar for which he wrote a paper

on Malraux's *La Condition humaine*. That novel was one of the great romantic touchstones of my early youth. Jones showed me a great deal I hadn't realized simply by correlating the plot curve and the private movements of the individual characters—once so hypnotic to me—with the unfolding military situation.) Hence, he is able to suggest objective contexts for this most thorough yet offered of American World War II fiction.

Almost of necessity, then, his approach is analytical, unsensational, very far from the urgency some of us might insist that the topic demands. After all, we have so many war novels because, jingoist and pacifist alike, we live in a world of constant warfare. So much of our experience is in the context of war that the politics and emotions of antiwar seem, in moments of weariness, only subtler, near-hysterical manifestations of the dominant social pathology (an observation suggested in slightly different terms in Malcolm Lowry's *Under the Volcano*).

The proportions are immense; it is almost just a quantitative matter. "To keep the study manageable," our author explains, "I omit novels about prisoners of war and the Cold War. The primary material is novels of World War II, Korea, and Vietnam." And as the material piles up, venomous reflection of the cold truth about the way we really live and who we really are (forget it most of the time though we may), it seems far more than the conventional rationalization of his career for this officer to assert: "As the later books reveal with startling clarity, the war novel has become one of the most logical ways of writing about life in the twentieth century." For is not war itself "part of the overall experience of life, perhaps not entirely normal, but something to be expected"? And then?—

> The predicament of war drives the protagonist deep into his own resources, forcing him to face himself and to examine his principles with unprecedented scrutiny. The intensity of the experiences detailed in these novels crystallizes individual values and produces self-evaluation, a most pervasive quality of the books as a group.

It is at once self-evident and surprising—and terrifying. People entering an army are in the same world as before—that is, in an extension and a manifestation of it, and a parody, and under certain circumstances (which we civilians imagine to be the real point of armies) a hideous example of power struggle *in extremis* that renders individual pain meaningless and individual life negligible. Such a range of experiences, such distortions of psyche and feeling, such explosions of privacy! How can we help being fascinated by all this re-possessing of what, to the men and women involved, is a complex of memories so alive that even the mindless stretches of tedium were *intensely* boring? We know only too well that our natures adapt to whatever our reality may be, and that they find values in it to absorb us: this or that practical advantage, friendships and loves and hatreds, "proofs" of oneself. To be in a concentration camp presents configurations similar to those of war—though in that ultimate expression of people who are processing other people for their own purposes, the Nazi extermination camps, we have an instance of "life in the twentieth century" whose victims could hardly learn to take it for granted.

That last sentence of mine touches on such complex matters that it doubtless needs infinite revision. The two kinds of totalitarian mobilization of poor, heedless humanity —military and mass-incarcerative—touch each other at many, many points. There was a sense in which Hitler's victims did take their predicament for granted—that is, saw that their worst, most deeply repressed memories of familial experience were being re-enacted in even more remorseless form than before. History, our fantasies, our very ideals trick us in too many ways. Yet we cannot believe that the past and the future simply mirror one another.

Peter Jones has spread the information about the fictions constructed out of modern American war experience before us. He has categorized the kinds of works they are and moved through them with empathy—an understanding reader who once went over the same terrain himself in a different life, as it were. And he tries to derive, or at least propose, certain moral and philosophical meanings that attach themselves to the enterprise of the novelists. In the course of praising one book, Anton Myrer's *Once an Eagle*, he asserts that war is "a timeless and universal phenomenon." He thinks that understanding this principle has helped Myrer's novels achieve more, artistically, than those of other novelists, and his reading of Kurt Vonnegut, Jr., has led him to place his discussion of Vonnegut at the end of his account of our war fiction—to an important extent because Vonnegut embodies the same principle in his work.

The assertion, or overriding conception, is a crucial statement of the implications of our war fiction. Though I cannot agree—I think the idea begs the human question involved—Jones is absolutely right to thrust the importance of these implications at us. On that issue of war's timelessness and universality depends the matter of whether humanity can at last act in its own interests rather than suffering abject subjection again and again to the "policies" of governments trapped by set rituals of response and decision.

These novels of war offer so compressed and distilled a view of actual people forced to live and die as though these blood rituals were an ineluctable law of nature that they are certainly grounds for a not very divine despair. We are compelled to recognize the all-pervasiveness of this burdensome assumption of the inevitability of recurring wars forever and ever. Therefore all the maintenance of huge armies, the amassing of weapons, the ministries of war or "defense," the smashing and distorting of love, and, of course, the actual killing and burning and ravaging that our unconscious selves keep company with day and night. But after the recognition of some kind of defeat man has suffered and of its immense psychic repercussions and its invasion of every cranny of polity and culture, can we not take our bearings "realistically"? Not to jump with joy at being permitted to see life in the raw, however miserable, close up (like the still-adolescent E. E. Cummings of *The Enormous Room*, who described imprisonment in a French detention camp during World War I) —although there's a certain point in that. But not to confirm the institution either, simply because it's grown so rankly and wildly and wrought havoc with our dream of Eden. There's a kind of despair that casts a cold, true eye over existing reality without for a moment voting for its permanence. We are in a disastrous world. Hence all the depression, displacement, manic laughter of victims at the "catch-22's" engulfing them. Novelists and poets know what to do: show it, project it, for what it is and how it feels. Is the next step just to accept it? Well, we shall see.

CONTENTS

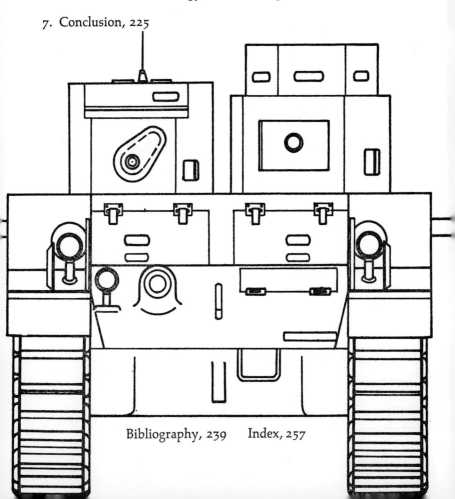

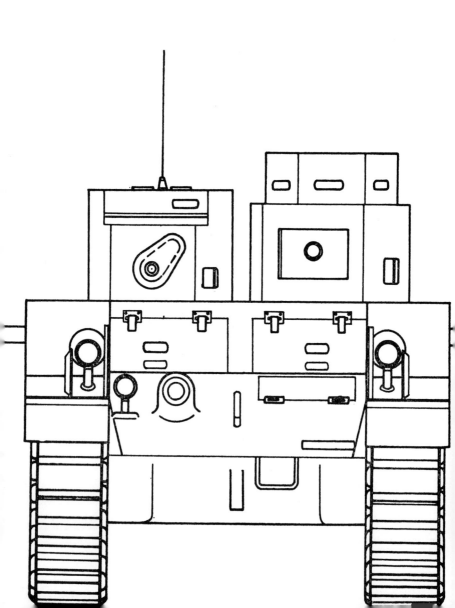

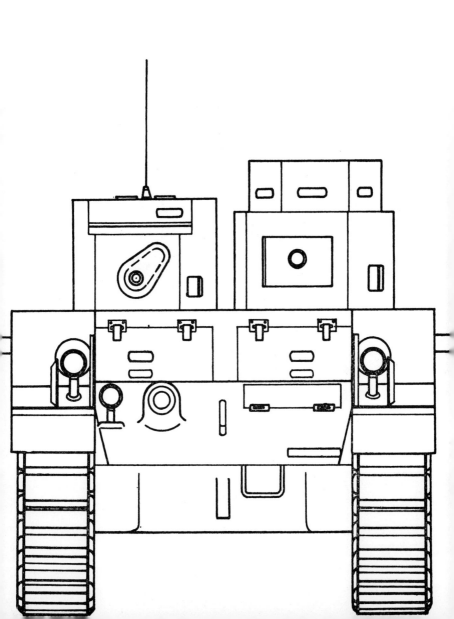

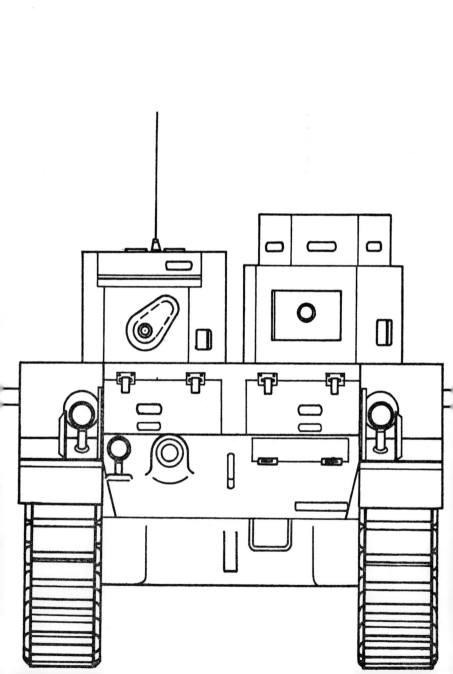

1.

INTRODUCTION

In 1954 Malcolm Cowley recognized and articulated a fact of literary history. In *The Literary Situation* he wrote: "There is no longer any doubt that many more novels have been written about World War II than about World War I, that more of them reach a certain level of competence or merit, and that, as a group, they compose a sounder body of work."[1] Cowley mentions having read some fifty books for his evaluation, which appeared well before the flood of American war novels in the late 1950s and the early 1960s. F. Van Wyck Mason included the works of some forty authors in his *American Men at Arms*, an anthology of the literature from World Wars I and II and Korea, published in 1964. But the selection criteria of anthologists are idiosyncratic; and critical surveyors have, in the main, bypassed all but the spectacularly successful war novels. This study, based on a comprehensive examination of a representative cross-section of the literature, attempts a fresh evaluation of the contemporary American war novel.

Many of the authors discussed here have done more than simply recast their own wartime experiences. This analysis stresses four dominant themes that issue from the entire body of works: first, the war novel as *Bildungsroman* (the novel of education); second, developing attitudes toward military commanders; third, relationships of sexuality and the violence of war; and fourth, impressions and explorations of the psychology of combat. The works covered include novels of World War II, Korea, and Vietnam, published between 1944 and 1968. To keep the study manageable, I omit novels about prisoners of war and the Cold War.

1. Malcolm Cowley, *The Literary Situation* (New York, 1954), p. 34.

Chapter 6 is a short study of Kurt Vonnegut's novels. It would be a mistake to survey the contemporary American war novel without including Vonnegut. At first, his primary vehicle was science fiction, but from *Player Piano* on, his books are authentic war novels. In Vonnegut's vision, war is an intrinsic element of the human condition, somehow inextricably related to technology and the idea that Progress really means something. Read in chronological order, his books show a definite movement away from science fiction, gradually becoming more concerned with war as the unifying motif.

Robert Ardrey and Sigmund Freud have written about innate human qualities that are responsible for war. Erich Fromm, in *The Anatomy of Human Destructiveness*, argues that wars are, and have been, primarily instrumental, arranged and precipitated by national leaders to enhance the national interest in some larger sense. Vonnegut shows that for whatever reason, war is an apparently unavoidable part of human relations, although destined to become unsupportable because of its widening consequences. In the prerevolutionary stages of *Player Piano*, a suddenly perplexed engineer asks, wonderingly, "Is progress bad?" In *Cat's Cradle*, the man who made Hiroshima possible and who ended the Earth by Ice, asks, "What is sin?" Millennia farther out in space, a Tralfamadorian robot from *Slaughterhouse-Five* punches his spaceship's starter button for the final time, igniting the Milky Way. With reason in the saddle and sin shot down, "What can be done, must be done." It's the death penalty in the San Lorenzo of *Cat's Cradle* for anyone caught playing footsie, literally. The same goes for galaxies when technology is part of the game.

As for aggression, violence, and sexuality, Vonnegut describes a statue of the discoverer of atomic power, a sculpture complete with a "shocking erection." His books show an integral, quirky relationship between technology and war, set against a background of consistent, calculated lunacy. He offers the thinking man's last refuge from the world: humor. Because of its unique qualities, Vonnegut's work must be treated separately. His statement is more fully articulated than any other, and it defies integration.

All of these considerations influence the structure and content of this study. Because my approach is thematic, some novels appear in more than one chapter. Furthermore, many of the texts are relatively obscure and not generally available. To produce an integral, self-contained appraisal, and to provide a substantive basis for my conclusions, I include rather more material on some lesser novels than might otherwise be appropriate.

Without question, the war novel has developed into a distinguishable genre: war is the matrix, forming the general background for particular action; it is a metaphor for the human condition, as in the novels of Hemingway and Anton Myrer. In the novels of education and those concerned primarily with commanders, war is part of the overall experience of life, perhaps not entirely normal, but something to be expected. And in some of the works dealing with sexuality and violence, war is the ultimate degradation of humanity, as in Ralph Leveridge's *Walk on the Water* or Mitchell Goodman's *The End of It*. The predicament of war drives the protagonist deep into his own resources, forcing him to face himself and to examine his principles with unprecedented scrutiny. The intensity of the experiences detailed in these novels crystallizes individual values and produces self-evaluation—the most pervasive quality of these books as a group. This theme is consistently reflected in the novels of combat, particularly Edward Loomis's *End of a War* and Tom Chamales's *Never So Few*.

The books covered by this study present an unusually wide range of literary quality. Many are first or only novels. But some are Pulitzer Prize winners, or were written by men who won Pulitzers for other books. Characteristically, ethical or ideational aspects dominate, subordinating other considerations. War is a compelling subject for literature, and the detached, objective author is rare, probably because of the qualities intrinsic to the subject matter. Almost invariably the books reflect the milieu in which they were produced. Many were published in the late 1950s or 1960s, a dozen or more years after the events that inspired them. Overall, the books display virtually every structural and stylistic technique, di-

rect evidence of the war novel's emergence as a suitable medium for expressing diverse human values and experiences.
As the later books reveal with startling clarity, the war novel
has become one of the most logical modes of writing about
life in the twentieth century.

Collectively, the books emphasize individual reconciliation to the ordeal of combat and adjustment to the general
pressures of war, recording immediate responses and varieties
of accommodation. Typically, the hero brings to his war experiences a set of apparently coherent and complete moral
precepts, which finally prove inadequate. The subsequent
process of revision and rationalization is often the true center
of the book. As James Cozzens illustrates brilliantly in *Guard
of Honor*, the military establishment is itself an ethical battle-
ground during periods of mobilization. Bureaucratic legalism,
with its set rules of conduct, clashes with the ideals of individuals who may possess and employ more subtle civilian distinctions, or who may not know or favor restraint.

As *Guard of Honor* emphasizes, the American armed
forces are not totally isolated from the world of civilian
life. The conservative, authoritarian structure of the military
establishment will eventually reflect shifts of ethical and social
codes within the culture it represents, though probably in
delayed sequence. This is a perspective often absent in the
war novels. In addition, military service may be the protagonist's first exposure to a world beyond the familiar—perhaps
his initial contact with a comprehensive and systematic code
of conduct and discipline—often the first shock he undergoes.

The war novel depicts men attempting to "seize the day"
before death erases them, or struggling to articulate their own
principles in a battle to retain rational integrity before the irrationality of death. Accordingly, psychological and sociological considerations are of fundamental significance. If Freud is
correct, the conscious recognition that death may be near
clashes with the inability of the unconscious to accept the idea
of personal extinction, producing profound, sustained tensions within the individual.[2]

2. Sigmund Freud, *Reflections on War and Death*, trans. and ed.
A. A. Brill and A. B. Kuttner (New York, 1918), p. 62.

Three earlier works constitute prototypes for contemporary war novels. In terms of structure, characterization, and exploitation of the genre's potential as a means of more general expression, they established precedents that still exert a strong influence. These books are: Stephen Crane's *The Red Badge of Courage*, John Dos Passos's *Three Soldiers*, and Hemingway's *A Farewell to Arms*.

The Red Badge of Courage is a novel of initiation and a synthesis of divergent motifs. Henry Fleming's rage in battle suggests Homeric wrath atrophied. He had envisioned war as a Greek epic, and his continual rationalizing is similar to Achilles', except that Henry remains deceived about the nature of war, expecting to survive it. Crane begins his story *in medias res*; uses animal imagery that evokes but contrasts sharply with Homer's beast similes (in battle Henry snarls like a "cur"); he inserts a *deus ex machina* in the form of the mysterious stranger who guides Henry back to the regiment; and he ends his story at a null point, between battles—structurally, all in the Homeric vein.

But the most significant aspect of the novel is its compound nature. Crane blends epic devices and a romantic protagonist with naturalistic action that reverberates with the advent of technology in warfare. Henry is amazed to find the "golden process" of nature undisturbed by human battle, and, seduced by the beauty of the natural setting, he is at the end still ignorant of nature's indifference. Once he begins firing, Henry works his weapon like "an automatic affair," functioning like a tradesman at work. Contemplating return to the fighting, he thinks of the armies as great machines, and decides to return to the "blue machine," though not without romantic visions of a gloriously heroic death "on a high place before the eyes of all." When the regiment falters in a later attack, it is a "machine run down." Machines as symbolic elements of war, their cataclysmic effect on the nature of warfare and on the attitudes of men who fight, are prominent themes in many contemporary war novels.

Crane combined several motifs in *The Red Badge of Courage*, creating the first modern war novel. The ironic clash of narrative voice with the thoughts and acts of the youthfully naive protagonist parallels the contrast between Henry's ideas of epic war and the modern battlefield on which he fights. His experiences are clearly in the pattern of initiation or education, the most consistent theme of the modern war novel. Dos Passos's *Three Soldiers* shows the direct influence of Crane's book, as do Richard Matheson's *The Beardless Warriors*, Irwin Shaw's *The Young Lions*, Anton Myrer's *The Big War*, Harry Brown's *A Walk in the Sun*, and numerous lesser novels. Crane's novel about the first modern war also reflects accurately the impact of technology and machine-age firepower. It is doubtful that any American who sets out to write of a young man going to war in the twentieth century does so without conscious reference to *The Red Badge of Courage*.

John Dos Passos's *Three Soldiers* also has exerted massive, sustained influence on subsequent war novels. Dos Passos introduced multiple protagonists, the theme of America as melting pot, and the pattern of following central figures from background phases in the United States to their final fates in war—all of which later became standard techniques in the war novel. He seized the machine motif and put it squarely in the psychological center, using chapter headings to focus attention on the effects of the great civilized war machine (a technique later used with sharp emphasis by Norman Mailer in *The Naked and the Dead*). Dos Passos's fated soldier, John Andrews, observes that "civilization [is] nothing but a vast edifice of sham, and war, instead of its crumbling, [is] its fullest and most ultimate expression." Thus, Dos Passos anticipated by some forty years the spate of books on psychology, sociology, cultural history, and anthropology, all wrestling with Freud's proposals about the primary attributes of civilization and of individual instincts about war and aggression.[3]

Andrews and the two other central characters are the first manifestations in war literature of the psychic split so prevalent in contemporary literature. Fuselli is an urban nonentity, but Andrews, an alienated, passive artist, and Chrisfield, a pathological Dionysian man-of-action, represent the most common form of the fracture. Chrisfield, prefiguring the

3. John Dos Passos, *Three Soldiers* (New York, 1932), pp. 224–25.

"natural" killer of later novels, hates all forms of authority. Frustrated and distorted by regimentation, excited by the violence around him in war, he concedes, "Ah got a bit of the devil in me." Again and again, sex and violence merge inextricably in his thoughts. On the same evening that he throws a grenade, thinking murderously of the enemy and his sergeant, Chrisfield is inflamed by the sight of a waitress, whose full-breasted body causes "his furious irritation [to] flame into one desire."[4] Later, in a nightmare, he wrestles "for his life, with Sgt. Anderson, who turned into a woman with huge flabby breasts."[5] Andrews is the author-artist-victim as hero, but Chrisfield is no less significant for modern literature. In him Dos Passos created an example of the perversion of nature, a natural "wild man" corrupted by civilization, a study in social pathology. Only Chrisfield evinces any taste for fighting, and his motive is revenge. Dos Passos depicted the uneasy relationships between the officers and men of an egalitarian society's army in a manner still alive in Shaw's *The Young Lions*, Jones's *From Here to Eternity*, and Anton Myrer's *The Big War*.

The theme of initiation appears frequently in contemporary war novels—throughout *Three Soldiers* (although it is applied to Chrisfield on whom it is lost), the novels of Shaw, Jones, and Myrer (mentioned above), and such works as *Catch-22* and *Why Are We in Vietnam?* It is also a theme apparent in Grail literature; Jessie L. Weston has analyzed the rite: "I think we shall not go far astray if we conclude that the test preceding, and qualifying for, initiation into the secrets of physical life, consisted in being brought into contact with the horrors of physical death, and that the test was one which might well end disastrously for the aspirant."[6]

Ernest Hemingway's *A Farewell to Arms* extended the war novel's horizons to include a philosophical dilemma. By the end of the book, there is a feeling of explosiveness under Lieutenant Henry's taut neutrality, the style described by

4. Ibid., pp. 167, 175–77.
5. Ibid., p. 193.
6. Jessie L. Weston, *The Quest of the Holy Grail* (New York, 1965), p. 90.

Erich Kahler as "an inversion of all the bitter experience and disillusionment of the generation," characteristic of Hemingway clarity. Omitting detail, social commentary, and "explicit psychology," Hemingway manages, says Kahler, to achieve a concentration that handles factuality "so pointedly that it becomes symbolic."[7] Few novels create the sharp impact of the lieutenant's recitation; few authors of modern war novels try to reproduce the Hemingway style. His use of dramatic structure, his exploitation of a biased and unreliable narrator, and his creation of an atmosphere of existential anxiety, however, provided patterns for subsequent writers.

Lieutenant Henry's sense of reason has been so brutally outraged by his wartime experiences that he is driven to calculated detachment. The irony and repressed hysteria that underlie his story grow from those experiences. The war itself is the supremely shocking example of the world's irrationality, drving him to repudiate it and retreat to neutral Switzerland. His life is a series of confrontations with the world, crises in which he resembles Albert Camus's Meursault. Lieutenant Henry lies easily to Catherine when she asks if he loves her. But the world intrudes: the man above him in the ambulance is allowed to bleed to death; the Italians are willing to execute him after Caporetto; Catherine and their baby are taken from him. All these events demonstrate that there is, finally, no retreat from the world.

Lieutenant Henry's final state is closely related to the statement made by the "great Italian thinker," Rinaldi, who calls reason the "snake" that led to expulsion from Eden. In *The Myth of Sisyphus* Camus defines the absurd as the opposition of man's reason and his longing for happiness against the "unreasonable silence" of the world's irrationality. "The irrational, the human nostalgia, and the absurd that is born of their encounter—these are the three characters in the drama that must necessarily end with all the logic of which existence is capable." Henry knows there is no Eden; at the end of his recitation, he could well be standing in the dark rain outside the hotel where Catherine and their child died. Like Meursault

7. Erich Kahler, *The Tower and the Abyss* (New York, 1967), pp. 98–99.

he is "emptied . . . of hope," facing a universe that regards him with something between the "benign indifference" cited in *The Stranger* and the vindictiveness of the gods who doom Sisyphus. Henry makes the only decision left: to continue the struggle with the world. Like Sisyphus returning to his rock, Henry knows that defeat is inevitable and that he can assert himself as man only by making the decision to continue.[8]

Rinaldi is right: man's destiny is not in Eden; but in the world. Choosing rationally, man establishes and maintains an opposition with the world that continuously defines him as man. During *A Farewell to Arms*, Lieutenant Henry moves far along the road to an education, setting the stage for the works examined in chapter 2, the war novels of education. Point of view, of course, is crucial to an interpretation of the war novel, as in much modern literature. The war novel is almost always an ethical forum, expressing outrage or describing a search for meaning in the dilemma of war. Narrator Boman of *The War Lover* and Mailer's merrily pathological D.J. of *Why Are We in Vietnam?* are no less engaged in that search for truth than is Lieutenant Henry.

The novels by Crane, Dos Passos, and Hemingway furnished a wide range of style, form, thematic content, and characterizations for succeeding generations of authors. In addition, two other men wrote with success of World War I: Thomas Boyd and Humphrey Cobb.

Boyd's *Through the Wheat* (published in 1927) shows the direct influence of Crane. Like Fleming, William Hicks enlists, hoping to see some action. Hicks's education, however, is more complete, with greater realistic detail: he is caught sleeping on guard duty; feels numbing fear in combat; sees unarmed men shot down in cold blood; is gassed; and finally goes insane during a heavy bombardment that kills his best friend before his eyes. Boyd shows a brief glimpse of an ambitious general who, devoutly seeking his third star, exhorts his troops to battle by promising them "Hell, Heaven, or Hoboken by Christmas." The novel concludes with a scene that suggests the final moments of *The Red Badge*: "An

8. Albert Camus, *The Myth of Sisyphus*, trans. and ed. Justin O'Brien (New York, 1955), pp. 21, 89–91.

ochre cannon-ball lay suspended in the soft blue sky. Efflorescent clouds, like fresh chrysanthemums were piled atop one another. . . ." The enemy approaches from an adjacent ridgeline as Hicks walks over ground strewn with bodies to get his rifle. The Germans draw "ever . . . nearer," but "no longer did anything matter, neither the bayonets, the bullets, the barbed wire, the dead, nor the living. The soul of Hicks was numb."[9] (More than thirty years later, in 1961, James Jones would explain this numbness in direct behavioristic terms in *The Thin Red Line*.) Not a wafer, but a cannonball, Boyd's sun bears witness only to war, and nature remains as indifferent as in *The Red Badge*. At first, the nineteenth-century style seems to reveal an author who doesn't really know his subject. But the ironic clash of style and diction with scenes of death and putrefaction is continuous, adding steadily to the final impact of *Through the Wheat*.

Corporal Tyne of Harry Brown's *A Walk in the Sun* climaxes his brief history of battle in an incident remarkably parallel to the last glimpse of Hicks. Both books reflect the influence of, or consciously invoke, the final scene of *The Red Badge of Courage*. But whereas Henry Fleming is deceived in appraising his career and immediate environment, and Hicks is fully resigned to death, Corporal Tyne faces an unresolved future, reflecting Brown's desire to portray an incomplete process, one closer to real experience. The progression from Henry Fleming through Hicks to Corporal Tyne's charge across an open field in Italy shows an increasing reticence among authors of contemporary novels to take firm, unchanging overt moral stands on the issues they raise, and their greater concern with creating an evocative situation, an "objective correlative" for the image or emotion they want to create in the reader's consciousness. Tyne's words, "It is so terribly easy," conclude the book. Like Thomas Mann's Hans Castorp, Tyne rushes forward to die or to live—not specified by either author.

Cobb's *Paths of Glory* (published in 1935) was a primary source for William Faulkner's allegory of war, *A Fable*. Cobb's

9. Thomas Boyd, *Through the Wheat* (New York, 1927), pp. 259–60.

book is a mordant commentary on the nature of war, un-
relieved by humor or ornamentation. He gives greater cov-
erage to general officers, who, like the man briefly revealed in
Through the Wheat, are characterized as ambitious, ruthless
men, bent primarily on furthering their own careers. Cobb
shows that war brings out the worst in all but the very best of
men. Like other books of World War I, this novel is vague on
affairs at high levels of command. Only scenes of small-unit
or individual action among men of lower rank are done with
any attempt at authenticity—the rest is allegorical.

Describing the death of a valorous young officer, Cobb's
prose shows signs of the "new factuality" announced by
Kahler in his discussion of Hemingway:

> There were two detonations, so nearly simultaneous that they
> seemed to be one. . . . A chunk of jagged, revolving metal was
> travelling with speed and precision in Paolacci's direction. It
> tore through his pelvis, carried the whole right hip away, and
> knocked him over the edge. . . . Later his eyes opened and his
> jaws relaxed. . . . [After moon-rise a rat climbed "noiselessly"
> over to the dead man.] Then it stepped forward daintily, jumped
> on the Lieutenant's chest and squatted there. It looked to the
> right and to the left, two or three times, quickly, then lowered
> its head and began to eat Paolacci's lower lip.[10]

Cobb's adverbs derive special impact from their placement
and the absence of other modifiers: "squatted" and "eat" strip
away the illusion created by the moonlight and "daintily,"
creating true horror. Both *Through the Wheat* and *Paths of
Glory* attempt to reproduce for nonparticipants the conditions
of battle in the apocalyptic struggles of World War I.

The novels of World War II and the later period are, as
Malcolm Cowley noted, more wide-ranging in both subject
and content. The techniques of Dos Passos and the breadth of
inquiry suggested by Hemingway are still influential, but
numerous other factors are also active. The subjective, auto-
biographical approach, intensely bound to personal experience, has given way to the application of virtually all variants
of literary style, structure, point of view, and characterization.

10. Humphrey Cobb, *Paths of Glory* (New York, 1935), pp. 45,
52–53.

Similarly, the focus of contemporary war novels reflects the impact of history, psychology, and other disciplines.

Clearly identifiable thematic elements link the novels discussed each of the next four chapters. Chapter 2, "The War Novel as *Bildungsroman*," deals with works that manifest features of the novel of education, as exemplified by Thomas Mann's *The Magic Mountain*, and the strains of archetypal rites of initiation, delineated in Jessie L. Weston's absorbing study, *The Quest of the Holy Grail. The Red Badge of Courage* and *Three Soldiers* conform to the pattern with surprising consistency, as do the five contemporary novels examined in this chapter. The later works also display the development of individual philosophies, and a chronological trend away from the theme of guilt in the cast of original sin or the residuum of religious-sexual guilt so prevalent in American literature during the 1950s. War amplifies and accelerates the overall challenges that life offers; surviving war, these young men are preparing for life in general. (An exception is James Jones's *From Here to Eternity*, no more a strict war novel than James G. Cozzens's *Guard of Honor*. But the rules established for inmates of the military establishment as Prewitt experiences it are gradually becoming more applicable to any man in the modern technological world. This is one of the primary reasons for the great attraction of Jones's romantic rebel-hero in the twentieth century.) Particularly relevant to the novels of education is Miss Weston's observation that the fundamental motif of Grail literature is the quest *manqué*, a task necessitated by a previous sin or error. It is young men who fight their nation's wars, which are precipitated by the collective flaws and failures of the generation in power. But going to war is almost always the first great "adventure" of life, the primary movement from home into the world beyond.

Chapter 3, "The Literature of Command," examines novels that explore the peculiar environment of flag-rank military officers, the admirals and generals responsible for the execution of wars. Several of the best contemporary war novels are in this category, the subject having attracted writers of the first rank. Mailer's *The Naked and the Dead*,

James G. Cozzens's *Guard of Honor*, and Anton Myrer's *Once an Eagle* represent the best of this group.

Among war novels, the novels of command are most explicitly devoted to the political and sociological repercussions of military affairs. The men who wield high command in wartime exude an attraction not dissimilar to that of the Aristotelian dramatic hero: the protagonists are powerful figures; their decisions exert direct, vital influence on the fates of myriad lesser men who labor under them on behalf of the state and of the civil populace that it represents. In this literature weak men do not achieve flag rank. Among those who do, the most menacing flaw is an indiscriminate lust for power beyond the well-defined limitations of military power in American society.

The novels of command tend to be dramatic in structure and in presentation as well. Dialogue is used to convey most key ideas, and there is consistent use of a "chorus" figure who presents the author's position or the conventions of society. Evidence of the split-psyche is persistent, manifested either in the contrasts between protagonist and antagonist, or by situations that force a choice between radically opposing courses of action.

Almost without exception, the protagonist's affairs are complicated by the intrusion into military affairs of political considerations and the influence of the "fourth estate," in some incarnation. From the consistent pattern of interplay among these three factors it is obvious that the increasing influence and direct power of the American military establishment during the years since World War II have not been lost on the authors.

Chapter 4, "Sexuality and Violence in the War Novel," deals with aberrations of human sexual response, either directly attributable to war or exacerbated by the conditions that war produces. The chapter's three primary themes are homosexuality, the interaction of sexual drives and the violence of war, and situations in which human beings engaged in fighting become intimately involved with the machines of war, to the extent of identifying with them or becoming subordinate adjuncts to the machines' greater function—destruction. Here, as in the novels of education, fragmentation of the psyche is manifest. A consistent pattern of pairing also emerges in many of the characterizations in the literature of command, with "good-light" and "evil-dark" figures embodying the dual aspects of human nature. Under the intense pressures of sustained combat, the social conventions, civilized inhibitions, and ethical conduct often give way to more primitive reactions.

These novels of sex and violence are near the center of contemporary American literature of the late 1950s and 1960s. Running throughout the works covered in chapter 4 is the broad, vigorous stream of Romantic protest against the machine age, opposed to the very concept of "progress." The distorting impact of technology on basic human responses to life figures prominently in these novels, which tend to be intense, subjective, grimly pessimistic appraisals of a desperate condition, amplifying John Andrews's speculation about the basic quality of civilization. Numerous descendants of the psychotic Chrisfield inhabit these pages. Among the works featured in Chapter 4 are Norman Mailer's *Why Are We in Vietnam?*, Irwin Shaw's *The Young Lions*, Anton Myrer's *Once an Eagle*, Glen Sire's *The Deathmakers*, and *The War Lover*, by John Hersey.

"The Psychology of Combat," chapter 5, examines novels that center on the conduct of combat. Their emotional range varies from the red rage of Big Queen in *The Thin Red Line* through the resigned, silent professionalism that typifies novels of the Korean War, to John Sack's absurd Dimirgian, nephew of Yossarian, in *M*. The main themes of these books are guilt and the variety of motivations for which men fight. Concerned primarily with men at the individual and small-unit level, many of these novels focus on gradations of loyalty, which is frequently the crucial, polarizing factor in a man's final decision about combat.

The primary sources in chapter 5 include—at one end of the spectrum of guilt—James Jones's *The Thin Red Line* and Sire's *The Deathmakers* and—at the other end—Edward Loomis's *End of a War*, about a young soldier who rationalizes his way through the moral maze of war. The studies of motivation range from the chaotic milieu of Harry Brown's *A Walk in the Sun*, through the opposing allegiances of Tom Chamales's brilliant first novel, *Never So Few*, to the disillusionment of David Halberstam's *One Very Hot Day* and the absurdity of John Sack's *M*. In general, the novels of combat are the least literary. The fact that most of them are of relatively recent publication, and that all of the works specifically about Korea and Vietnam fit into this category, indicate a shift in emphasis. The authors of these novels dwell intently on the fact of war and disregard all but the essentials engulfing the man who fights.

Among contemporary American war novels, the influence of a comparatively small group of literary and philosophical figures is striking. Freud's theories of man and his civilization are widely represented. Erich Kahler's *Man the Measure* and *The Tower and the Abyss*, along with Leo Marx's *The Machine in the Garden*, raise the issues of man-versus-machine, echoing the tradition of Carlyle, Emerson, and Thoreau. Other prominent influences are Whitman, Melville, Faulkner, and, representing a French literature that caught the spirit of the age before other national literatures, Camus and Sartre.

The problem of the ethical "ought" dominates many of these novels; orthodox Christianity is of diminishing importance, colliding with personal beliefs compounded from the works of Plato, Kant, Spinoza, Nietzsche or from variants of existentialism. But seldom far from the foreground of any of the war novels is the predicament of the individual who attempts to conduct himself in accordance with any rationally coherent set of beliefs.

Twentieth-century technology, which is continuously shrinking the earth, forces mankind into more intimate mutual awareness and interdependence. Technology also produces conditions that aggravate existing tensions in human relationships. War has been virtually incessant during recorded human history, but in this age we are instantly aware of every minor skirmish and major encounter around the world. Whether human nature is dynamic or is a constant ratio of qualities, war, with its destructive potential expanded to the indefinable limits of technology, has become a logical metaphor for the plight of "civilized" society in the twentieth century. Acutely aware of their times and fully attuned to literary traditions, these authors are what Sartre calls "engaged." They seek to point out a moral or to explicate aspects of one paradoxically fascinating aspect of human endeavor—war. Their combined efforts have produced a body of literature which demonstrates that the war novel is a medium appropriate for exploring universal human problems.

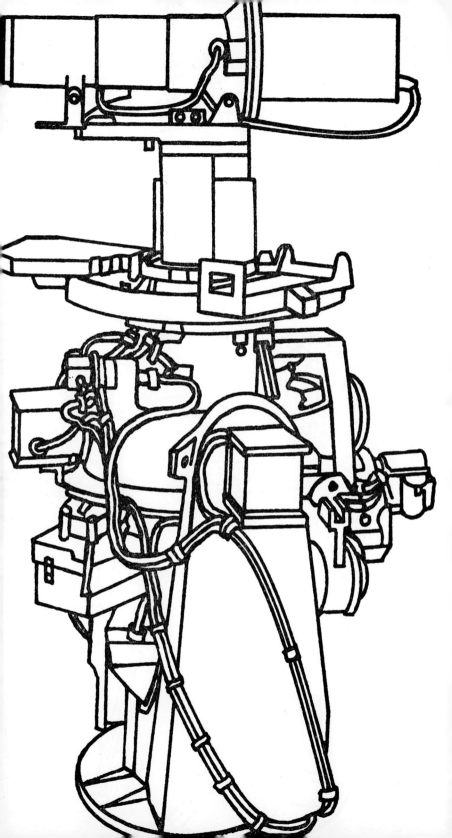

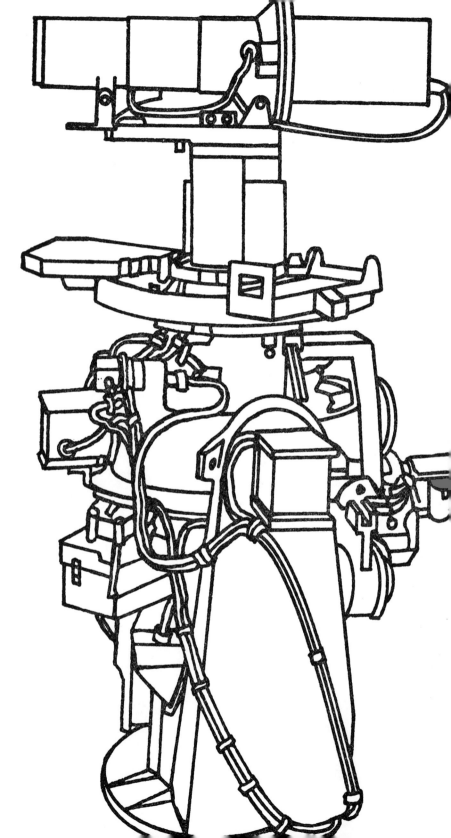

2.

THE WAR NOVEL AS "BILDUNGSROMAN"

Five books best exhibit the war novel as *bildungsroman*: James Jones's *From Here to Eternity*, Anton Myrer's *The Big War*, Richard Matheson's *The Beardless Warriors*, Joseph Heller's *Catch-22*, and Norman Mailer's *Why Are We in Vietnam?* Although their books do not depict combat, both Mailer and Jones demonstrate the growing parallel between modern technological warfare and the quality of contemporary life. Civilization grows increasingly dependent on technology in war and in peace. Waging war, nations exploit the ultimate possibilities of science to further military and political goals. In the twentieth century, therefore, with the boundaries between "war" and "peace" nebulous and ill-defined, the war novel is a logical medium for writing about life.

Wars are fought by young men. As suggested in the introduction, *The Red Badge of Courage* and *Three Soldiers* parallel remarkably the primary aspects of Grail literature rituals. Jessie L. Weston notes that the presence of death intensifies the appraisal and appreciation of life, and that the experience of initiation often ends badly for the quester.[1] In *From Ritual to Romance*, Miss Weston stresses the relationship between the quest and a need to restore vitality to the king or fertility to his wasted lands.[2] A young man fighting his nation's battles is an obvious analogue to the aspirant who seeks the Grail: both are motivated by a cause greater than themselves. "The final stage," writes Miss Weston, "is initiation into the higher Secret of the Mysteries, that of regenera-

1. Jessie L. Weston, *The Quest of the Holy Grail* (New York, 1965), p. 90.
2. Jessie L. Weston, *From Ritual to Romance* (New York, 1957), p. 23.

tion and spiritual life."[3] Each of the novels discussed in this chapter expresses a version of the events detailed above.

These novels are most accurately placed in perspective by remarks of Thomas Mann, in a commentary on *The Magic Mountain*. In a 1953 article for the *Atlantic Monthly*, Mann praised a paper by Howard Nemerov as having given him new insights into his own book. Nemerov's theme was "The Quester Hero: Myth as Universal Symbol in the Works of Thomas Mann." Agreeing that Hans Castorp is a variant of the Grail Seeker, searching for meaning in life and finding his answers in the proximity of death, Mann refers to the traditional ordeals at the Chapel Perilous. "And after all," he says, "what else is the German Bildungsroman (educational novel) . . . than the sublimation and spiritualization of the novel of adventure? . . . Probably these rites were originally rites of initiation, conditions of the permission to approach the esoteric mystery; the idea of knowledge, wisdom, is always bound up with the 'other world,' with night and death." Correlating Grail themes to his novel, Mann explains that "the magic mountain is a variant" of the "Chapel Perilous," and Hans an initiate investigating the mystery of life.[4] The twin themes of initiation and education merge in *The Magic Mountain* as they do in each of the following contemporary war novels, although in widely diverse arrangements.

As Mann employs the word, education accommodates numerous events, ranging from Private Hackermeyer's lessons on night patrols to Robert E. Lee Prewitt's visions of life and choice. Anton Myrer's Alan Newcombe learns that all experience belongs to a single category; Captain Yossarian gradually comprehends his responsibility as a human being; and Mailer's D.J. gets his final instructions from the "deep beast" of nature: "Go out and kill. . . ."[5] All of these young men move through situations that force them to basic decisions about the enigma that lies at the center of the Grail romances

3. Weston, *Quest*, p. 90.
4. Thomas Mann, "The Making of *The Magic Mountain*," quoted in *The Magic Mountain* (New York, 1964), p. 728; hereafter cited as *Mountain*.
5. Norman Mailer, *Why Are We in Vietnam?* (New York, 1967), p. 203; hereafter cited as *Why*.

and of *The Magic Mountain*: "the mystery that is man."[6]
Uses of the convention are provocative. Hans abandons the
security of his mountain sanitarium for the battlefields of
World War I, but Yossarian uses his hospital sanctuary as
a springboard for desertion to neutral Sweden, and D.J. mutters feverishly during his farewell dinner in Dallas, "Vietnam,
hot damn."[7]

These novels of initiation reflect both contemporary and
traditional motifs. In every case, either there is violent tension
between father and son or else the father is absent, maintaining an American literary tradition that runs from Leatherstocking through Huck Finn and Hemingway's Lieutenant
Henry to Prewitt of *From Here to Eternity*. A sense of specific
guilt or an echo of the general alienation that pervades modern
literature animates each of these novels: Matheson's Private
Hackermeyer feels somehow responsible for everything that
goes wrong around him; Alan Newcombe of *The Big War* is
conscious of an innate difference between himself and other
people; Jones's Prewitt has a deep feeling of personal guilt
that grows from religion and a promise to his mother; Yossarian knows he is out of place in an absurd world at war with
itself; and D.J. feels fundamentally alien to the polluted world
that technology and corporate greed are methodically destroying.

The process of education, irrevocable acts or irreversible
decisions, instances of initiation and maturation, and moments
of revelation—each novel discussed in this chapter stresses
these points. The themes of initiation and quest, of course,
are basic to all the war novels, but the use of traditional forms,
the adaptation of existing conventions, and the extension or
variation of accepted literary practice informs each work with
a unique set of values, blended from harmony and discord.
Matheson adapts Crane's classic tale to a modern setting;
Jones places his romantic rebel's naturalistic decline in a philosophical structure of tragedy; Anton Myrer's *The Big War*
recalls both Dos Passos's *Three Soldiers* and Homer's epics;
Heller sets his picaresque hero adrift in a chaos of absurdity

6. *Mountain*, p. 729.   7. *Why*, p. 208.

that reflects both Kafka's ridiculous bureaucracy and Camus's sense of the absurd as a confrontation between man and the world (set forth in *The Myth of Sisyphus*); and Mailer's tale blends black humor, the tall story, the romantic view of man and nature, mythic overstatement, and an extension of Faulkner's technique (evident particularly in "The Bear").

The Magic Mountain serves as a touchstone, after the method of Arnold, primarily for matters of theme and structure. Mann presents virtually all of the possibilities inherent to the *Bildungsroman*, superbly articulated. None of the following novels raises explicit questions of philosophy with even approximate lucidity, but similar issues impinge on the action of each, however tangentially. Powerful imperatives of experience coerce the youthful protagonists hurriedly to their conclusions, without benefit of years of long debate between proponents of opposed schools, such as afforded Hans by humanist Settembrini and absolutist, authoritarian Naphta.

Hans leaves his retreat for war, perhaps wondering about the implications of his great vision, wherein he dreamed of man's "courteous and enlightened social state, behind which, in the temple, the horrible blood-sacrifice was consummated."[8] The narrator of *The Magic Mountain* regards Hans with an ironic, avuncular condescension, though not without approval. Will the universal "extremity of fever" into which Hans so generously throws himself produce a wider realization of Hans's epiphany in "Snow"?[9]

In each of the following novels, young men come to final conclusions, no more assured of their validity than Henry Fleming or Hans Castorp. The contemporary prose does not communicate the elevated detachment of Mann's narrator; instead, there is a continuing sense of the author's personal involvement. The greatest thematic difference, however, between these novels and *The Magic Mountain* is that the education takes place during combat, except for Prewitt and Mailer's D.J. But, as Heller's novel brilliantly demonstrates, there is increasingly slight differentiation between military regimentation and the discipline imposed by a technological bureaucracy. Private Hackermeyer concludes, by observation

8. *Mountain*, pp. 495–96.   9. Ibid., p. 716.

and experience, that everybody is a free agent. Cause and effect explain everything to his satisfaction, though he may well be deceived. Killed by the thing he loves, Prewitt learns that "The Malloy" was right about God, and perhaps right also about reincarnation. Prewitt's visions and the lessons learned by experience reinforce his preconceived convictions.

In Anton Myrer's *The Big War*, Danny Kantaylis affirms with his death the intuitive knowledge that in a moral dilemma, a man really has "no choice"—that there is only one way to act. Jay O'Neill verges on understanding that some sense of commitment is necessary, and Alan Newcombe learns imperfectly that all experience in the phenomenal world belongs to the same category. Unable to integrate learning and experience successfully, he is killed.

The final two books mark a shift in orientation. Heller's Yossarian rejects in its totality the absurdity of the world, accepting only his own judgment as a moral criterion. Through experience he gains an insight into the absurd, which covers all his experience. Like Hans, Mailer's D.J. thinks he understands the nature of things. Sardonically, completely aware of its import to him, D.J. accepts the next reel in the tape of his life: "Vietnam, hot damn." Whatever it is, the "deep beast" that runs his life is irresistible.

Private Hackermeyer of *The Beardless Warriors* (published in 1960), is a product of his time. Life in the machine age makes him susceptible to training but alienates him from other people. Anxious to "do well" as a soldier, he is motivated by both conscience and the social fear of demonstrable inadequacy. In brief, violent days of combat Hackermeyer learns that a man who survives his first exposures to war can, if he is apt, assimilate enough knowledge to survive indefinitely. This perception is central to the development of the tempered optimism with which Hackermeyer contemplates his future at the conclusion of the novel.

In content, if not in execution, *The Beardless Warriors* consistently recalls *The Red Badge of Courage*. Like Crane, Matheson begins his story *in medias res*, depicts his hero reacting to a series of battles in a short span of days, marks his changing attitudes, and shows him at the end a young man confident of his own survival. But there are differences. Though Hackermeyer experiences the red rage of battle, he is always aware of his own isolation on the battlefield, and he is desperately intent on trying to do what he has been trained to do. Only the voice of Sergeant Cooley links Hackermeyer to the world outside his foxhole. Those foxholes mark another crucial departure: Hackermeyer learns first in his education to dig often and deeply. The holes from which he fights emphasize the terrible isolation of combat.

In battle Henry Fleming begins almost immediately to fire his weapon like "an automatic affair," conscious of vague "battle phantoms" swirling about him. In Hackermeyer's first combat:

> The rifle felt incredibly heavy. Its barrel end kept sinking. Hackermeyer propped his left arm rigidly. He heard popping noises all around him and wondered vaguely what they were. He squinted through the sights and hitched the rifle over until a lumbering black-booted figure entered his line of fire. . . .
> Suddenly the war telescoped into a private duel between the German and himself. He held his breath. Only his heart pounded unchecked in the fixity of his body as he hitched the barrel over a third time, then a fourth. Abruptly he gave up trying to track the German soldier. . . . Moving the rifle again, he braced it. When the German crossed his sights, he pulled the trigger.[10]

Matheson's style produces the effect of the Military Handbook. Hackermeyer remains rationally aware, painfully conscious of every movement, deliberately going through the prescribed sequences. Shooting the enemy is the final performance of a methodical, much-rehearsed training routine.

Hackermeyer's education into the secrets of warfare is fast and violent. A series of foxhole "buddies" advance his education and initiate him into the mysteries. Young Foley, complaining that war does not make sense, fails to clean his rifle. In the first skirmish a fatal shell fragment seeks him out at the bottom of his hole, where he lies, terrified. Linstrom is totally undisciplined, attempting to cope with combat by ignoring it. In an incident that recalls Henry Fleming's encounter with the corpse in the forest chapel and Chrisfield's first

10. Richard Matheson, *The Beardless Warriors* (Boston, 1960), pp. 61–62.

sight of death, Hackermeyer loses track of Linstrom, who has consistently refused to do his share of digging. Looking for Linstrom, Hackermeyer checks the area around his foxhole after a heavy bombardment, but finds only "colorless slime" dripping from some shattered trees. His last companion is Guthrie, whose cynical humor almost obscures the fact that he is a superb soldier. Though seriously wounded, Guthrie survives, because he has "earned" it by being a good soldier —cause and effect. Thus, Hackermeyer learns the mortal necessity of obeying orders.

Anxieties and the true motive for his quest arise from one of the most persistent common denominators in modern literature, consistently reflected in the war novel: the deterioration of the family. Years of his father's drunken abuse have imbued Hackermeyer with a sense of guilt, and after being drafted he feels vaguely responsible for everything that goes wrong in the squad. Neither sex nor religion affects him significantly. He does not brood over killing the enemy; it is his job as a soldier. Combat enables Hackermeyer to prove he is competent. And in Sergeant Cooley he finds a surrogate for the sullen, alienated father who had rejected him, whose death leaves him utterly alone in the world.

The thrust of Matheson's book—and perhaps its most serious defect—as a presentation of combat, is that Hackermeyer sees a logical pattern in his experiences: men die because they are incompetent or because they seek death. Realizing this, he is able to retrieve himself, heroically saving his surrogate father from death in combat.

Saving Cooley's life is Hackermeyer's own passage into manhood, the key to his future. Visiting Cooley in the hospital he is at first relieved that Cooley will be spared further combat, then terrified by the realization that Cooley will no longer be with the squad. "You come out whenever you're ready, son," says Cooley, inviting him to visit after the war. His future secured, Everett Hackermeyer has now become Everett Cooley, a squad leader, a man, after only sixteen days of combat. Consciously imitating Sergeant Cooley he welcomes his replacements, some older than he, confident that he has learned what Cooley knows about combat and about life. This is Hackermeyer's first command: "All right. . . . *Come* on, children."[11]

Crane's Henry Fleming is commonly alluded to as "the youth," or "the young soldier." Henry lives his romantic adventure in a realistic setting that is incompatible with his illusions. Deceived by a sunbeam, he assumes that the worst is over, that some divine fiat assures his survival. Crane's studied detachment from Henry's predicament emphasizes that "the youth" is seriously deceived in his final optimism. There is no similar contrast between Hackermeyer's perception of events and other possible interpretations. Hackermeyer concentrates only on the fact that he has survived. Cooley's promise takes on the same significance as Henry's "golden ray of sun." The author's empathy for his subject is manifested in *The Beardless Warriors*; there is no conflict of style with events, of tone with events, as in *The Red Badge*. Hackermeyer's predicament is revealed not by style, but by the pattern of his experience and his own analysis of it.

Mailer's General Cummings, in *The Naked and the Dead*, observes that "the natural role of twentieth-century man is anxiety."[12] Going further, Camus generalizes the statement, saying that man inhabits an absurd universe, but longs for reason and happiness."[13] Camus agrees with Heidegger that only intense preoccupation with affairs "of the world" can distract the "lucid man" from flashes of anxiety that will turn into perpetual anguish and despair. Perhaps because Hackermeyer is still young, and only recently initiated into life, his world seems to operate rationally under rules of cause and effect. In a society strongly influenced by the Protestant assumption that good people do well in the world, Hackermeyer is animated by the fear of being inadequate. Bereft of faith in God and alienated from nature and from his fellow man, the individual must rely on and be sustained by faith in himself. A soldier, who remembers his training and

11. Ibid., pp. 336–37.
12. Norman Mailer, *The Naked and the Dead* (New York, 1948), p. 177.
13. Albert Camus, *The Myth of Sisyphus*, trans. and ed. Justin O'Brien (New York, 1955), pp. 20–21.

follows orders, survives. This is the lesson that Hackermeyer learns. He assumes the burdens left by his predecessor, his symbolic father, with an equanimity that comes from having learned that lesson well, however insufficient it may prove in the future.

This is one view of warfare: an aspect of life that must be endured along with the rest. Doing the "work at hand" well can deter disaster. This notion reflects a moral similar to that of Beowulf, that fate is apt to favor the man who keeps his head, and that a man's greatest duty lies in loyalty to his friends.

Anton Myrer's early novel, *The Big War* (published in 1957), blends Homeric epic with several aspects of Dos Passos's *Three Soldiers* in detailing the education of Alan Newcombe. The book's three protagonists, its ethnic mixtures, its snatches of song and verse, and its numerous literary allusions, suggest Dos Passos as influence. Newcombe, like John Andrews, is an artist—at least potentially—at war. But Myrer's framing device is Homeric epic. His major characters are obvious analogues for classical counterparts. Once their identities are established, certain patterns are predictable. But the clash of philosophies implicit in this combination of motifs promises provocative variation. Immersed in literature, Newcombe would like to believe that life is an epic and war a heroic adventure, but he learns differently.

Myrer's characters demonstrate three distinct reactions to war, three ways of coping with life. Irishman Jay O'Neill is an orphan, but he is untouched by experience; he is a happy sensuous animal, sufficiently cunning to avoid deep involvement. In contrast, Danny Kantaylis evinces characteristics of both Hector and Ulysses. A veteran of Guadalcanal, Danny is already devoted to the war, accepting whatever fate befalls him. Jay talks incessantly, but says nothing; Danny thinks deeply, but rarely speaks. Alan Newcombe is rich, educated, and abstracted from life by years spent in carefully selected schools and with comfortable family friends. The Newcombes are at home with the Lowells, buttressed by father's financial interests and mother's cultural activities. Consequently, Alan Newcombe brings to his basic training a philosophy compounded of his gleanings from learning, quite ignorant of experience. Highly intelligent, over-bred and under-responsive, he carries the bulk of the story in the process of reconciling his preconceptions with the realities of life in war. Jay O'Neill picks his way nimbly through the maze of combat, an adequate fighter but nothing more, and Newcombe gropes for some correlation between the theoretical knowledge of his university education and the hell of war, while Danny Kantaylis stoically accepts each day's trials. Like Odysseus he subordinates himself to the imperative of the greater social good.

Language gives *The Big War* a special quality. Myrer is obviously fascinated with word-play. Using Newcombe's sensitivities as the primary vehicle for telling the story, Myrer generates a prose that is sometimes too ornate, but always effective, never without a sense of intelligent direction. As he exploits the resources of language in depicting Newcomb's reactions, Myrer's stream of allusion sometimes spills inappropriately into the speech of inarticulate Danny and non-scholarly Jay.

Minutes before his death, Danny reflects on the principle that guides him: "It was the one fearful, incontrovertible fact of life. . . . You tried to do well, do all that was asked of you and maybe at certain times a little bit more . . . and went down, after hanging on as sturdily as you could. That was life; accept your responsibilities, try to harm as few people as possible, and hope for the best . . . and meet your destiny as cleanly as possible, anyway."[14] As the squad moves through its patrol they sight a formation of Japanese led by a tank that has penetrated their lines and threatens the rear of the battalion. Like Achilles at the moment he hears of Patroklos' death, Danny instantly mourns his own death, knowing that for him there is no choice: "He was filled with mounting, choking rage then with the saddest, weariest, most forlorn resignation he had ever felt. . . . We got to get it. Got to. No choice."[15] Seizing a demolition satchel, he runs to the tank and throws himself under its treads.

14. Anton Myrer, *The Big War* (New York, 1957), pp. 365–66.
15. Ibid., pp. 367–68.

As Newcombe's education in war unfolds, the testimony of his senses battles his outraged intellect in episodes that recall both Henry Fleming's battle rage and Hackermeyer's deliberate struggle to reproduce training sequences. Superimposed over all is Newcombe's obsessive compulsion to think in literary analogies, the malaise of which Dos Passos's John Andrews complains to Genevieve Rod. Literature gives Newcombe objective distance, an intellectual refuge from the fact that combat is happening to him, personally. Preparing for his first combat he checks his weapon; intellect rejecting the significance of the event:

> Newcombe pulled a clip out of his belt. Savage teeth, well aligned.
> His rifle looked strange to him, curiously proximate and bright. Why was that? Never had it possessed so many corners, so many facets of gleaming metal—an amazing . . . complexity that nearly dazzled him. This was better, though; movement was better. . . . He rubbed vigorously at the bolt with his sleeve, looking about. Now remember. . . .[16]

Action releases the tension, gives the brain a respite. His memories of the landing are an impressionistic montage of incongruous actions, "a slowly dreaming whirl where time stood still and drunken. . . ." But Newcombe responds, detached though fighting for his life. Instincts assume the role abandoned by reason, as external events and his own reactions vie for Newcombe's attention:

> Low: Fire low and squeeze 'em off.
> The gun kicked him, kick, kick, kick: he pressed in toward the recoil with his shoulder, a fierce affection: brass bubbles flipped past his eyes' scan. . . . Another clip. Quick. Jay was shouting something. They were puppet figures—jerking along on arms and legs, jerking stiltlike. . . .[17]

Newcombe is finally forced to a decision about experience and reality, based primarily on a short, intense love affair. The squad is briefly in reserve, and Newcombe's mind is filled with memories of men shot to pieces before his eyes, of the odor of burning flesh, but "the sickening montage of recent experience" was due to "subjective imagination." But what *is*

16. Ibid., pp. 250–51.   17. Ibid., pp. 280–81.

reality? As he gratefully eats warm bread and drinks hot
coffee for the first time in days, Newcombe thinks suddenly of
Helen, realizing for the first time that the warm bread, the
horror of combat, and his marvelous idyll with Helen are all
part of the same fabric of experience: "And if this was reality,
then so was *that*—wasn't it? . . . Accept it all: accept it
all, both terrors and delights. What other conclusion was
there?"[18] After Danny's death he tries to write Andrea, but
sees his communication collapse into empty, impersonal elegi-
ac formulae:

> He bent forward all at once and covered his face with his
> sleeve. Weep no more, kind shepherds, weep no more, for
> Lycidas. . . .
> . . . Help us. Get thee apart and weep. All dark and comfortless.
> There was no way. Words were nothing. Words, his vocation
> and his passion, melted away in the face of that torn and bloody
> form.[19]

Unlike Nick Adams, cerebral Newcombe cannot choke back
his thoughts. On patrol, Newcombe mounts a small rise that
affords him a view of the ocean across the island, and his curse
returns: "Thalatta . . . he moved toward it, his eyes on the
pulsing glitter of the sea."[20] From a clump of bushes that he
should have checked, a burst of machine-gun fire cuts Alan
Newcombe down. War is not an epic adventure; it is death.
He had written to Helen that he was sure that no human
events were necessary, not even war; it was the romance of
the idea of war, "Errol Flynn in brief, Errol Flynn," that was
to blame. Newcombe had learned the "Secret of the Mysteries," but, in Miss Weston's words, this test ends "disastrously for the aspirant," because his learning is imperfect.[21]
Only Jay survives. Danny met death because he would not
avoid it; Newcombe learned his lesson poorly, and was killed;
Jay remains "ignorantly, fanatically" sure of his survival.

Myrer's modern-dress *Iliad* is a superb example of the
modern war novel. The combat action blends verisimilitude
and impressionistic impact, and his analogues are deftly created. Myrer combines Achilles with Paris in Lieutenant

18. Ibid., p. 317.   20. Ibid., p. 430.
19. Ibid., p. 398.   21. Weston, *Quest*, p. 90.

D'Alessandro; Kantaylis is a composite of Hector and Odysseus.

The predominant tone of *The Big War* is acceptance or resignation, for which Danny Kantaylis is the consistent model. Family tumult is present to some degree, but the basic issue is larger than the family, even larger than the state. There is no sense of guilt attributed to any figure; to be ignorant of life is guilt enough. Myrer's women are idealized representations of the idea implicit in Goethe's "eternal feminine."

One voice who might speak for all three figures—Jay O'Neill, Alan Newcombe, and Danny Kantaylis—is Sartre, in this discussion of human responsibility:

> First of all, man exists, turns up, appears on the scene, and, only afterwards, defines himself. . . . Thus there is no human nature. . . . Man is nothing else but what he makes of himself.
>
> . . . .
>
> Subjectivism means, on the one hand, that an individual chooses and makes himself, and, on the other, that it is impossible for a man to transcend human subjectivity. . . . In fact, in creating the man we want to be, there is not a single one of our acts which does not at the same time create an image of man as we think he ought to be. To choose to be this or that is to affirm at the same time the values of what we choose, because we can never choose evil. We always choose the good, and nothing can be good for us without being good for all. . . .
>
> If . . . we exist and fashion our image at one and the same time, the image is valid for everybody and for our whole age. Thus our responsibility is much greater than we might have supposed, because it involves all mankind. . . . Therefore, I am responsible for myself and for everyone else. I am creating a certain image of man of my own choosing. In choosing myself, I choose man.[22]

In Sartre's view, conscience and intuition are superior to intellect as a guide. Ironically, his argument echoes the same insistent desperate optimism, predicated on a similarly "good" will, that pervades the thought of Kant, whom Sartre repudiates on the subject. Explaining himself on the issue of self and mankind, Sartre again parallels Kant's explication of the

22. Jean-Paul Sartre, *Existentialism and Human Emotions,* trans. B. Frechtman (New York, 1957), pp. 15–18.

categorical imperative: man is not only a person who chooses, says Sartre, "but also a lawmaker who is, at the same time, choosing all mankind as well as himself." [23]

The three final books discussed in this chapter demand closer analysis and show more clearly the war novel as *Bildungsroman*. The first is James Jones's *From Here to Eternity* (published in 1951). Jones's Robert E. Lee Prewitt is a striking figure, marked like Hackermeyer by guilt linked to his mother's death. For Prewitt the passage into manhood is impossible, his initiation fatal. Prewitt, in his thirties, is no farther along the road to understanding than teen-aged Hackermeyer. Prewitt comes out of Harlan County, Kentucky, bearing the burdens of a stern religious heritage and an insupportable promise to his dying mother. "Promise me you wont never hurt nobody unless its absolute a must, unless you jist have to do it." Those words bind Prewitt's naturally rebellious soul to an inevitable war with the world. As Prewitt leaves home, his father is in jail and his mother dead, "and since his father had beaten him again just two days before . . . he did not figure his father counted. . . ." [24] Once Prewitt breaks the vow to his mother, his guilt is absolute, his fate is fixed. No motive can meliorate the consequences, and every act carries him more surely to his death.

From Here to Eternity is a unique mixture. A rebellious contemporary American demigod pursues a career of naturalistic decline, framed within the general learning-curve of classical tragedy. During his brief life, Prewitt learns bitterly, both from experience and from a series of visions that grow out of his head-long collisions with the institution into which he has delivered himself, the army. His "Chapel Perilous" is, first, the company kitchen, where he learns that every man needs something outside himself to cling to, and second, the stockade, where he listens intently to a man who "teaches" him about the evolution of God. Dying, he is gratified to

23. Ibid., p. 18; of Immanuel Kant, *The Philosophy of Kant*, trans. Carl J. Friedrich (New York, 1949), pp. 180–81.

24. James Jones, *From Here to Eternity* (New York, 1951), p. 16; hereafter cited as *Eternity*.

realize that experience confirms his original theory about human will and choice.

A romantic rebel, Prewitt is anachronistic, an individualist in a rigidly hierarchical bureaucracy. The powerful influence of his mother and the negative residue of a once-potent religion combine with his army experiences in the way circumstances work on Mann's "simpleminded hero": the ordinary stuff of which he is made undergoes a heightening process that makes him capable of adventures in sensual, moral, intellectual spheres he would never have dreamed of "outside the Army."[25]

Like Lear, Prewitt makes his fatal decision before the novel's opening action: he deliberately insists on a transfer to Captain Dynamite Holmes's "G" Company, knowing there will be pressure for him to box. He also knows that he will not box, and that trouble is, therefore, unavoidable. But when another bugler is selected to play the important ceremonies, Prewitt's sense of propriety is offended. He demands a transfer. He quit boxing when he accidentally blinded another man, and will on no account violate his oath again. Prewitt could remain in the bugle corps with easy duty, but he commits the irrevocable act, for reasons he cannot himself fully comprehend or articulate:

> The reason was, he wanted to be a bugler. Red could play a bugle well because Red was not a bugler. It was really very simple, so simple that he was surprised he had not seen it standing there before. He had to leave the Bugle Corps because he was a bugler. Red did not have to leave it. But he had to leave, because he wanted most of all to stay.[26]

Playing "well" was not good enough. Whatever you do must be done superbly or not at all; there can be no compromise. Prewitt's moral sense and inflexible pride of accomplishment will not allow him to stay where his worth goes unrecognized. But deeper than that is his subconscious drive to punishment and conflict. Why had he broken the vow to his mother in the first place?

Prewitt's decline follows a predictable path. As the book

25. *Mountain*, pp. 725–26.   26. *Eternity*, p. 8.

opens, he is on the verge of moving to "G" Company. The transfer costs him his rating, consequently his extra pay and his girl. Now he challenges Captain Holmes and "G" Company. Book 2 ("The Company") ends with Prewitt's memorable rendering of taps—his open challenge to the army at large. In Book 3 ("The Women") Prewitt meets Lorene (Alma), undergoes "The Treatment," which is Holmes's retaliation for his refusal to box on the "G" Company team, and finally, he cowers in the bushes as the MP's drag Maggio away, howling, to the stockade. In Book 4 ("The Stockade"), Prewitt becomes a kept man, is caught in the "Queer-Chaser" roundup, helps create the "Re-enlistment Blues," fights and conquers Bloom, decks Platoon Guide Galovitch, is framed, arrested, tried, convicted and sent to the stockade, undergoes four months of Major Thompson's hospitality, is released from the stockade, and kills Fatso Judson in a fair fight—making his own death a necessity. In Book 5 ("The Re-enlistment Blues"), Prewitt tries to return to the army and is slain by it.

Gide says of Oedipus that his tragedy begins at the moment he realizes his guilt and the hopelessness of his situation. So it is with Prewitt. Actively seeking to maintain conflict between himself and the world, he acts to perpetuate the confrontation, until the moment of his death. His predicament culminates in the slaying of Fatso Judson, the perfect expression of his position in the world. Prewitt knows from the moment he breaks his mother's death-bed request that he is guilty, and he devotes the rest of his life to insuring that his punishment will result.

Prewitt is a superlative doer. Playing poker or pool, shooting, bugling, composing music—he can do anything he wants, but he drives himself to defeat, almost by design. Prewitt makes things happen. His fists confirm Bloom's decision to kill himself. He is responsible for Maggio's arrest, but his example enables Maggio to escape from the army with a "Section-Eight" discharge. He forces Fatso Judson to fight and kills him easily, on Fatso's own terms. His influence over Alma is so great that she is ready to stay in Hawaii, abandoning her cherished dream of a return to respectability. His

presence in the stockade hastens Malloy's departure from it.
And most important, he forces the army to kill him.

Prewitt's education consists of three visions about free
choice and life, as well as advice from Maylon Stark and
tutorial precepts from "The Malloy," guru to the stockade
elite. These preliminary initiatory steps are followed by the
"higher Secret of the Mysteries," as he lies dying.

Prewitt muses over his fate one morning, minutes before
reporting for KP duty. "Busted" to a straight-duty private,
he tries to understand what has happneed to him since the
transfer, and why it has happened. His life appears to him in
a metaphoric vision as a one-way staircase, leading down from
his former position on an upper step.   1947562

> He had taken that step of his own free will; he knew that then,
> and now, in ruminating back, he knew it now. But it was, he
> also knew, an own free will that while it allowed him choice had
> only one alternative for him to choose from. If this was so, and
> he was quite sure that it was so, then that had not really been
> the first step at all, that quitting of the Corps, and there was
> no first step anywhere but only another mythical bannister-
> meeting point shading off above him into God knew how long
> before he was ever born. *Yet those steps were not haphazard,
> they were well built and well proportioned, all of a piece and
> solid. They would never fall out from under you. They had been
> put there. Each step was a decision that was not a decision, part
> of a plan, each with its subsequent steps that were not sub-
> sequent steps* [emphasis added].[27]

They were not subsequent steps, of course, because God, or
the devil, had placed them there for Prewitt at the time of his
predestination. The vision helps Prewitt handle the trouble-
some issue of responsibility. Like the chorus in *Oedipus Rex*
following Jocasta's blasphemies, Prewitt looks desperately for
a sign that he is not alone, that some power imposes order on
his life. He is understandably troubled by the realization that
he is trapped in a world he did not make, in a life for which
he may be held responsible. Like Camus's Sisyphus, Prewitt's
only choice is to be either active or inert.

Here, as in *The Thin Red Line*, Jones intrudes into the
thoughts of his character in an augmentation that merges

27. Ibid., p. 184.

narrative and interior monologue. Driven to elemental considerations of time and space—"Fixt Fate, Free Will, Foreknowledge absolute"—Prewitt is uncomfortable. His vision
somehow leads him to consider time, but he is no better
equipped than Milton's rebels to understand a being operating
free of time. Here, as in the subsequent visions, Prewitt is
"almosting it," haunted by spectres from a religion he no
longer consciously acknowledges. The "free will" that Prewitt
appears to exercise in the decision to move along the staircase
operates like Spinoza's scheme of divine necessity, which
Prewitt later encounters, somewhat transmogrified, emanat-
ing from "The Malloy" in the stockade. This first vision introduces wide-ranging possibilities, and most obviously, a
concept dimly recalled from his childhood.

First Cook Stark offers a practical expedient. Prewitt
can escape both the wrath of Captain Holmes and "the Treatment" by joining forces with Stark in the kitchen. Resorting
to such a sanctuary is the only practical course of action. The
cook also plants the germ of Prewitt's new religion: "In a
world like [this], theres only one thing a man can do; and
thats to find something thats his sam, really his and will
never let him down, and then work hard at it and for it and it
will pay him back. With me its my kitchen. . . ."[28]

The second vision occurs during a lull after Maggio's
arrest and the flurry of questioning about "queers." Prewitt
knows that it was primarily his aggressive inquisitioning of
Hal and Tommy on the subject of homosexuality that precipitated Maggio's wailing challenge to the MP's:

> Only when Kid Prewitt appeared on the scene, like a catalyst
> poured into a tranquil beaker, did the mixture begin to boil and
> explode. Angelo had not been tainted by the queers; it was only
> when Kid Galahad Prewitt had stepped in looking for the Holy
> Grail with moralistic fears and questionings that Angelo had
> suddenly felt guilty enough, or tainted enough, to do something
> drastic. There were times when Prewitt felt a special quality
> that seemed to force everyone he touched into making dramat-
> ic decisions about their own lives, no wonder people did not
> like him to be around. . . . Enter Kid Galahad Prewitt. The
> action precipitates. The conflict of fear rises flapping from the

28. Ibid., p. 211.

depths like a giant manta ray, looming big and bigger, looming huge, up out of the green depths that you can look down into through a water glass and see the anchorcable dwindling in a long arc down to invisibility, up from far below that even, flapping the two wingfins of choice and the ego caught square in the middle. And they had to choose, had to face it, and which ever way they chose they still got hurt.[29]

Prewitt describes his own position: free to choose, unable to deter the consequences. Pride and necessity shape his choices, but he knows it is always better "to face things" regardless of the consequences. He is on a quest for the Grail, but it is neither stone nor dish, it is death.

This time the author is too much in evidence. Prewitt might have heard about Sir Galahad during his childhood encounters with religion; the manta is apt and could be derived from his Hawaiian experience but the variation of Eliot's simile from chemistry, though appropriate, is not within Prewitt's likely ken. Mystical insight cannot be held responsible for scientific detail. Faulkner sharpens the precision of terminology and supplements a vocabulary to express subtleties of thought for nominally inarticulate characters, but here Jones wanders outside credible experience. Curiously, Prewitt thinks that "they" have to choose, not yet aware that it applies to him as well.

Prewitt's final "Chapel Perilous" is "the Hole." Enduring solitary confinement in Major Thompson's stockade, he puts into practice Jack Malloy's method of meditation, learned from "some Yogi books." The vision here prepares Prewitt for his terminal lesson, taught him by Malloy. Concentrating, he achieves literal ecstasy, floating free of his body "there on the bunk," conscious of a connecting "jism cord" which meant death to break. Then he floats away from the stockade:

But wherever he went there was always his end of the jism cord stretching away in the ballooning black distance back to the other of him back there. . . . and he could understand many things that had always upset him and bothered him, it was as if for the first time he had gone off the world like a spaceship and could really see all of it, and realize how each of it all had its

29. Ibid., pp. 410–11; for other aspects of this conversation, see pp. 110 ff.

own private point, and that nothing was ever wasted . . . and
that more than anything else it was like a small boy going to
school every day, maybe he did not want to go but he had to go
anyway, and if he does not learn one lesson one day it still isnt
wasted because the wasted day helps him learn much quicker
the next day. . . .[30]

This hint of reincarnation and immortality clashes with Prewitt's memory of desolation at the moment of his mother's
death, as he watched, unbelieving, while she died before his
eyes.

Forced increasingly to make the most of his own resources, Prewitt achieves his final initiatory vision under conditions of maximum stress and privation, a mystical withdrawal from repugnant surroundings, spirit triumphant over
matter. More than in either of the two preceding instances,
Prewitt is in a state of trance, mortification of the body easing
the release of spirit. Instead of watching, dormant, he is now
spiritually active, gaining for the first time a positive perspective, a new objectivity about his own and all human affairs.
And this is a more genuine presentation of Prewitt, couched
in his terminology, in similes he would be apt to employ. The
run-on, unpunctuated passage emphasizes the flow of his subconscious thoughts. Prewitt concludes by returning to the
motif of his first vision: a grand plan does account for all;
nothing is wasted. In a way, it is a most comforting and convenient interpretation for him.

Prewitt's visions, true to his character, become clearer
and more optimistic with adversity. Insisting on his transfer
from the bugle corps, Prewitt makes it clear that he will be a
bugler his way, or not at all. In the stockade he decides that
to be a man he must live exactly according to the dictates of
his conscience, or not live at all. A unique blend of guilt and
the spirit of Sisyphus animates Prewitt. He acts so that the
confrontation between him and the world is in a constant
state of crisis; in so doing, he approaches the finale of his
search for a new religion and its God.

First there was the one-way staircase and the path to predestined defeat. But the surging manta ray flapped wings of

30. Ibid., p. 579.

alternative choice, though the choices may have offered equally adverse consequences. In "the Hole," Prewitt realizes that
to be human is to choose, and to act in accordance with that
choice. He wonders whether cutting the cord of life brings
freedom or another chance to learn lessons failed in the preceding cycle, but he is reconciled to the fact that he must
follow his personal daemon. He still has to contend with the
need for punishment. All paradoxes are resolved by three
shots in the dark a few days after Pearl Harbor.

Like Hans Castorp laboring in the snow, Prewitt is now
very close to completing his vision of life and death, needing
only "The Malloy's" teaching to augment Maylon Stark's
advice and the illumination of his own visions.

By interspersing Prewitt's insights into the human condition throughout the novel, Jones focuses to a greater degree
than a casual first reading might reveal on the theme that a
man is not truly human until he stops drifting. He must take
stock of himself, try to understand his principles, then anchor
himself with the dictates of conscience. And Prewitt cannot
shake the residual feeling of guilt that is virtually the sole
remnant of his religion. So his actions are always calculated,
consciously or unconsciously, to maintain friction between
him and the world. He is defined by his actions.

Malloy completes Prewitt's education. Teacher to the
stockade elite, his philosophy is a scrambled blend of Epictetus, Thoreau, Marx, Darwin, Jack London, and the Bible;
his God is "growth and evolution." Hebrew vengeance and
Christian forgiveness have given way to the modern God of
acceptance. Since life is trial and error, inaction is the only sin.
"Logic and evolution" demand that a new age will come.
Malloy calls himself the rock to which the stockade-keepers
are sentenced for life, but his philosophy is also tattered. He
confides to Prewitt that his present run of bad luck is the
result of some terrible thing done in ages past.[31] (This from
the new God of acceptance!)

Jones introduces Spinoza into the novel, centering the
question of its meaning upon the philosophical paradox of
freedom and necessity. Teacher Malloy tries to talk Prewitt

31. Ibid., p. 647.

out of his announced intention of killing sadistic Fatso Judson. Pointing out that Fatso merely performs his function, Malloy emphasizes the idea of resignation with a loose reshuffling of a line from Spinoza's "Of Human Blessedness": "He said," quotes Malloy, "Because a man loves God he must not expect God to love him in return."[32] Just before his own departure from the stockade, Malloy repeats the line to Prewitt, adding this crucial gloss:

> "When a man has found something he really loves, he must always hang on to it, no matter what happens, whether it loves him or not. And," he said with an almost religious fervor, "if it finally kills him, he should be grateful to it, for having just had the chance. Because thats the whole secret."[33]

Here is Maylon Stark's central concept, grown harsher, with punishment explicitly promised. Malloy does extract the idea of resignation from his text, but it is ludicrous that his philosophy of an evolutionary deity should be anchored by a passage from Spinoza. Malloy undoubtedly misses the point of "because" in the quotation. Spinoza defines the intellectual love of God as "joy attended with the idea of God as its cause, that is to say, the love of God . . . in so far as we understand that He is eternal. . . ."[34] The same passage from "Of Human Blessedness" has this central statement: "He who loves God cannot strive that God should love him in return. If a man were to strive after this, he would desire that God, whom he loves, should not be God, and consequently he would desire to be sad, which is absurd."[35] Spinoza insists that nothing in the world is contingent, that human prayer asks the perfect being to alter His ways to accommodate human understanding, a thesis in direct opposition to Malloy's. For Spinoza, human freedom consists of an acceptance of limitations in the light of God's infinite perfection; like Epictetus, he wants things to happen just as they happen.

But Prewitt has the last element of his education: he has

32. Ibid., p. 660.
33. Ibid., p. 664.
34. Baruch de Spinoza, *The Philosophy of Spinoza*, trans. and ed. Joseph Ratner (New York, 1954), pp. 362–63.
35. Ibid., p. 364.

found his new religion, his new God. The army fulfills perfectly the prerequisites laid down for him by both Stark and "The Malloy." The army is his, in a special way. He loves the army and knows that he is doomed to be a thirty-year man. The army takes care of him, supports him, takes consistent note of his transgressions and punishes him, is the object of his love—and it most assuredly does not love Private Robert E. Lee Prewitt. In his world, the army is both church and God, the stockade its chapel. The pains of retribution satisfy Prewitt on several levels. At war with society, adrift from his religion, Prewitt needs a pattern to follow. The army provides that pattern.

Prewitt's God kills him. On his way back from Alma, trying to return to "G" Company, he is accosted by the military police. Technically a deserter, he is not known as Fatso's killer. A general amnesty is in effect, and a telephone call to First Sergeant Warden could have solved his AWOL problem, but, as usual, Prewitt acts with stubborn independence. He breaks away from the MP's, easily eluding them in the dark. When the spotlight comes on, however, he realizes that his God is angry; he stops, turns, and is struck by three shots fired at random in the dark.

Dying, Prewitt remembers Malloy's parting admonition. He concludes wryly, "Well, I learned it, Jack. I learned it." Prewitt feels no anger toward the MP's. They acted properly, with skill and dedication. "And these were the Army, too. It was not true that all men killed the things they loved. What was true was that all things killed the men who loved them. Which, after all, was the way it should be."[36]

When it comes, death is like the vision in "the Hole," familiar and comforting. He sees double in the same way, realizing that it really is not going to end, that what he had thought once long ago, before his mother's death, was true after all: there will be an endless chain of "decidings." "That made him feel good, the being right."[37]

Predestination, chance, or free will—Jones offers no conclusive proof for any as the cause of Prewitt's death. Given his character and predispositions, however, Prewitt's fate is

36. *Eternity*, p. 789.   37. Ibid., p. 791.

predictable from the moment of his transfer. He was a match-less soldier whose ability in every area earned respect—even from Fatso Judson and the guards, from First Sergeant Warden, from everybody who knew him. Prewitt is more than merely rebellious; he is driven to establish and maintain a state of opposition with the world. It reassures him that he is a special person, and it provides the security of limits and punishment that his residual sense of guilt demands, that his impotent religion cannot administer. Joining "The Profession," Prewitt finds God and church in one. He loves everything about the army, from the sensuous pleasures of firing during range week to daily barracks life, the routine of close-order drill, and all the off-duty avocations of the soldier. To extend his own logic, manifested in his request for a transfer, Prewitt had to make the army kill him because he wanted more than anything to be a soldier.

Prewitt's conception of himself was a vision of the super-lative soldier, the perfect warrior, to whom all the normal rules somehow did not apply. His own standard was almost impossibly high; if he could not be the best, and be acknowl-edged as the best, he would rather not be at all. This sentiment is complicated by Prewitt's incessant need for punishment, and his search for God. In the army he finds the answers. It is "something he really loves," and "it finally kills him," according to "The Malloy's" formula.

In spite of some weaknesses, *From Here to Eternity* is the best modern American war novel, one of the finest novels of the twentieth century. Jones does not have consistent success with dialogue, especially with Sergeant Warden. With the ex-ception of Prewitt, the characters are two-dimensional stereo-types, and, as has been noted, the women are not credible except as exaggerated types. Both Karen and Alma personify the enduring, infinitely resilient quality that human life per-sistently manifests. The novel's point of view shifts back and forth from that of the omniscient observer to interior mono-logue, leaving book and author virtually inextricable. Com-menting on this quality of the novel, Maxwell Geismar writes that Jones absorbed knowledge of the army "through his rebellious bones."[38] Mailer's integration of techniques from Dos Passos and Hemingway produces what Geismar refers to as "lit'r'y" polish and excellence. But his political treatise, *The Naked and the Dead*, remains an occasional piece, a call to arms against the imminent dangers of postwar fascism. Jones's great achievement delineates perfectly the plight of a single modern man trapped in the impersonal turbulence of society's transition from the weakening institutions of the past to the technological bureaucracy of an apparently omnipotent rationalism.

The spirit of the novel is best expressed in the rendition of Prewitt's final taps:

> The first note was clear and absolutely certain. There was no questioning or stumbling in this bugle. It swept across the quadrangle positively, held just a fraction of a second longer than most buglers hold it. Held long like the length of time, stretching away from weary day to weary day. Held long like thirty years. The second note was short, almost too short, abrupt. Cut short and too soon gone, like the minutes with a whore. Short like a ten-minute break is short. And then the last note of the first phrase rose triumphantly from the slightly broken rhythm, triumphantly high on the untouchable level of pride above the humiliations, the degradations.
>
> He played it all the way, with a pause and then hurried rhythm that no metronome could follow. There was no placid regimented tempo in this Taps. The notes rose high in the air and hung above the quadrangle. They vibrated there, caressingly, filled with an infinite sadness, an endless patience, a pointless pride, the requiem and epitaph of the common soldier. . . .[39]

Prewitt's final taps bears the unique mark of the man who plays it. Here, Jones finds the perfect similies, extracted from life in the service, perhaps not wholly translatable to anyone who has not lain in his bunk as a private soldier and listened quietly to this daily *memento mori*. Jones's vocabulary, varying sentence length, and use of consonants and vowels to control the prose rhythm match this passage perfectly to its subject. Emotionally, too, Jones catches the primary qualities

38. Maxwell Geismar, *American Moderns* (New York, 1958), p. 238.

39. *Eternity*, p. 218.

of the bugler in his playing. Prewitt the soldier stamps his personal mark of excellence and ineradicable individuality upon every act a soldier performs. The men who hear the last taps recognize his spirit modulating a routine call that normally means simply that it is time to turn off the lights. Prewitt manages to fill taps with all the elaborate complex of meanings that normally accrue only at funerals. By reminding men of the ultimate significance that reposes in aspects of life that they have come to take for granted, he reminds them of what it means to be human, and to be aware of it.

In this novel Jones successfully universalizes the experience of one man. Prewitt in the army personifies man in the modern world. His life and the lessons he learned were preparation for death, the traditional vocation of the tragic hero. Refusing to surrender his individual prerogatives, Prewitt retains in triumph over the naturalistic crush of events his invincible sense of human dignity. He remains to the end unconvinced that "what a man is dont mean anything at all."[40] James Jones's achievement is likely to loom larger as years pass because he expressed, almost a generation before it became a fact of American life, the crisis between the individual and the institutions that dominate society. Prewitt's astonishing intransigence is compounded of the tragic flaw, religious guilt, and a new element: he personifies the irrational romantic asserting himself against an increasingly monolithic technological society.

The three works examined so far—*The Beardless Warriors, The Big War,* and *From Here to Eternity*—are securely founded in traditional forms and themes. Their philosophic tones range from romantic intuition to pragmatism and existential humanism. But Joseph Heller's *Catch-22* (published in 1961) is in a class by itself. Other authors have used some of the elements that constitute Heller's masterpiece, but none approaches its convoluted complexity. In *Cannibals and Christians* Norman Mailer opines that a hundred pages randomly eviscerated from Heller's book would in no way impair its

40. Ibid., p. 210.

effect.[41] Richard Lehan and Jerry Patch complain in a critique of the novel that it should have been more scrupulously edited.[42] Both remarks suggest misreading, confirmed in the case of Lehan and Patch by other comments.

Catch-22's themes surface in apparently random snatches. It is a novel of education, and some of Mann's words on *The Magic Mountain* are helpful. Like Hans, Yossarian is a "shrewd but simple" searcher, perhaps even a "guileless fool," in quest of the Grail.[43] Too, his contemplative retreat is a hospital. Unlike Hans, Yossarian begins his adventure with a fictitious ailment (an imitation Prometheus in a really absurd universe?), but at the end Yossarian leaves the hospital, for the first time willingly, after a career of superlative malingering. If man is matter, a hospital is the only efficacious church. Elevated by the spiritual intensity of his experience, seer Yossarian gazes raptly at Snowden's dying body and finds it "easy to read the message in his entrails." The grim secret is that man *is* matter.[44] In *Catch-22*, the pervasive aura of Snowden's death and this final revelation affect Yossarian like Castorp's daily contact with the dying patients, his glimpse in the fluoroscope at the skeleton of his doomed cousin, and his shattering vision in the snow. Both Hans and Yossarian evoke Wordsworth's confirming vision on Mt. Snowdon at the conclusion of *The Prelude*, in each case ironically inverted.

The philosophical milieu of *Catch-22* differs radically, of course, from that of *The Magic Mountain*. Hans leaves the mountain sanitarium, in obedience to his "blood," to fight his nation's war; Yossarian flees the hospital and the insanity of war to his responsibilities as a rational human being. Yossarian finds himself, like Camus's hypothetical man, longing for reason in the face of the world's irrationality. The absurd is born of that confrontation, Camus says; it cannot exist if

41. Norman Mailer, *Cannibals and Christians* (New York, 1966), p. 117.
42. "*Catch-22*: The Making of a Novel," *Minnesota Review* 7 (1967): 239.
43. *Mountain*, pp. 724–28.
44. Joseph Heller, *Catch-22* (New York, 1961), pp. 429–30.

either element is absent.[45] Unlike Sisyphus, Yossarian opts out. Lehan and Patch comment on this element of the absurd, also mentioning the "ridiculous" absurd in Kafka's "over-structured and bureaucratic world where existence must be validated by an I.D. card." Irrationality and bureaucracy are omnipotent in *Catch-22*, and war is but an aspect of the greater absurdity, incorporating both elements—in execution and planning, respectively.

The themes in *Catch-22* parallel the idea of a shrewd fool, which immediately attaches to its picaresque hero. The incremental revelation of Snowden's death, the career of Milo Minderbinder, Orr's escape and his mysterious pact with the whore who beat him on the head with the heel of her shoe, the real nature of "Catch-22," and the myriad of lesser but supportive and coherent elements all maintain the novel's unique air. The separate gobbets combine to form a comprehensible form, displaying the requisite shape and substance of an absurd creation. Heller's treatment of time also sustains the feeling that all of the novel's multitudinous actions are happening, now.

It is difficult to track simple detail through the pages of *Catch-22*. This explains why Yossarian is referred to by one commentator as a navigator rather than a bombardier. He is the primary Yahoo, the one who actually toggles the bombs, a fact crucial to his final decision. One critical slip, which would bring a knowing smile to Yossarian's face, is Lehan and Patch's mistake in attributing to gallant, love-lorn Nately the murder of poor Michaela, the dim-witted, unattractive whorehouse maid. Aarfy kills Michaela; stupid, affable, vicious—he is the paragon of combat aircrewmen.[46] Also, the reader knows by the end of chapter 24 exactly why Yossarian shows up naked to receive his medal—not, as Lehan and Patch maintain, only at the novel's end.[47]

Let us trace the initiate's progress. Simple, he cannot understand why the fact that "they are trying to kill everybody" should assuage his personal anxieties in combat. His

45. Camus, *Sisyphus*, pp. 21–23.
46. *Catch-22*, pp. 361, 384–85, 408.
47. Ibid., p. 255.

career as a hospital patient frames Yossarian's education. In "real" time, as opposed to novelistic sequence, the first bit of truth comes at Lowry Field during an early stage of his chronic ailment. Incensed and scared when a strange set of parents mourn him as their son, a dying soldier, he is brought up short by the doctor's impatient rejoinder: "Of course you're dying. We're all dying. Where the devil else do you think you're heading?"[48]

Before Yossarian learned discretion, prior to the opening incident of the novel, he led his flight over the target for a second time, braving flak to win a DFC and a promotion to captain.[49] On a subsequent "milk run" the flak strikes back, and he acquires the validating wound of the hero, more authentic in this case than the pseudo-Promethean liver: "I lost my balls! . . . I lost my balls!"[50] But his scream is premature. Not exactly in the tradition of von Eschenbach's Parzival, nor as tragic as Jake Barnes, Yossarian is neither separated from his manly parts nor even rendered impotent. His bloodied nether limbs sustain a minor but adequate wound in the thigh, sufficient to secure hospitalization for his memorable encounters with Nurse Duckett.

His last excursion to the hospital crystallizes Yossarian's determination. Initiated by liberal gouts of Snowden's blood on his uniform, he vows never to wear a uniform again. After Nately's death, he walks backward, gun at the ready, determined to fly no more missions. Nately's ubiquitous whore, by this time an obvious personification of life itself, pursues Yossarian relentlessly. Her stab in the arm, following his tacit agreement to accept the trip home, sends him to the hospital for the final time. There he learns of Orr's epic voyage by life raft through the Straits of Hercules to Sweden, and is ecstatic. Yossarian patiently explains to Major Danby that the escapists, the true escapists, are those who allow the malign bureaucracy to run their lives; the strong man chooses to live on his own terms: "There's nothing negative about running away to save my own life."[51] Both species of the absurd are trying to deprive him of his life. Yossarian opposes the flow of ex-

48. Ibid., p. 181.
49. Ibid., p. 135–38.
50. Ibid., p. 284.
51. Ibid., p. 440.

ternal events in a manner almost worthy of Sisyphus, while incidentally keeping body and soul together.

Catch-22 is a hysterically funny book. Its black humor recalls Swift and the pages of the *Anatomy of Melancholy.* As Burton's Democritus points out, in a mad world, laughter is the only feasible response. The fighting men of this novel are direct descendants of the soldier as defined by Gulliver: "a Yahoo hired to kill in cold blood as many of his own Species, who have never offended him, as he possibly can."[52] Heller's is the humor of Mark Twain, the substratum of GI humor. In "Soliloquies on Masks," George Santayana notes that the comic response can handle situations too bleak for tragedy. Humor offers a safety valve for pressures that might otherwise unbalance reason.[53]

Dunbar's philosophy and Yossarian's reaction to Snowden's death demonstrate this qualitative relationship. Dunbar loved to do things he disliked and to associate with people he loathed because the resultant utter boredom made time slow down excruciatingly, thereby lengthening his life. So he played ping-pong and cards, and explained the intricate relationship of time and space to clods like Yossarian and Clevinger.

> You're inches away from death every time you go on a mission. How much older can you be at your age? A half minute before that you were stepping into high school, and an unhooked brassiere was as close as you hoped to get to Paradise. Only a fifth of a second before that you were a small kid with a ten-week summer vacation that lasted a hundred thousand years and still ended too soon. Zip! They go rocketing by so fast. How in the hell else are you ever going to slow time down?[54]

Looking at twenty-year-old Snowden's dying body Yossarian sees the answer to Dunbar's first question. Defeating all philosophers and their systems, death solves the time-space problem emphatically, if not neatly. At the instant the flak entered his body all space collapsed to a point of flickering conscious-

52. Jonathan Swift, *Gulliver's Travels and Other Writings*, ed. Ricardo Quintana (New York, 1958), p. 200.

53. George Santayana, in *Classic Essays in English*, ed. J. Miles (New York, 1965), pp. 314–21.

54. *Catch-22*, pp. 38–39.

ness within Snowden's expiring brain, and he is older than Lear, older than any living thing. With friendly efficiency, Yossarian treats the wrong wound, assuring Snowden that everything will be fine. Opening the flak-jacket, he sees "God's plenty" as the young airman's insides slither to the floor. It isn't the terrible carnage that bothers Yossarian. Snowden had stewed tomatoes for lunch, and Yossarian cannot abide stewed tomatoes. Turning aside, he vomits: "Ripeness was all."[55] In *Catch-22* the laughter is invariably tinged with hysteria, manic with vented frustration.

Some of the novel's humor derives from straight responses to complex questions, some from situational humor. When Milo asks what happened to Snowden, Yossarian answers: "He got killed."[56] And when Yossarian finds himself rolling around on top of Nately's whore, desperately defending himself from her knife, he is suddenly aware of an amorous rhythm to her writhing. Off-guard for a moment, he soon realizes that as one of her hands slips into his pants, the other gropes on the floor for the knife: "She still wanted to kill him!"[57] Literally, she still holds him personally responsible for Nately's death; symbolically, such is life. *Catch-22* is most serious when it is most comic.

A major element of Yossarian's environment stresses the total dehumanization of individuals by the imponderable processes of the technological bureaucracy that conducts the war effort. An accident of fate made (Major) an officer; the seamless logic of his name and rank precludes further promotion, or reduction. Doc Daneeka's "death" demonstrates the impact of data-processing efficiency, as does ex-PFC Wintergreen's status as one of the most powerful men in the theatre because of his access to the mimeograph machine. General Peckem's numerous suggestions that bombing lies under his jurisdiction (since it is indeed a very Special Service) results in all combat forces being transferred to that command, but only after Peckem's conniving gets him reassigned and General Scheisskopf commands Special Services. The war is no respecter of persons; its machine-logic takes words only at

55. Ibid., pp. 428–30.   57. Ibid., pp. 386–87.
56. Ibid., p. 257.

face value. Yossarian himself is the principal fugitive, unable to commit the irrevocable act until he learns there is no alternative. When he refuses to rejoin the air war, "he is jeopardizing his traditional rights of freedom and independence by daring to exercise them."[58]

The women of *Catch-22* are degraded, systematically. Nately's whore achieves symbolic stature, but only because she is the reverse image of Goethe's "eternal feminine." She does not lead Yossarian, she drives, pursues him. Life, as she demonstrates, will eventually kill you. She was generally bored, as were the men around her; and when Nately began to adore her most passionately, he lost her. Mrs. Daneeka readily joins the bureaucracy in authenticating her husband's death, because her fortune takes a dramatic turn for the material better at his "demise." Nurse Duckett remains "Nurse," despite her valuable and passionate attachment to Yossarian, who leaves her without regrets. Her chief merit is that Yossarian enjoyed making love to her with clothes on, more than to the vigorous naked whores of Rome. The whores personify the complete debasement of hope, creativity, and life itself. Aarfy's thoughtless, incidental murder of Michaela is a point of emphasis. All of the women, including frustrated Mrs. Scheisskopf and "marvelous" Dori Duz, are reduced to the purely recreational facet of their sexuality. Only the solace of their "divine fulcrum" attracts masculine attention in a world at war, intent on self-destruction.

Like any novel with ambition, *Catch-22* raises pithy questions of philosophical import: in wartime why do some live and others die? (chapter 8); what system is it that dispenses rewards, and punishments in the world? (chapter 17); if God is good and omnipotent, why is there pain in His universe? (chapter 18). Yossarian's education, however, is essentially completed during his quest to Rome, where he realizes the truth of that chameleon concept, the most irregular rule—Catch-22. Though he needs the final nudge of Orr's escape to give him the courage to act, he finds in Rome the answer to that tantalizing question.

58. Ibid., p. 396.

Minna Doskow rightly calls Yossarian's trip to Rome a descent into hell, in the classic tradition.[59] Successful, he brings from his encounter in Marchese Milo's personal Nighttown the sure knowledge that there is "no such thing" as Catch-22: "Catch-22 did not exist, he was positive of that, but it made no difference. What did matter was that everyone thought it existed, and that was much worse, for there was no object or text to ridicule or refute, to accuse, criticize, attack, amend, hate, revile, spit at, rip to shreds, trample upon or burn up."[60]

Ostensibly, consciously, intending to rescue "Nately's whore's kid sister," he brings back the vital knowledge that Catch-22 is the most powerful force in human affairs: it is an idea. The idea grows by logical extension in bureaucratic society, where people are trained to surrender their human prerogatives to processes and institutions. Each of the eight manifestations of Catch-22 that Yossarian encounters in the novel develops from that thesis. But the variant he hears in devastated Rome drives him to conclude that he inhabits a world in which power is the only morality. Sitting in the ruins an old woman tells Yossarian, "Catch-22 says they have a right to do anything we can't stop them from doing."

During the last hospital scene, the final pieces of the puzzle fall into place. Orr deliberately got himself shot down all those times so he could practice his final escape. The Roman whore pounded him on the head with her shoe because he wanted her to kill him. Orr's plan was unsuccessful, however, so he had to escape. Nately's whore lurks in the hallway, ready for immediate pursuit, but Yossarian knows now that he is totally responsible for his actions. The war is ruled by capricious irrationality—in the person of the new commanding general, Scheisskopf—and by the international, profit-motivated corporation—represented by Milo Minderbinder's new combine—which now includes even ex-PFC Wintergreen and all participants on both sides in the war. Education complete, Yossarian obeys the rational imperative.

59. "The Night Journey in *Catch-22*," *Twentieth-Century Literature*, 11–12 (1965–67): 186–93.
60. *Catch-22*, p. 400.

His previous exits from the hospital were executed under protest. Limping dramatically or protesting a malfunctioning organ, Yossarian had been reluctant to depart the sanctuary. Now he leaves, gladly. But unlike Hans Castorp, Yossarian heads for a refuge. How else can weak rationality cope with omnipotent insanity?

It is important to realize that *Catch-22* is not simply a blackly humorous, absurdly ingenious antiwar novel. Heller makes the point himself. In an interview devoted primarily to his play, *We Bombed in New Haven*, he mentioned *Catch-22*: "I'm not interested in the subject of war. I wasn't interested in the war in *Catch-22*. I was interested in the personal relationships in bureaucratic authority. It distressed me to see *We Bombed in New Haven* described as an anti-war play."[61] In Heller's play it is "inevitable" that people bomb themselves. In *Catch-22* Milo's famous bombing contracts reflect the same inevitable result of the alliance between business, bureaucracy, and misguided nationalism.

More than any of the novels previously discussed, *Catch-22* demonstrates the fact of alienation in the world. Not religious, sexual, or social guilt, but the fundamental alienation of people from both human reason and emotions. Yossarian's family problems are not an issue; neither are his country's national objectives. Vowing to live forever or die trying, he makes his own separate truce with the world, content to leave it, in his quest for a place where humanity can prevail. And, as Orr's success attests, the human mind is adequate to the task of saving itself.

In the twentieth century, war has become more pervasively a normal adjunct of life, so that writing about war is a way to write about life, prompting Heller's careful description of *Catch-22*. Technology is largely responsible for this, as is "progress." Both have magnified the impact of war on world society simply by increasing man's available power and providing him with world-wide instantaneous communications networks—the latter introducing what Marshall McLuhan calls the tribal complex into global relationships.

61. Quoted by Israel Shenker, *New York Times*, December 22, 1968, D1.

Anxiety and suppressed hysteria are rampant in *Catch-22*. In *Why Are We in Vietnam?* Norman Mailer has produced an American original, a work that carries these qualities to a ribald pinnacle of intensity. In tone, its genealogy can be traced back through the traditional romantic concern of technology versus nature, as delineated in Leo Marx's *The Machine in the Garden*, but in other respects *Why Are We in Vietnam?* is a native. Mailer combines elements of mythic hyperbole, the traditional frontier tall story, the venerable theme of initiation into nature and the mysteries of manhood, and America's involvement in Vietnam. It is a war novel in that it discusses a theory of the genesis of war. The thesis is that "progress" has developed a society and technological power-base in the United States that makes war a veritable necessity, and Vietnam just another place to go shooting.

Mailer mixes politics with art. Although genius in one area does not confer infallibility in another, in this study Mailer's politics will go unchallanged. He has, as usual, captured a vital characteristic of our age, which is structured and presented as the education of D.J. and Tex Hyde.

The book's sharp impact is due to a wild blend of style, structure, tradition, and precedent. The diction and style of Henry Miller and William Burroughs are Mailer's surface materials. His philosophical point of view stems from the Emersonian idea that through Nature man can somehow become reconciled to God and to his own nature—a concept Faulkner refuted at length. The novel's overall structure, however, is an adaptation of Faulkner's motifs and techniques, which consecutive readings of *Why Are We in Vietnam?* and "The Bear" will affirm.

Using a knife, Boon Hogganbeck killed the last great mythic bear within the contiguous United States in approximately 1940. Substitute "grizzer" for Old Ben, cast the others with appropriate regard for thematic resonances (discords, occasionally), and Mailer's book instantly assumes a stature and complexity beyond D.J.'s feverish recitation. Mailer's use of his predecessors' work compares with a talented priest of the mysteries intoning a germinal "O-o-m-m-m" in the Marabar Caves.

Faulkner goes into terrific detail, tracing the tangled pattern of racial mixture and human misery caused by white sexual license. The Jellicoe (D.J.'s) family bush is no less tangled and tawdry. And, as everybody knows, the inevitable mixed-blood, Tex Hyde, is a better man than D.J. will ever be, even though he is forever tainted with his mother's "sort of vile polluted cesspool Eenyen blood like Mexican. . . ."[62] It is more than faintly possible that Jellicoe genes lie submerged in the Hyde "slicky shit" gene-pool. The D.J. (Dr. Jekyll at times)-Tex Hyde relationship is complicated, something like a combination between that of Ike and Cass Edmonds and that of Lucas Beauchamp and Zack Edmonds.

Most of Faulkner's devices are here: the continuous S-curve of narrative time that eventually closes back on itself, revelation by bits and pieces, a "barmy" narrator, torrents of sexual excesses, racial hybridization, interior monologue, and even an adaptation of the Faulknerian "frozen-moment" technique of stasis, out of *Don Quixote*. But the hyped-up world of *Why* has no time for tableaux, so the action can only be slowed, something like the dreamy passage of Ike's great buck. Encountering "grizzer," D.J. and father Rusty hear the cannon-roar howl, and are "frozen like prisoners in the searchlight," the roles of hunter and hunted rudely reversed:

> And Rusty fired from behind and that animal didn't stop, it kept coming on down like a twelve-foot surf of comber bamming right for your head, and D.J.'s heart and his soul sweet angel bird went up the elevator of his body and all balls but flew out before he slammed bolt and fired again at grizzer not ten yards away flame of the muzzle meeting flame from grizzer's red flame ass red mouth, grizzer kerwhonked half in air from the blast, took leap, hop, howl, one mad bound off the trail, leaving awake of hot caves, gamy earth, fur went by so near, yeah, one flash of blood on his honey hide, and then he went booming down that mean crazy slope of the ledge, twisting D.J.'s neck, so fast was the move.[63]

Why Are We in Vietnam? is the detailed reminiscence of eighteen-year-old D.J., as he sits at table with Tex Hyde during a banquet the evening before their departure as draftees to see the "wizard, in Vietnam." Mailer uses inter-

62. *Why*, pp. 17–19.   63. Ibid., pp. 140–41.

chapters for D.J.'s editorial commentary; D.J. (disk jockey, delinquent juvenile, Dr. Jekyll) speaks as if taping the entire book, or as if everything is "on-tape" for humans before they are programmed to "decide." The central motif is the American mania for violent action, culminating in the epic hunt for "grizzers" in Alaska, the only remaining American frontier.

In the mainstream of tradition, D.J. is initiated by blood into the cult of violence, witnesses the mystery of death, finds communion with a kindred spirit, and undergoes a series of tests. He becomes, for better or for worse, a man. Mailer is as adept as Heller in using tradition against itself: his greatest satiric twist concerns the American tradition of hunting and our national obsession with weapons. Millionaire Rusty has decreed a hunting trip, and all hands scurry about to equip themselves. Their collective arsenal could easily have reversed the outcome at the Little Big Horn. "Well, now here, let's give a rundown on the guns for those good Americans who care. And those who don't, shit, they still get a chance to encounter a lot of meaningless names and numbers which they can then duly repeat at cocktail parties for new name grabbers."[64]

Thus, chapter 5 opens with a list of shoulder-fired armaments that runs, with absolute plausibility, for more than two pages, listing such seductive details as "Weatherly Magnum," "Winchester Model .270," "Weaver K-3," "Unertl," and "lever-action deer gun." For the fully initiated there are calibers from .250 to .404; alluring bullet-masses like 180 grains, scope powers and provocative muzzle velocities, "extra high up over 3 thou,"—all guaranteed to entice and mesmerize the ardent gun buff, and to establish the speaker's inside knowledge.[65] Mailer's shift in this novel from boxing metaphors to the sexier jargon of interior ballistics is a most logical one, considering the special subject of this piece.

Oddly enough, the quality of the man runs inversely proportional to the size of the weapon he carries. The smallest caliber man in the group is Rusty's number-one assistant, who is anxious to "expedite his dangerously dull slick-as-owl-shit ascent of the corporation ladder," but who trembles at the

64. Ibid., p. 77.   65. Ibid., p. 79.

thought of confronting "grizzer" with anything less than a nominally potent atom bomb. Accustomed to hunting only in the "office jungle," he plays the game, acquiring the most heroic weapon built since the Siege of Granada. He has:

> —get in line to look at it—from a white-haired riverboat string-tie type of an ex-oil well promoter, some friend of his wife's shiftless uncle's boss, a third-string Dallas Mafia type (don't even look how that gun got around to there or the Ford Foundation will be up and along for gropes) this gun being a used, indeed banged-up, African rhinoceros-hippo-elephant-soften-the-bullet-for-the-lion double-barrelled .600–.577. . . . Jeffery Nitro Express carrying a 900 grain bullet for shot #1, a 750 grain for shot #2, and a recoil guaranteed to knock a grand piano on its ass.[66]

D.J.'s education in the North begins immediately. Guide Big Luke can drop anything with a .250 rifle, and he is as much a man of the woods as Sam Fathers, but his worth is determined finally by the fact that he is also like "the President of General Motors or General Electric . . . he'd weigh just as much as Charley Wilson or . . . McNamara. . . ."[67] Half-breed Tex Hyde gets the best kills, and Rusty's assistants hit their game consistently in the rump, a phenomenon that D.J. gleefully attributes to "homeopathic magic, man." Virtually hitless, Rusty begins to slide.

D.J.'s insights become increasingly acute, particularly after the initiation, a hip extension of Sam Fathers's modest application of blood to Ike McCaslin. Whipping out a cup, Big Luke offers each boy a cup of the (wolf) blood to drink, then buries the head with accompanying ritual jabbering, imploring the wolf not to stir the "grizzers" up against them. Mailer's description captures the raunchy combination of untamed sexuality and wild power of the North that invests the animal's blood with "a taste of fish, odd enough, and salt, near to oyster sauce and then the taste of wild meat like an eye looking at you in the center of a midnight fire, and D.J. was on with the blood, he was half-sick having watched what Tex had done."[68]

66. Ibid., pp. 81–82.   68. Ibid., p. 69.
67. Ibid., pp. 46–47.

The relationship between father and son plays an important role in D.J.'s development. His parents are newly rich, gross, and possessed of sexual endowments beyond belief, a bit strange in their employments. Father and son steal away from the party for a private seance with "grizzer," each badly needing a kill to reinforce his sagging prestige. White man, American, Texan, industrialist, conservative, middle-aged stud and father—Rusty has yet to prove to the assembled party that he is as good as God intended him to be. D.J. is simply battling Tex's record of success. They encounter bear tracks that indicate "some fast dark boxcar size of beast [is] moving around somewhere in relation to them."[69] D.J. smells death and remembers when, as a hapless five-year-old, he interrupted his parents making the beast with two backs. Only his mother's intervention saved his life. Now, Rusty again earns his son's undying enmity by lightly claiming that it was his shot that put their nine-hundred-pound "grizzer" away. Feeling homicidal under mounting pressure to take vengeance on his father, D.J. wakes Tex in the night and they steal away together.

Mailer's description of this randiest of all initiations relegates the others to pale obscurity. Ike McCaslin left behind watch and compass, but these boys start out virtually mother-naked, plodding up the slopes of the Brooks Range to commune with the North. They relent slightly, but take only necessities, no weapons. Climbing, they are slowly freed of the "mixed shit" of their civilized lives. White-hot fear in the face of nature sears it away. Mailer warms to his task, citing Goethe, Maxwell, Rousseau, Volta, the earth's magnetic field, super-conductivity, and the perpetually ringing circuits that cryogenics have made possible—all lashed together by a vocabulary redolent of Burroughs and Miller, and cemented by sexual metaphors in every line. Tuning in to their long-forgotten natural frequencies the boys feel a surge of—something. D.J. reels off their experiences in terms of a sexual, magnetic over-volt-charged force-field (oversoul, updated) centered at the earth's poles.

69. Ibid., pp. 135–36.

Prior to his epiphanies, Ike saw Buck and the Bear. But now Nature shows her power less subtly. To these boys it's Darwin modulated by de Sade and Krafft-Ebing. In rapid succession they see the parade of Alaskan wildlife: wolf vs eagle, grizzer vs caribou, fox, ram, and the stately moose— featuring three agons of stark will and lust for killing. Like a psychodelic visual distortion of Job's seance with God, the message comes through, loud, Man. God *is* a beast.[70]

Saturated by the powerful forces of nature under the poles, steeped in and permeated by the over-gauss of the force-field of Earth, the boy's fractured adolescent minds are welded to a new manic perfection. The experience provides the final animal voltage necessary to send them over the military crest of manhood, even by stern "Takes-ass" standards. Each biting his finger (they have no knives), the two become blood-brothers. "All passion spent," they return to camp and the expedition returns to Dallas.

All this was two years ago. The boys were charged, but by what? As narrator D.J. reminds the reader, "You never know what vision has been humping you through the night."[71] This passage preserves the text of their communication from beyond: ". . . Prince of Darkness, lord of light, they did not know; they just knew telepathy was upon them, they had been touched forever by the North . . . and the deep beast whispering Fulfill my will, go forth and kill. . . ."[72] At the fiercest pitch of their experience, D.J. realized with a shock that "God was a beast, not a man."

Mailer explains the Manichean nature of their initiation by referring directly to their environment and their human heritage. A passage from Emerson's "Nature" supplies the necessary perspective for evaluating the seriousness of Mailer's rebuttal.

The problem of restoring to the world original and eternal beauty is solved by the redemption of the soul. The ruin or the blank that we see when we look at nature is in our own eye. The axis of vision is not coincident with the axis of things, and so they appear not transparent but opaque. The reason why the world

70. Ibid., pp. 180–97.   72. Ibid., p. 204.
71. Ibid., p. 208.

lacks unity, and lies broken and in heaps, is because man is dis-
united with himself. He cannot be a naturalist until he satisfies
all the demands of the spirit. Love is as much its demand as
perception. Indeed, neither can be perfect without the other. In
the uttermost meaning of the words, thought is devout, and
devotion is thought. Deep calls unto deep. But in actual life, the
marriage is not celebrated. There are innocent men who worship
God after the tradition of their fathers, but their sense of duty
has not yet extended to the use of all their faculties. And there
are patient naturalists, but they freeze their subject under the
wintry light of the understanding. Is not prayer also a study of
truth,—a sally of the soul into the unfound infinite? No man
ever prayed heartily without learning something. But when a
faithful thinker, resolute to detach every object from personal
relations and see it in the light of thought, shall, at the same
time, kindle science with the fire of holiest affections, then will
God go forth anew into the creation.[73]

The last chapter of *Why Are We in Vietnam?* begins with
a sentence that indicts the "parsimony and genuine greed of
all those fucking English, Irish, Scotch, and European weeds,
transplanted to North America, that sad deep sweet beauteous
mystery land of purple forests, and pink rock, and blue water,
Indian haunts from Maine to the shore of California, all
gutted, shit on, used and blasted, man, cause a weed thrives
on a cesspool. . . ."[74] Mailer describes the pollution of the
North American continent by the filth and waste of the "new-
comers," who have distorted even the magneto-psychic-
telepathic field that unites the poles and should unify all men.
Their collective lusts and prayers of greed surge through the
ether: "—oh, God, let me hump the boss' daughter, let me
make it, God, all going up through the M.E.F. [magnetic-
electric field] cutting the night air, giving a singe to the dream
field, all the United Greedies of America humping up that old
rhythm, turning the dynamo around, generating, just cut
through that magnetism and go, boy, and God got to give it
to the Greedies . . .—so the Devil feeding them from one side
and God having to juice man from the other."[75]

During the 1830s Emerson saw the growing hostility between man and nature, but asserted that the innocent, patient

73. Ralph W. Emerson, *Selections from Ralph Waldo Emerson*,
ed. Stephen E. Whicher (Boston, 1960), p. 55.
74. *Why*, pp. 205–6.   75. Ibid., p. 206.

naturalist of good faith could redeem himself by repairing his own disunity of self, thereby achieving "redemption of the soul." Mailer's vision of the initiation of young men into the world of the twentieth century is blackly pessimistic, cloacal. The disunity is irrevocable; there is only slight communication. Rusty and D.J. communicate only when locked in competition, competition bordering on mortal combat, always in the presence of death or with the imminent possibility of death. The machine age has shut man off from himself, altering the once-beautiful face of nature so that the final line of communion with the transcendental spirit is utterly useless, clogged with garbage.

D.J. and Tex are young enough to retain an essential susceptibility to the message of unravished nature, but their experience is terrifying. Reconciliation is no longer possible. Perhaps once a "foster-child" of earth, as Wordsworth wrote, man, in Mailer's vision, is now an abject prisoner of a system he has perverted with his own offal. Emerson said that all materialists will become idealists, and that no idealist could become a materialist. His optimistic forecast is drowned out by the chop of "Cop Turd" blades, the thunder of gun-fire, and the chatter of radios. The boys saw in the face of nature only the raw power, none of the beauty. Spiritually maimed, though somewhat aware of it, they wait for the next action: "We're off to see the wizard in Vietnam."[76]

Using Dallas as a microcosm of modern America, Mailer evokes memories of the violence that killed John F. Kennedy. Militant radicals, police power, and industrial wealth at its worst combine to create the milieu wherein D.J. and Tex are produced. "Toynbee coefficient" disastrously low, the man of modern "syphilization" (a most logical variant of Melville's "snivelization") talks and acts only in terms of violence and the grossest sexuality. He has no faith either in himself or in God, Who is presumably busy fending off the perpetual Manichean challenge. The only hope lies in things and in action.

Mailer's novel expresses in explicit contemporaneous language a conclusion described in Leo Marx's *The Machine*

76. Ibid., p. 208.

in the Garden (subtitled, *Technology and the Pastoral Ideal in America*): "American writers seldom, if ever, have designed satisfactory resolutions for their pastoral fables. The power of these fables to move us derives from the magnitude of the protean conflict figured by the machine's increasing domination of the visible world."[77] The interaction of man, technology, and nature has in some way irreparably distorted communication beyond the "visible world." In Mailer's version nature itself is so afflicted that only the "deep beast" speaks to man: "You never know what vision has been humping you. . . ."[78]

Strong signature characteristics of the *Bildungsroman* link these five novels. All of the protagonists are questers. Thomas Mann's remarks on *The Magic Mountain* demonstrate the virtually inseparable relationship between the Grail motif and the nominal *Bildungsroman*. In four instances the immediate environment is a wasteland, either the midst of war, or in the case of D.J. the product of progress. And it can be supported that Prewitt too inhabits a wasteland—certainly in the moral sense.

There is surprising consistency from book to book on two salient qualities. Without exception, the questers proceed incrementally in their acquisition of knowledge, prompted by visions or moments of revelation, and each visits the "other world" of "night and death." Hackermeyer reaches two moments of crisis in caves: his pact with Cooley and the nightmare, after which he prays for death. His passage into the other world occurs when he is knocked unconscious during an attack, then comes to, and, finding that he is now behind enemy lines, exchanges uniforms with a dead German. He returns to triumph, with a prisoner in hand and the destruction of a German mortar-crew to his credit. And in the process of saving Cooley he is knocked unconscious, nearly killed, awaking literally to a new world.

Prewitt's visions are crucial to his progress. The third and

77. Leo Marx, *The Machine in the Garden* (New York, 1968), p. 364.

78. *Why*, p. 208.

most important comes to him in "the Hole," where he lies effectively dead for three symbolic days. Dying, he realizes that there is to be an endless chain of "decidings" in the world of death, confirming the hint of his earlier experience. Alan Newcombe's trial of passage from literature to life is marked primarily by his joltingly intense affair with Helen and the moment that he is forced to correlate the face of war, the taste of bread, and his memories of Helen as all belonging to the same category of experience: to desire Helen is to accept the rest. The war on Fanerahan is a place of trial and death, as any war is a place of "night and death," to use Mann's characterization.

The last two works are remarkable for their explicit adherence to the overall pattern, as mutually defined by Miss Weston and Mann. Yossarian's great moment of revelation and of decision comes in his last visit to the hospital, obviously his "Chapel." Peering at Snowden's mangled body, he becomes a priest, marked with the blood of this human victim. And, as Miss Doskow points out, his quest to find "Nately's whore's kid sister" is a descent into hell. Like Prewitt he retrieves the core of the truth he seeks. *Why Are We in Vietnam?* is a veritable catalogue of the initiatory pattern. D.J. seeks to "help" the old king (Rusty), and though he does not save his life, as Hackermeyer does for his surrogate father, D.J.'s rounds into "grizzer" do much to improve the old man's vitality and prestige before he returns to the "CCCC-and-P" wasteland. Previously marked with blood (the wolf's), D.J. helps in the primary task of the Alaskan quest: to slay the great beast. Mailer's inventory of weapons, and the detailed discussions thereof, are worthy of the hoary tradition of Anglo-Saxon weaponry-anatomizing. Finally, Mailer makes it plain that Alaska is "another world," although not in the exact sense of Mann's definition.

The role of humor in this group of novels is intriguing. Each of the protagonists qualifies as guileless, or as shrewd fool. Hackermeyer's story, however, is utterly without humor except for some remarks by Guthrie, the only one of his close companions to survive the war. Prewitt's contact with humor is the gallows variety of the stockade. Basically simple, he remains impractical, even idealizing his beloved whore, who like Nately's indifferent love, is bored unto death with him until his ordeal. But Maggio's tough humor sees him through and out of the Army. Jay O'Neill provides some comic relief in *The Big War*. He, too, survives, but over-educated Newcombe and stoic Danny Kantaylis are killed.

Heller and Mailer both exploit the potential of black humor expertly. Consider the ritual wound of the Quester: Yossarian sustains a close call in the thigh; and D.J., though unmarked by the Alaskan ordeal, bears on his posterior the permanent imprint of Rusty's dentures—a scar that commemorates an epic football confrontation (modern gladiatorial jousting) on the lawns of home. Mailer's epic satire and catalogues of mythic exaggeration, Heller's ironic distortion of traditions, his clever use of specialized jargon like "special services," the absurd logic of the dying-soldier gambit—all hint at the condition best reflected by the grotesquely distorted figures that inhabit their novels: the human predicament may well have passed the point of no-return.

Both novels illustrate powerfully man's alienation from the world and the alienation of individuals from each other. In these books, the traditional cohesive forces in society are either totally absent or vitiated to the point of being inconsequential. Prewitt's Calvinistic spectre is the only substantial vestige of conventional religion to be found. Hackermeyer's guilt is attributable solely to his performance in the world. In Yossarian's world the family is not worth mentioning, and the church is a dim, fading caricature, personified by the chaplain. Men like Luke, the super-guide and expert killer, are priests of the modern mysteries. In *Catch-22* and *Why Are We in Vietnam?* technology literally explodes on the scene, fragmenting society beyond repair.

The novels also reflect a changing social and literary milieu in both structure and point of view. As the philosophical tone shifts from confident pragmatism to resignation to exuberant hysteria, structure and plot give way in precedence to characterization and incident. Earlier novels, the epic, and traditional romanticism are replaced by the absurd, by hyperbole, and by black humor. And D.J.'s hammering "Intro

Beep" commentary pounds out the warning of the schizoid split-psyche, the questionable narrator who so frequently dares readers of modern literature to believe—one way or the other—the tale recited to them.

When dealing specifically with a father-son relationship, the modern American war novel maintains and perhaps heightens the traditional literary representation of strife and irreconcilability. Fathers are not merely negligent or absent; some actively persecute their sons, although society itself also contributes to the problem. Among this group of novels, the manifestations are numerous. Hackermeyer and two of the young men who are killed beside him are from broken homes, and each suffers from a father who has abdicated his responsibilities. When Prewitt leaves home after his mother's death, he is content to let his father stay in jail. In *The Big War*, Jay O'Neill is orphaned in infancy by an automobile accident; Alan Newcombe's father is totally absorbed in financial affairs; and Danny's father is senile. Mailer's Rusty and D.J. "go at it hammer and tongs." In having D.J. almost decide to kill the old man rather than the "grizzer," Mailer simply accentuates the problem inherent in the modern American situation.

The war novel consistently sustains this thesis of American family life. Deceived by everyone around him, the protagonist of David McCuish's *Do Not Go Gentle*, learns that his father was involved in an adulterous relationship for several years. Years in the mines kill the father prematurely, but Norm remains bitter. His critical failure in combat is that he fails to save his bullying squadleader, an obvious analogue for his dead father. Evincing signs of the pathological rages that possess Dos Passos's Chrisfield, Norm renounces life and returns to combat, finding refuge in its close relationships. Private Willy of Boyd Cochrell's *The Barren Beaches of Hell*, also orphaned by the automobile, survives combat untouched because he has learned to expect nothing but trouble from life and nothing but disregard or treachery from people. And so it goes. Leon Uris's *Battle Cry* is virtually the only war novel to depict a happy resolution of the problem. The least significant work of this group, and apparently written with the movies in mind, *Battle Cry* shows Danny Forester returning from the holocaust of the Pacific war, wounded but intact, perhaps salvaged by his firm family ties.

Like Huck Finn, Ike McCaslin, Augie March, Chief Broom of Ken Kesey's *One Flew over the Cuckoo's Nest*, and "Giles Goat Boy, Son of WESCAC,"—these protagonists endure the rigors of initiation into American life, characterized by morbid variations of the struggle of father and son to understand each other. If not orphaned or abandoned young, they watch the male parent decay before their eyes or are tormented by him until the final break occurs.

Major aspects of both Mann's definition of *Bildungsroman* and Miss Weston's delineation of Grail literature abound in each of the war novels. Of particular relevance is this passage from *The Quest of the Holy Grail*, which parallels almost exactly Mann's comments on the essence of *The Magic Mountain*:

> Regarded, then, from the ritual point of view, it seems clear that the Grail Quest should be viewed primarily as an initiation story, as a search into the secret and mystery of life; it is the record of an initiation *manqué*. The Quest, properly speaking, begins only when the hero, having failed at his first unpremeditated visit to the Castle to fulfill the tests to which he has been subjected, sets out with the deliberate intention of finding the vanished Temple of The Grail, and fulfilling the conditions which shall qualify him to obtain full knowledge of the marvels he has beheld.[79]

Of all the secular literature to which the phrase "initiation *manqué*" can be applied, none is more suitable than the fictional theme of a young man going to war, though a slight modification is required. As the Grail hero attempts to restore vitality to the old king and fertility to the land, so young soldiers in every age are sent to indemnify with their lives the mistakes and sins of preceding generations, whose acts precipitate the crises that only blood can resolve.

79. Weston, *Quest*, p. 95.

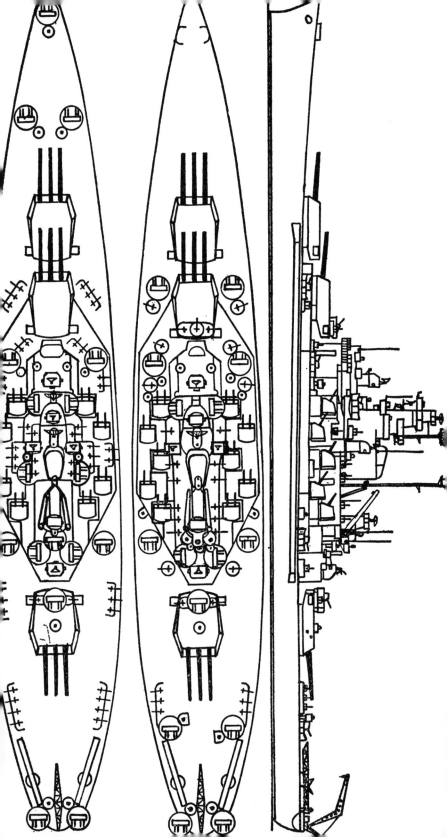

3.

THE LITERATURE OF COMMAND

The major novels of World War I deal primarily with enlisted men and junior officers. Hemingway's Lieutenant Henry; Dos Passos's beleaguered artist, John Andrews; Faulkner's dying pilot, Donald Mahon; the sacrificed battalions of *Paths of Glory*; Hicks, the persevering, inconspicuously gallant hero of *Through the Wheat*—these are men who fight without knowledge of the larger political issues, men who are ignorant of strategy. Their art and end is tactics: individual and small-unit struggles for survival. They fight to defeat the enemy, to preserve their own lives, and to gain the immediate objectives specified in their orders.

Many of the better war novels written since World War II, however, focus on the high-ranking military commander. Whereas in the early novels general officers were merely undifferentiated, functionalized creatures of the environment that wars inevitably produce, these later works portray commanders whose personal and professional attributes, augmented by the enormous power of the modern armies they command, produce implications that reach beyond the battlefield, implications sometimes not dissipated by war's end.

As technology and weaponry advance, the fact that modern war is an exercise of total national power increasingly becomes part of the consciousness of anyone who writes about war. So it is not surprising that many of the better war novels written in recent years should center upon military commanders, figures who wield the ultimately uncompromising power: military force. In *Aspects of the Novel*, E. M. Forster suggests that a great part of the interest in the "people" of novels lies in the fact that the reader, speaking of the conventional novel at least, may derive some solace from a creation that does "suggest a more comprehensible and thus a more manageable human race . . . [giving] the illusion of perspicacity and power."[1] The illusion is one in which both reader and writer are free to participate vicariously.

Contemporary novelists of the first rank have been attracted to the subject of command. James Gould Cozzens won a Pulitzer Prize in 1949 for *Guard of Honor*, which brought proper attention to his work for the first time. The novel's complex plot and intricate network of human relationships emphasize his concern with mature, upright, ethical men caught between the ideal and the actual in human affairs. Norman Mailer's *The Naked and the Dead* appeared the same year. (His best work subsequently has dealt with social and political commentary, merely emphasizing the true thrust of his first novel.) Herman Wouk won a Pulitzer Prize in 1952 for *The Caine Mutiny*, which combines the novel of education with a perceptive description of the human and environmental forces converging on men who exercise wartime command. Thirteen years after winning a Pulitzer Prize for *The Late George Apley*, John P. Marquand turned his analysis of upper middle class society to the army, with *Melville Goodwin, USA*, published in 1951.

Two journalists have also published novels of commanders, based essentially on their own experiences. James Bassett was Admiral Halsey's public relations officer for most of World War II. A lifetime newspaperman, Bassett was a political analyst for the *Los Angeles Times* when *Harm's Way* was published in 1962. Melvin Voorhees wrote *Show Me a Hero* (published in 1954) as the result of his experiences as deputy information officer for the Eighth Army in Korea. Both books are superior war novels, obviously influenced by the interplay of strong personalities with the unpredictable matrix of military and political forces during war.

The novels of command develop two primary types of commander. The first, and most common, is a nominally benign figure, perhaps endowed with almost superhuman will, who is motivated by laudable, purely professional and patriotic considerations. The second type exhibits sinister tendencies: he is cerebral and too conscious of the potent po-

1. E. M. Forster, *Aspects of the Novel* (New York, 1954), p. 64.

litical implications of military power. Some commanders of this second group entertain specific political ambitions; others simply try to use political influence to enhance their own military careers. The truly malignant seek to merge political and military power.

In some of the novels of command there is a clear contrast between officers; in others only one type appears. I have categorized the novels to be discussed by the dominant tendency of each work. In some cases, such as with Brigadier General Slater in James Jones's *From Here to Eternity*, a brief cameo incident is sufficient to establish the parameters. In the first category—that of the benign, patriotic commander—I include *Guard of Honor* (1948), William W. Haines's *Command Decision* (1946), *Melville Goodwin, USA* (1951), *Show Me a Hero* (1954), and *Harm's Way* (1962). The second group—the sinister and cerebral commanders—includes *The Naked and the Dead* (1948), Stefan Heyn's *The Crusaders* (1948), and *From Here to Eternity* (1951).

Several other books frame this section. *The Caine Mutiny* (published in 1951) is a perceptive study of individual reactions to command; it also describes the maturation of Willie Keith. I include it here because it examines wartime command at an intermediate level and emphasizes the flaws that prevent men from rising to the eminence of flag rank, or even preclude their survival at lower levels. *The Caine Mutiny* is a logical place to begin examining books that chronicle the development of generals and admirals. A discussion of Anton Myrer's second war novel, *Once an Eagle* (published in 1968), concludes this chapter. It places in opposition "good" and "evil," as personified by two general officers, in a culmination of trends indicated in the preceding novels. Myrer surveys the history of military power in American foreign policy, while studying closely the kind of man most likely to succeed in the modern world.

The novels of command display several common denominators. Almost without exception the man who achieves flag rank is, compared to other men, exceptionally strong-willed and confident. Following a contemporary novelistic pattern characteristic of "success" in other fields, commanders frequently forfeit marital concord and sexual tranquility as "hostages to fortune." The "good" figures are generally more than merely adequate sexually; the "evil" characters are almost uniformly disturbed sexually or are virtually asexual.

These novels are consistently dramatic in structure and technique. Nominally concerned with the climax of a series of actions, they also adhere to other attributes of Aristotelian drama. Within the scope of their movements, flag officers are powerful and their judgments crucial. Defects of character or errors in judgment invariably produce serious consequences. Events build toward a climactic act or decision, from which flows the dénouement, a revelation of the results. Information accrues through dialogue or variants of the interior monologue, a contemporary equivalent of the soliloquy. Pure narrative description is minimal, and judgments are generally those of a limited observer, merely a participant in the action or a bystander on the sidelines of the main events. Since novels have become the characteristic genre of our century, it is not surprising to see many signs of epic and dramatic conventions appearing in these novels of powerful and attractive wartime figures. The necessity of choice and the individual's struggle in determining his final course is consistently near the center of each novel's action. The effect is to emphasize the enormous responsibility that accompanies great power.

In contrast to the novels of World War I, these works exhibit a uniform awareness of power in nonmilitary manifestations. The flag officer personifies the most obvious power: military force. His actions, indeed, the mere fact of his existence and the need for it, make him a focal point for political pressures or influence, and for the collective interest of the "fourth estate." This triad of power appears in virtually every command novel, though political factors are pervasive. The press, or literary figures, and politicians represent society; they may confer standards of conduct or merely comment on action, like the choruses of Sophocles or Euripides. The personality and private life of the commander also influence the situation, but these (and all other) considerations are subordinated to military affairs, his immediate concern.

The change in milieu explains the shift in emphasis from the novels of World War I. The scope and duration of America's involvement in World War II, along with the exponential growth in the power of modern weapons, made military commanders the subject of more continuing interest than in any period since the Civil War. The intermittent wars in Korea and Vietnam and a generally inflammable world situation have sustained that interest.

The novels are, of course, fiction, and none of their characters is a direct reproduction of an actual commander. Certain definite associations, however, can be established. In *Once an Eagle,* the exploits of General Sam Damon on two occasions parallel specific acts of general officers whose direct action in close combat influence the course of a battle: Lt. Gen. Robert L. Eichelberger at Buna-Gona in the Pacific war, and Maj. Gen. William F. Dean in helping to prove the efficacy of newly developed antitank weapons against the North Koreans at Taejon. Melvin Voorhees's Lt. Gen. Lark Logan echoes the sentiments of Lt. Gen. Matthew B. Ridgeway's letter to the Eighth Army in January 1951, speculating about the quality of American life and America's ability to succeed against sustained, determined opposition. The dedication of James Bassett's novel about a hard-nosed fighting admiral mentions Adm. William F. Halsey.

But the two most prominent patterns in modern war novels as a body are those derived from Gen. George S. Patton and Gen. Douglas MacArthur. Patton's flamboyant mannerisms, his impressive record of combat command, and his uncompromising refusal to muzzle his remarks about peers and superiors imprinted his name in the American consciousness. Such literary figures as General Farrish of *The Crusaders*, John Marquand's Melville Goodwin, and General Beal of J. G. Cozzens's *Guard of Honor* reflect aspects of the Patton image.

General MacArthur is the most striking figure in modern American military history. Having performed with unique brilliance at every level of command from first captain of the corps of cadets to chief-of-staff of the army, he "returned" to the Philippines, presided over the reconstruction of Japan, and commanded the United Nations forces in Korea. From the audacious landing at Inchon, he moved north, close to the border of China. His subsequent easy arrogation of Olympian prerogatives in exercising the authority of his command is history, as are his public evidences of political ambition. Characters in several novels evoke his memory: Mailer's General Cummings, General Logan's supreme commander in *Show Me a Hero*, and General Massengale of *Once an Eagle*.

Patton and MacArthur appear to have contributed most prominently to the literature of military figures. Stereotypes or caricatures derived from obvious facets of their reputations and public performances apparently served to polarize the thoughts of authors who may have written without specific commanders in mind, but who sought to universalize their statements on warfare and its impact on society.

Such statements, however, have not been confined to fiction. In March 1969, historian Arthur Schlesinger, Jr., essayed to put the nation on the *qui vive* concerning what he termed the "new warrior class" in the United States. In an article written for *Harper's Magazine* Schlesinger quotes J. A. Schumpeter, who suggests that the instinct for physical combat is fading in the modern world, and that national proclivities toward imperialism are becoming similarly attenuated. Schumpeter defines imperialism as "the objectless disposition . . . to unlimited forcible expansion." His prime example is ancient Egypt, where the armies, originally organized and motivated by conventional national motives for aggression, eventually created wars to justify their own existence and to perpetuate their own domestic supremacy. From this development grew the elite warrior class. Schumpeter concludes that the affluent and virtually self-sufficient United States is the nation least likely to manifest aggressive tendencies in the twentieth century.[2]

Mr. Schlesinger challenges Schumpeter's premise on the grounds that it fails to consider the effects of a protracted Cold War between massive industrial states. Such subtle but

2. Arthur M. Schlesinger, Jr., "USA/USSR: The End of the Age of Superpowers," *Harper's Magazine*, March 1969, pp. 41–49.

deadly conflict "might," Schlesinger contends, "produce new structural elements and organizational forms oriented towards war, *a new warrior class*, a new form of imperialism" (emphasis added).[3] As proof, he enumerates instances of crucial presidential decision-making, from the administration of Franklin Roosevelt to the Kennedy era, stressing the increasing influence of military advisers and a corresponding decline in the prestige of civil aides. There is a new imperialism, Schlesinger warns, and the "active carriers" of the new menace are "most particularly our military leaders . . . who . . . have conned both executive and legislative branches of the government into voting enormous military appropriations, and into building enormous military installations, largely irrelevant in the missile age, all over the world. . . ."[4] Not impugning the motives or the essentially good will of the warriors, Schlesinger agrees that their reasons are purely military, adding that it is their particular inclination to "invoke the emotions of virility and patriotism to strengthen their cases."

The validity and coherence of Schlesinger's argument are not at issue here. A strong public assertion that the condition exists, however, is of more than passing interest. The fact that an influential historian and adviser of presidents should enunciate the warning is particularly significant.

Many of the novels discussed in this chapter include implicit expressions of a similar apprehension, more clearly articulated. The greatest threat comes from a highly intelligent, flag-rank officer with ambitions beyond the military, who sees the enormous potential of political power. The difficult process of establishing a balance between the two forces is a continuing, clearly defined issue. Mr. Schlesinger's remarkable hypothesis merely emphasizes that the issue, raised in literature, is not merely the stuff of literary supposition; it is a part of the contemporary dialogue among major elements of American society.

The Caine Mutiny serves as an admirable prologue to a discussion of the literature of command. Concerned with the lower echelons of command, this novel touches on numerous

3. Ibid., p. 42.   4. Ibid., p. 43.

areas common to novels of flag-rank officers. Those who command the *Caine*, including Willie Keith himself, confront the same basic issues, though on a smaller scale.

Although there are well-handled spots of humor in *The Caine Mutiny*, this is a serious book. The humor ingratiates Willie to the reader and emphasizes his initial approach to life. Not really a picaro, Willie sees the world much as some of Conrad's memorable figures do. The wartime experience changes him. Like Conrad, Wouk uses a ship for background and unity—here a small warship. It is an ideal setting: there is no escape from incessant contact with men under constant duress, no relief from or for the man who commands.

Closing his military career, Willie muses about Commander Queeg, beginning to understand: "Our disloyalty made things twice as tough for Queeg and for ourselves; drove him to his worst outrages and made him a complete psychological mess. . . . Queeg conned the *Caine* for fifteen months, which somebody had to do, and which none of us could have done."[5] Though he still sounds like Holden Caulfield, Willie matured aboard the *Caine*; he learned the burdens that command imposes.

Six men commanded the *Caine*. Commander de Vriess drove his crew to consistent tactical excellence, but was blunt, profane, and grossly remiss in discipline and maintenance. Maryk acted only after continuous goading by Tom Keefer. Though his motives were irreproachable, his act of seizure ended his hopes for a naval career. Thinking back, Willie is now not sure that Queeg would not have acquiesced to reason in a few additional moments, or that the change of course was truly a necessity. The "marvelous academy man" who replaced Maryk revitalized the *Caine* for Tom Keefer's brief tenure, confirming the hope that things occasionally work the way they ought.

Willie finds the experience puzzling. In comparing the civilian world he left and the universe of the navy, he, like Lewis Carroll's Alice, has difficulty discriminating illusion from reality. In the opening chapter, "Through the Looking

5. Herman Wouk, *The Caine Mutiny* (New York, 1951), pp. 463–64.

Glass," Willie's mother delivers him to the navy in a Cadillac. Spoiled and pampered, Willie epitomizes his nation. He is another in the long line of protagonists in modern fiction whose fathers have slighted their responsibilities. At the novel's end, immediately prior to the decommissioning ceremony that turns the *Caine* to official scrap, Willie reads in the *Pensées*: "Life is a dream, a little more coherent than most."[6] Moving back into mother's Cadillac he finds that like Alice's kitten, she is unchanged, still uncomprehending. She would have Willie return completely to the life interrupted by the war. The war, her husband's death, and everything about the external world fail to make any impression on her. But Willie is different. Wouk's use of the "Alice" gambit is effective, more so because of its ambiguity: which is the "real" twentieth-century world?

Of all those he observed, Willie profits most by the wild inconsistencies of literatus Tom Keefer. In their first serious conversation Keefer dazzles Willie with his philosophy of naval organization and operations: an ingeniously conceived system of fragmented functions that enables a few "brilliant boys" at the top to rise uncontested to high command on the efforts of the legions who toil ignominiously beneath them. But when Willie inherits the code files from Keefer, he finds that the novelist concentrated on his book, merely stacking decoded messages randomly in drawers.[7]

The Keefer brothers are a study in contrasts. The split psyche, the fragmentation of twentieth-century man, the simple fact that there are two alternatives in any moral dilemma—Tom and Roland demonstrate it well. Of Roland, who dies struggling to save his ship from fire, Tom says ambivalently, first, that he had good instincts, and then later, that the military schools he attended must have had something to do with his performance. Tom murmurs with prophetic irony that a man never knows until he is challenged how he will react. Having driven Maryk to the point of keeping a book on Queeg, he abandons Maryk's projected visit to the admiral at the very threshold, aboard the mighty *New Jersey*: "Can't you feel the difference between the *New*

6. Ibid., p. 482.　　7. Ibid., p. 224.

Jersey and the *Caine*? This is the Navy here, the real Navy. Our ship is a floating booby-hatch. Everybody's asiatic on the *Caine*, and you and I must be the worst of all, to think that we could get away with pulling Article 184 on Queeg. Steve, they'll ruin us. We haven't got a chance. Let's get out of here."[8] Keefer had campaigned with Maryk using substantially the same approach as with Willie. When he rants about two navies, even Maryk sees the logical inconsistency: "You can't have it both ways, Tom. That's like Queeg."[9] This is the first time Keefer is explicitly compared to Queeg; the second comparison is his own.

At every direct confrontation Tom Keefer folds. He is silent when Queeg asks if he concurs in Maryk's seizure of command. Keefer's true substance, or lack of it, stands in stark relief at his abrupt departure from the bridge during his first, and last, command. "Lord" Tom forgets his responsibilities as a captain, as a commissioned officer, as a man. Clutching the precious symbolic words of his novel, Keefer leaps. Retrieved after his eloquent act, he attempts to salvage some vestige of dignity by rationalizing:

> I feel more sympathy for Queeg than you ever will, unless you get command. You can't understand command until you've had it. It's the loneliest, most oppressive job in the whole world. It's a nightmare unless you're an ox. You're forever teetering along a tiny path of correct decisions and good luck that meanders through an infinite gloom of possible mistakes. At any moment you can commit a hundred manslaughters. An ox like de Vriess doesn't have the imagination to be bothered by it—and more, he has a dumb, oxlike sure-footedness for the right path. Queeg had no brains, but he had nerves and ambition. . . .[10]

To Keefer's devious, opportunistic mind, command is a veritable hell. Totally subjective, he sees it only as exposure and vulnerability. Roland had good instincts, de Vriess was an animal. But even Keefer is finally forced to glance into the abyss. Calling himself "Old Swandive," he acknowledges his kinship to the man he helped destroy. Leaving the *Caine*, the "iron poltergeist" sent to haunt him, Keefer's last words to Willie are: "Don't forget one thing. I jumped."

8. Ibid., p. 310.   9. Ibid., p. 311.   10. Ibid., p. 459.

Queeg was certainly pathetic, but events sought him out remorselessly. He was virtually without experience in vessels of the *Caine* class, but he refused de Vriess's offer of help. Queeg's first commands from the bridge exhibited astonishingly bad judgment, producing damage to another ship and creating the occasion for his first false official report. It was a typical Queeg tour de force. Though no single act could possibly justify Maryk's final action, the accumulation of Queeg's petty insanities, his moral bullying, and his apparent cowardice became too much to bear.

Wouk uses lawyer Greenwald to make two points about traditional military characteristics. Like Cozzens's Judge Ross, Greenwald is the voice of reason. Reading the naval court-martial board the way an observer in *Guard of Honor* appraises the "locker room" camaraderie of the collected army officers, Greenwald challenges their code. He presents this special syllogism: naval officers are not cowards; naval officer Queeg acted like a coward; therefore, naval officer Queeg must have been sick. As Greenwald knew it must, the board takes the alternative, enabling him to salvage both Queeg and Maryk. And at the party his bitter summary includes a reminder that Queeg is not representative of the navy, "a lot of them sharper boys than any of us, don't kid yourself, best men I've ever seen, you can't be good in the Army or Navy unless you're goddamn good."[11] Filling his allotted role of providing perspective, Greenwald alludes to the challenges of combat command. Inept, unintelligent, and perhaps cowardly, Queeg had nevertheless "guarded the coals" for years and had bought time for the reserves to train. Moreover, it took fifteen months of combat patrol and its unremitting tension to erode completely the veneer of conditioned response and bureaucratic, institutional procedures, revealing the nonentity beneath.

Willie is the "last captain of the *Caine*." Studying himself, he admits that it was Queeg's apparent cowardice that made him support Maryk's move. At the moment of decision, Queeg turned querulous and Keefer chewed his lip in silence, while Maryk formally relieved Queeg, and Willie confirmed

11. Ibid., p. 442.

his support of Maryk. Again on the bridge of the *Caine*, when Keefer jumped, Willie stayed. His cool, sure handling of the situation saved the ship. Subsequently Wouk stages Willie's formal rite of passage, undercut by the ironic humor that pervades the novel. All things restored, Willie smokes the promotion cigar of a now-dead sailor, Horrible. A tired, hungry warrior, Willie calls for food, "anything, as long as it's meat." Reflecting on Tom's leap and his own job of damage control, Willie realizes his own maturation: "Willie Keith crushing the stub in the ashtray was not the Willie who had lit the cigar. That boy was gone for good." [12]

Like Alice, he returns form his experience and tries to evaluate it. In his own case, a nice balance has been struck. Reprimanded for his complicity in the mutiny, Willie also carries in his records a Bronze Star, memento of his fight to save the *Caine*. And a sort of logical necessity also prevails in a wider sense. Maryk's naval hopes are dashed, but he is manifestly better suited to commercial fishing, to which he returns. Queeg loses his command but will retire from a shore assignment, rewarded for his years of service, harming nobody. Officers like "Iron Duke" Sammis and de Vriess will not rise above intermediate command, the best logical employment of their talents. The "marvelous academy man" personifies the excellence to which Greenwald referred in his summary. Keefer escaped outwardly unscathed, but his last words to Willie indicate the burden of inescapable self-knowledge.

Willie's reaction to command is an intriguing contrast to that of Queeg and Keefer, but the differences are more subtle than one might expect. Willie feels his personal identity shrink, subordinated to the demands of the greater responsibility. Less free than before, he is sensitive as a "young mother" to the general tenor of operations, his nerve-ends stretching to encompass "all the spaces and mcahinery of the ship." Whereas Keefer referred to command as the function of an animal, Willie feels like the "brain of a composite animal, the crew and the ship combined." He is not driven from them; they become an organic part of his responsibility. He

12. Ibid., p. 457.

does not even sleep as heavily as he had before. But, "the reward for these disturbing sensations came when he walked the decks. Power seemed to flow out of the plates into his body. The respectful demeanor of the officers and crew thrust him into a loneliness he had never known, but it wasn't a frigid loneliness. Through the transparent barrier of manners came the warming unspoken word that his men liked him and believed in him."[13] Willie is an eager and effective vital organ of the archetypal technological megamachine, as harmonious and benign in his functioning as Mailer's General Cummings and John Hersey's War Lover are malignant.

At the end of the novel, Willie is confident and competent. The grim but consistent pattern of his naval career wins out over his mother's regime of tan Cadillacs and a carefully mannered existence. Conrad is behind many scenes of *The Caine Mutiny*. The double, Tom-Roland Keefer; Tom Keefer's dumb refusal to act when he should, and his eloquent leap, with his rueful self-analysis; and above all, the merging of that austere code of necessity and man's struggle to cope with it—all evoke the atmosphere of Conrad's tales, but with a comic diffidence. Willie is convinced, though Wouk retains reservations, that Keefer's leap demonstrates the essential impotence of words, visions, and pretensions before the irrefutable testimony of action.

Wouk touches virtually every major area that is uniformly a matter of interest in contemporary war novels, insofar as they deal with military command. Pondering his own first-hand knowledge, Willie Keith, a civilian, might become more than idly curious about the more vital details of that "marvelous academy man," who obviously typifies the figure of success in the demanding environment of top-echelon service command. The following novels of command crystallize a set of attitudes, consistent among novelists, about the nature of such a man.

James Cozzens's *Guard of Honor* demonstrates the complex interaction of civil and military elements in a society mobilized against an external enemy. As Chester E. Eisinger correctly observes, "Judge" Ross is the ethical center of the

13. Ibid., p. 477.

novel.[14] Prudent and imperturbable, he is the vigilant arm of civil ascendancy, moderating the actions of an irrationally willful military power-structure. Most of the career military men are nominally competent within the narrow scope of their duties, well-intentioned but inept outside of official capacities.

Cozzens provides General Beal with a supporting cast of grotesques, whose laudable motives consistently produce events that keep their superior in trouble. (Although necessary to the plot, their lack of credibility is a significant weakness of the book.) Despondent as the last of his prerogatives are trampled, Colonel Woodman finds that not even Scotch and the uniforms of the past can console him. His suicide brings yet another general from Washington. Colonel Mowbray's exquisitely dull mental processes are animated by traditional loyalty to his commander. Because Mowbray ignored a crucial memorandum, and because a jumpmaster who should have known better allowed his men to leave the aircraft late, several men drown. Mowbray's arbitrary edict on the separate but equal officers clubs brings from Washington the inquisitive eyes of General Nichols, who also witnesses the disastrous airdrop. Benny Carricker's punch breaks the nose of the Negro pilot who almost killed all of them in the general's plane. His action was impulsive, and disastrous.

General Beal resembles more than anything else a personification of Carlyle's unconscious heroic genius. Sophisticated Captain Hicks notes with generous condescension the vital nature, but limited scope, of Beal's moral precepts. Uncomfortable at seeing the Air Corps "blowing our own horn," Beal indulges in public relations only because ordered to do so. Easily reading Beal's mind, Hicks "knows" that Beal does not question his credo "Duty-Honor-Country," and is totally unaware that "Country" might be a "delusive projection of the individual's ego," "Honor" no more than a "hypocritical social sanction protecting the position of the ruling class," or that "Duty" could be "self interest" com-

14. Chester E. Eisinger, "The American War Novel: An Affirming Flame," *Pacific Spectator* 9 (Summer 1955): 272–87.

plicated by concepts of "Honor."[15] Hicks is like Judge Ross
once was. Fresh from civilian experience, he knows nothing
of the traditions behind the motto, and is led by his own
cynical presuppositions to regard it as an empty phrase, a
convenient catalogue void of substance.

Like *Command Decision*, *Guard of Honor* shows the
culmination of diverse forces acting within small compass over
a matter of hours. Cozzens, however, is more skillful than
William Haines in presenting the inseparability of military
and civil affairs, and in showing how events "outside" affect
military life. Woodman's suicide, Benny's punch, the segre-
gation complex, the crashed attack bomber, the drowning, the
incident of the reporter—all focus attention and pressure on
Beal, who appears to be sincerely concerned only about the
condition of his protégé, Carricker. But men like Carricker
are the cutting edge of the weapon Beal commands; in war,
only warriors matter.

Guard of Honor is a complex novel. Though observing
unities of time and place, its plot is labyrinthine, tracing apparently disparate actions that finally merge at Beal's air base.
Cozzens follows one set of characters to the verge of an event,
and then abruptly changes to another; the technique is good
for maintaining interest, but it is occasionally tiresome. A
period of stasis in the birthday airdrop is just one example.
Colonel Ross has a few moments' respite from "panting after"
the regulars whose "messes" he is doomed to clean up, and
he luxuriates in reminiscence. The scene parallels Captain
Hicks's critique of General Beal, as Ross remembers the foi-
bles of his own mentor, Judge Schlichter. It was Schlichter's
curse that he came to enjoy too much inserting passages of
literature into the proceedings of his court, perhaps frustrated by actual scenes that he could not control.

Concluding that the old man lacked sufficient nerve for
the struggle, Ross riffles through his memory, seizing primarily on lines from the final chorus of "Samson Agonistes,"
as if in unconscious preparation for the impending crisis:

15. James G. Cozzens, *Guard of Honor* (New York, 1948), pp.
67–68.

"All is best though we oft doubt/What the unsearchable dispose/Of Highest Wisdom brings about,/And ever best found in the close. Oft He seems to hide His face, But unexpectedly returns, And to His faithful champion. . . ."[16] That Ross murmurs these words with the paratroopers dropping from the sky is too contrived. It is, however, appropriate that he should cite "Samson." Ross's tireless exertions prevent General Beal from pulling the temple down on himself. After all, balance must be maintained. "Judge" Ross is, in effect, a god out of the machine. Superhumanly active, he is ubiquitous. Not only does he figure in every major resolution, but most of the minor ones are also influenced by his judgment. He helped dispose of the crashed attack bomber, helped solve a problem for the engaged WAC, and took note of Mrs. Beal's connubial difficulties. But "Judge" Ross remains a personified principle rather than a credible character. As the author's spokesman, he is the ethical center of the novel, but is too obviously so. The novel's pattern of events and consequences sustains its didactic tone sufficiently to permit a more human, more credible judge.

Cozzens's novel vividly illustrates the essential unity and the paradoxical incompatibility of civil and military ways, normal human contact complicated by mandatory military prerogatives and traditions. Captain Collins thoroughly detests Lieutenant Edsell, but is moved to defend his actions in the case of the Negro reporter simply because the accuser ventures into Collins's official domain. Botwinick's dilemma over the crashboat memorandum has already been mentioned. Lieutenants Edsell and Phillips are motivated in their campaign for Negro rights at least as much by animosity toward the army as by a liberal sense of justice. A civilian employee leaks developments of the army's racial problems to the local paper increasing the pressure on Beal. Lieutenant Turck experiences a major problem as an "emancipated woman": a WAC officer who also wanted to become a doctor, her encounter with the symbolic snake, first in the barracks area and then in a dream, symbolizes her intrusion into traditionally

16. Ibid., p. 524.

male reserves. And Captain Andrews's frail wife collapses virtually at first contact with the army.

The pattern is consistent. Cozzens shows that in wartime professionals must depend on amateurs, who may do well or badly. Civilians in uniform, these reservists bring preexisting attitudes and prejudices with them, so that institutional military conservatism must oppose the more liberal ways of society "outside" at almost every turn. *Guard of Honor* is a novel of manners, with a scope of action and detailed human relationships that engage the reader's interest completely. Most of the characterizations, even the remote secondary figures, are fully realized as individuals. Though he does perpetuate a pejorative image of the military commander as a curiously hampered genius, Cozzens explores the complex unity of the society he depicts.

Cozzens's generals are a matched set. Nichols is the intelligent, cool staff manipulator. His airy references to the Quebec conference imply the political influences that exert more than a tangential effect on very high ranking officers. Like Ross, Nichols is fully aware that compromise is a necessity of civilized life. This leaves General Beal, who may be considerably more observant and perceptive than his associates are prepared to believe. He absents himself from crucial negotiations because he is not a diplomatist. He possesses the almost invaluable ability to sense when it is best to do nothing, or leave matters to those equipped to handle them. Nichols and Ross speak the same language, so Beal lets them work together. Playing to the hilt his image as a man of action, he motivates others to help him.

Beal will always count heavily on the good men around him to do what needs to be done. It is a priceless asset. His obsessive interest in Benny merely symbolizes the fact that his interests center on fighting the war, as Hicks noticed. War creates Beal's unique milieu, as he reminds Ross: "Even Jo-Jo knows they could do without him before they could do without me. That's not boasting, Judge. There's a war on. Jo-Jo can talk to Mr. Churchill; but the war, that's for us. Without me—without us, he wouldn't have a whole hell of a

lot to talk about, would he?"[17] Nichols's reputation as GHQ
enforcer is based on cold, brilliant performance, powered by
unflappable reason; Beal's easy assurance and open manner
inspire others to help him, naturally. He is a natural, gifted
warrior. Both men are perfectly matched to their roles, in-
comparably superior to the colonels who toil beneath, except
for Judge Ross, who symbolizes the rule of civil law to which
both must accede.

The motifs raised by Cozzens provide the substantive
core for four other significant war novels: *Command Decision; Melville Goodwin, USA; Show Me a Hero; and Harm's
Way*. The protagonist of each is a prime example of the unconsciously "good" soldier, who moves essentially untroubled
by moral dilemmas through the maze of decisions that other
men cannot negotiate unscathed.

In each of these books a finely tuned moral balance prevails. Haines's General Dennis is forced to yield to political
pressure, but in turn gains a concession that enables him to
win the air battle and thereby his next star and a larger command. Melville Goodwin confesses his infidelity to his wife,
who arranges in her customarily astute manner his next command. General Logan of *Show Me a Hero* is given his chance
at combat command in Korea, but is hamstrung by policy.
What Homer would call "deadly destiny" searches him out.
He has paid for professional success by divorce and by the
alienation of his only son, whose actions provide an enemy
with material for blackmail, forcing Logan to retire. Admiral
Torrey of *Harm's Way* loses his family by divorce and his
son's death in combat, but he gains success in combat: *quid
pro quo*. In each case the commander is the focus of strong
simultaneous pressures, exerted by family, politics, the news
media, contemporaries and superiors, and by the demands of
war itself.

The best presentation of this theme occurs in *Command
Decision*, as General Dennis's fist fells a meddling and cor-
rupt politician. Dennis's superior thinks of the repercussions,
and an observing reporter sees the two men as separate manifestations of the same sort of power, the army as a "projected

17. Ibid., p. 630.

form of a deeper malignance. It was not the weaknesses, the faults, the mistakes of armies; it was their existence that proclaimed the tragedy of mankind."[18] The man who wields power is transmuted by it. Broadcaster Skelton's conclusion about General Goodwin is that "there was a metal in him that life had never tarnished. . . . He was a stranger from a strange world which we could never touch."[19]

That the problem of command could be more complex is suggested by the later two books. In *Show Me a Hero*, General Logan's chief-of-staff cites the requisites for a successful commander, prefiguring Logan's eventual fall:

> If he's learned by then not to worry about the others he clambers over and often kicks downward in the process; not to fret except for publication about militarily acceptable casualties on his side; not to tell part or all of the truth when it would damage his career to do so and when he can fail to do so and retain an honorable appearance; not to get out of line with a fellow who has more authority or influence; not to neglect to flatter, ingratiate, and cajole all who can help him but cannot be ordered to do so—when he learns and ruthlessly practices or takes advantage of all that, he is very likely to be a successful major commander.[20]

And Bassett's Admiral Torrey is astonished at the impact on other men of the stars that suddenly elevate him. Observing an unscrupulous contemporary, he is sobered by the phenomenon of power:

> . . . at the ease with which rank lifts a man above the necessity of *requesting*, or once having attained his wants, of even thanking the donor, unless he were of a mind to display his imperial appreciation. Yet the power inherent in his two stars sobered him. He'd known some officers to whom power became an end desirable in itself, as they rose in rank, rather than remaining a useful tool that could work miracles when properly wielded. Blackjack Broderick was one of these. For such men there seemed to be a kind of diabolical fun in power; to be able to

18. William W. Haines, *Command Decision* (New York, 1947), p. 219.

19. John P. Marquand, *Melville Goodwin, USA* (Boston, 1951), p. 594.

20. Melvin Voorhees, *Show Me a Hero* (New York, 1954), pp. 138–39.

flick the wrist, cock the eye, crook the finger, nod the head, or shrug the shoulder—while your subordinates hunted desperately for the occult meaning behind those fleeting gestures. *Military power is the absolute power which even money can't buy*. It's denied to politicians, when you get right down to it, unless you rate the President a politician—and his supreme authority comes only in wartime when he's Commander-in-Chief of all the Armed Forces and therefore a military man himself (emphasis added).[21]

The obvious thrust of these incidents is to emphasize the temptations attendant to the exercise of power. And as Torrey realizes, military force is human power in its most arbitrary and uncompromising form. The forces of intellect, persuasive rhetoric, personal magnetism, moral suasion—all are variants of a graduated and indirectly coercive power. But military force is something beyond—a difference not of degree, but of kind. So it is appropriate that in the twentieth century, when technology has taught the world to think the unthinkable, novels about men who direct the concentrated force of entire nation-states in time of war should appear; the chosen vessels of the new faith must be the best kind of men.

The preceding novels are primarily concerned with men whose interests centered on problems within the military structure. Central figures who encountered the phenomenon of political power and influence being exerted upon the armed forces reacted with distaste, and, for the most part, disillusion, at the deviations from sound military considerations which political intervention imposed. The protagonists are essentially good men, often limited to a narrow genius for commanding soldiers in battle, men unfit for the intrigues and maneuverings of civilian life.

General Dennis reacted with his fist to congressional hypocrisy; General Beal departed the scene of compromise, leaving negotiations to other, subtler men; Melville Goodwin's stark simplicity is almost primeval, totally without artifice. Though he is acutely aware of the alternatives open to him, General Logan's unyielding sense of "right" denies any alternative in a moral predicament. Rockwell Torrey ob-

21. James Bassett, *Harm's Way* (New York, 1962), pp. 311–12.

serves the corrupting influence of power, acutely aware of all his prerogatives.

In *The Naked and the Dead*, Norman Mailer shows the final stages in the evolution of a Faustian monster, judged in the context of a free society as envisioned by these novelists. General Cummings might well have had his personal commonplace book carefully crammed with epigrams from Clausewitz, whose most famous sentence, "War is the continuation of policy by other means," was implicit in the genetic code that defined Cummings.

Following closely the genesis of the German general staff system, Walter Goerlitz cites other key elements of Clausewitz's theory, corollaries to the above.

> War, he emphasized, was the statesman's last expedient. How dangerous it was if a false policy hoped, by the use of warlike means, to attain ends that were contrary to nature. True, he demanded that in time of war the military commander should be given a seat in the Cabinet. He should not, however, have unlimited power. *His judgment and counsel should merely ensure that statesmen reached the correct decisions.* As against this, he held that the principle of moderation distorted the character of war. An essential condition for the war of annhilation was "a state system penetrated by the very highest consistency" (emphasis added).[22]

The passage hardly needs explanation. This is known as "voting with the bayonet." Textual purity relative to Clausewitz's original language, or the matter of translator's freedoms with the original are not really germane. The point is that this paragraph emphasizes exactly the situation that encompasses Mailer's obsessed general. Such thought processes are the hallmark of the sinister commanders developed by the modern American war novel, of whom Cummings is the prototype.

The primary theme of *The Naked and the Dead* is power. The novel delineates a hierarchy: the power of man over man, the power of military force, the power of political thought and polemic, the inexorable power of events on the lives of men. Ambitious, intelligent General Cummings is the central

22. Walter Goerlitz, *History of the German General Staff*, trans. Brian Battershaw (New York, 1957), pp. 62–63.

figure, the most gifted wielder of power. Sergeant Croft is a miniscule counterpart whose career demonstrates the same principle operating through a lesser agent, with correspondingly less refined responses. Lieutenant Hearn is the confused, undisciplined liberal, reluctantly converted by the efficiency of Fascist energy and determination, aligned during the last hours of his life to the ways of Croft and Cummings. Major Dalleson is the forceless nonentity through whom necessity displays its ineluctable power.

From the welter of comment on *The Naked and the Dead*, two remarks about the novel are most helpful. In a 1962 article in *Encounter*, Diana Trilling notes that the book "takes its ultimate stand, not in art, but in doctrine. As much as it is a drama of human motives, Mailer's first novel is a political document. . . ."[23] She points out that the army is not merely a hateful institution that dehumanizes men: "This army which, in the name of historical necessity, captures, rules, and destroys the common life of humanity, is modern society as Mailer sees it. . . ." Extending this thought, S. H. Hux calls "this army" a "paradigm of society; society and nature are pitted against the self."[24] As in *Catch-22*, the military machine is merely a manifestation of the larger basic malignancy, seen also by correspondent Brockhurst in *Command Decision*.

Miss Trilling's remark, however, must be modified. Structure is uniformly important, almost central, to the novels considered in this chapter. In *The Naked and the Dead*, Mailer's art—the nearly absolute control of structure and characterization—explains both the novel's success and much of its criticism.

General Cummings's island campaign is a completed action, confined both in time and space with Aristotelian unity. Cummings on the island is like Faust in his study, seeking to "learn the things that hold / The world together at its core, / So [he] may potencies and seeds behold."[25] The action

23. Diana Trilling, "Norman Mailer," *Encounter* 19 (November 1962): 48.

24. S. H. Hux, "American Myth and Existential Vision" (Ph.D. diss., University of Connecticut), p. 183.

25. Johann Wolfgang von Goethe, *Faust*, trans. Charles E. Passage (New York, 1965), pp. 19–20, ll. 382–85.

moves as Cummings directs it. Like a ship, airplane, or military unit, the island serves to unify the action. Characterizations are dictated by the predetermined sociological conclusion toward which Mailer is heading. The secondary characters are types, designed to depict the effects of social catastrophe. Almost without exception they are failures, lacking self-confidence and the ability to act independently. Intimidated by the general catastrophe that produced the Great Depression, they are at their most vulnerable, ripe for domination and guidance by the forces of reaction, personified by Cummings.

Mailer examines a crucial time, always keeping the end clearly in sight. He preforms his characters and places events to generate a consistent internal logic. The "time machine" and chorus breaks carry Dos Passos's practice a step further; here there is no semblance of random occurrence as in *Manhattan Transfer*, no apparently rambling or arbitrary insertions as in *U.S.A.* All parts are tightly interlocked.

Mailer's events occur in carefully controlled order and rhythm. Part 1, "Wave," is a general prologue. It sets the locale, introduces most of the cast of characters, and launches the action. Part 2, "Argil and Mold," is all General Cummings's. His battle-plan unfolds, he counters Japanese actions, disposes of Hearn, and decides to send "Recon" on its futile mission. Except for two important events, part 3, "Plant and Phantom," deals with the patrol's disastrous adventures. Chapter 6 is devoted to Cummings's firing of the howitzer and his resulting attempt at philosophical synthesis. Chapter 11 details Major Dalleson's reluctant conquest of the Japanese remnants. Part 4 is "Wake," the turbulent aftermath of violent action, and a requiem. Cummings contemplates the debacle that was to have provided the foundation for his rise to power, resolving to try again after the war, through politics and influence. The division slaughters the Japanese who remain; Major Dalleson turns to the climaxing achievement of his career: the plan to improve classes in map reading by superimposing the military grid system over the imposing contours of Miss Betty Grable. Fittingly, Dalleson has the last words: "Hot Dog!"

The chorus interludes comment on the eternal subjects of soldiers' conversations: "Chow Line," "Women," "The Million Dollar Wound," "Rotation," and the "mute chorus," "On What We Do When We Get Out." Complete with stage directions, these breaks not only heighten the dramatic effect, they produce an air of hopeless and ironic foreknowledge, as if the soldiers know in advance what is going to happen.

The "time machine" sections focus attention on the central figure alluded to in the preceding section, a reference or incident generally negative in tone, reinforcing the air of defeat. Red Valsen's section follows the chapter in which he fails to clean his weapon and fails to execute Croft's command about firing an insurance round into a fallen Japanese soldier, almost at the expense of his life. Gallagher learns of his wife's death prior to his segment; Wilson's turn comes after the revelation of his venereal infection; Brown weakens under the strain of leading the litter-party before his section; and Lieutenant Hearn is examined immediately following the humiliating lesson of the cigarette butt in General Cummings's tent.

Only Croft and General Cummings are introduced in a manner at all positive. Croft's machine-gun fire decimates the attacking Japanese as "Recon" defends its portion of the riverline: "he could not have said at that moment where his hands ended and the machine gun began. . . ."[26] Cummings is portrayed at a moment of insight into his own predicament, realizing that "in the final analysis there was only necessity and one's own reaction to it."[27]

Appraising his chief, aide-de-camp Lieutenant Hearn tries to account for Cummings's impact. Brilliant, but with "spotty" intellect, the general's outstanding asset is his "almost unique ability to extend his thoughts into immediate and effective action."[28] Hearn learns the portent of his analysis shortly before his assignment to a subservient slot on the "fear ladder," having heard Cummings confide that man's greatest urge is toward omnipotence: "Man is in transit be-

26. Norman Mailer, *The Naked and the Dead* (New York, 1948), p. 152; hereafter cited as *Naked*.
27. Ibid., p. 402.   28. Ibid., p. 77.

tween brute and God."[29] Like Faust, Cummings would be
God, with whom, as everybody knows, thought and act are
one. Believing in evolution toward that eminence, Cummings
had referred to himself as a division commander as the "lord
of my little abbey." Awaiting the "renaissance of real power,"
Cummings would wait through this period, "the middle ages
of a new era."[30]

Firing the howitzer is a transcendent experience for Cummings. A Fascist and a reactionary, he is obsessed with power
as the key to the secret that tempted Faust. Fascinated, Cummings tries to impose universal significance on the damped
parabola that is the trajectory of an artillery round. He is a
twisted Magister, making of the shell's trajectory a symbolic
correlative which subsumes all, behaving like the ultimate
Glass Bead Game that Hermann Hesse uses to mock the German obsession for synthesis. And it is, after all, the quintessential German of whom Cummings thinks in his musings.[31]

His personal application of the infinitely informative
curve is unpleasant: the projectile is the career of Edward
Cummings, propelled by the expanding energies of his bound-
less ambition. Impeded by death (gravity) and societal inertia
(wind resistance) the shell will be pulled from its ideal path,
to fall short. Having thought of Spengler's curve of cultural
development, Cummings might well have recalled Nietzsche's
assertion that "a production of good and healthy aristocracy"
is the sole justification for any society.[32] Earlier, waiting for
the shell's impact explosion, Cummings experienced the
fruition of his megalomaniacal delusion. He is momentarily
God, the island his universe. He thought, and the battle plan
was formed. Everything tends toward power for resolution:

> All the deep dark urges of man, the sacrifices on the hilltop, and
> the churning lusts of the night . . . weren't all of them contained
> in the shattering screaming burst of a shell, the manmade thun-
> der and light? . . . The troops out in the jungle were disposed in
> the patterns from his mind. . . . All the roaring complex of odors
> and sound and sights, multiplied and remultiplied by all the
> guns of the division, was contained in a few cells of his head,

29. Ibid., p. 323.   30. Ibid., p. 85.   31. Ibid., pp. 569–71.
32. Friedrich Nietzsche, *Beyond Good and Evil*, selections, trans.
Helen Zimmern, in *Ethics*, ed. Oliver Johnson (New York, 1958), p. 263.

the faintest crease of his brain. All of it, all the violence, the dark coordination had sprung from his mind. In the night, at that moment he felt such power that it was beyond joy; he was calm and sober.[33]

Later his intellect informs him of the failure, but his will cannot accept it, nor can he yet feel its weight. But he is puzzled by his relation to the battle and to the division he commands. He compares himself to a man who presses a button and then hopefully "waits for the elevator."[34]

Cummings's history, as Mailer assembles it, gives the general good reason to believe in the power of Necessity. The grandson of a man who formally relinquished his Presbyterian beliefs merely to please his wife, Cummings senses the spectre of predestination. Apparently born with his proclivities fully developed, he is powerfully moved by his first taste of combat, the sight of men moving to an appointed time and place to grapple with death: *"There were things one could do.* To command all that. He is choked with the intensity of his emotion, the rage, the exaltation, the undefined and mighty hunger."[35] Mindful of his deep but unarticulated purpose, Cummings marries "well," if almost incestuously. Although impressed by the tenets of Catholicism, he refuses to convert because it would be impolitic to do so. His wife personifies his goal: success. During an early frenzied bout of love-making, he rages: "I'll take you apart, I'll eat you, oh, I'll make you mine, you bitch."[36] The frustrated bearer of an intense, inchoate desire, Cummings's attributes, history, and personality reappear in varied forms in subsequent war novels.

A complicated set of interlocking correspondences link Cummings, Croft, and Hearn; the issue of self-knowledge separates Hearn from the other two. Croft is almost surprised when he shoots the prisoner, and is startled to hear his voice telling Hearn the lie about the pass.[37] Similarly, Cummings is shocked to realize after exiling Hearn to "Recon" that the platoon has a most hazardous mission impending. Just as

33. *Naked*, pp. 566–67.   36. Ibid., p. 416.
34. Ibid., p. 560.   37. Ibid., pp. 195–96, 581.
35. Ibid., p. 415.

Cummings overcomes Hearn with "inordinate power," so Croft confronts Valsen with the simple prospect of death, when Red manifests rebellious tendencies on the mountain. Just as Croft feels that the fatigue of the other men held him back from conquering Mt. Anaka, yet also realizes that he could not have succeeded without them, so Cummings puzzles over the paradoxical inertia of his unpredictable troops. Croft matches Cummings's fury on a parallel but lesser plane. Croft, too, has sexual excesses that underline his alienation. Because the attack on the riverline genuinely frightened him, Croft vented his rage on the unfortunate prisoner. Having made the fateful admission to him ("my wife is a bitch"), Cummings eliminates Hearn, reminding him of mythic divine intervention. The effect on their victims is equally deadly, their release is identical: Croft and Cummings differ only in scope.

Only Hearn achieves an understanding of himself, and he is astounded to find that Cummings's remark about his reactionary nature is true. In tracing the steps of Hearn's political conversion, Mailer indicates that the potential for madness lies within each man, and that it can be brought to fruition by external circumstances. Hearn found himself spewing Cummings's ideas in a letter and realized that "there were times when the demarcation between their minds was blurred. . . ."[38] Forcing Croft to apologize for killing the bird, although Croft is perhaps on the verge of killing him, the lieutenant understands how Cummings felt "when he had obeyed the order to pick up the cigarette butt."[39] Slowly, the true motives behind his actions emerge. He had come on the patrol full of the subconscious need to prove something to Cummings, desiring "not revenge but vindication." The intensity of the ambush, the specific feeling of power in controlling the patrol's reactions, had changed even that. "Wishing it could happen again," he now understands Cummings, and the reason for Croft's staring at Mt. Anaka; Hearn is, himself, "just another Croft." He remembers Cummings's assertion that liberals like himself wanted to remake the world, "but they never admit they want to make it in their

38. Ibid., p. 392.   39. Ibid., p. 532.

own image." The truth reveals itself to him by stages: "It had been there all the time, partially realized, always submerged. It had a jingle to it. . . . Not a phony but a Faust."[40]

Hearn is basically like the other two, susceptible to the seductive pleasures of controlling other men, pitting himself against a situation of violence and possible death. Aware now that he is merely using the patrol as a personal test, he knows that he should turn back, but "there was the inner smirk. *He ought to, but he wouldn't.* The shock, the self-disgust that followed this was surprising, almost sickening in its intensity. He was almost horrified with this sick, anguished knowledge of himself."[41] What Cummings and Croft were by nature, he had become. Hearn knows himself now, and his physical death is merely a formal validation.

After the anticlimactic mopping-up on Anopepei, Cummings is temporarily a beaten man. He realizes that mere "vulgar good luck" allowed Dalleson to do what he had failed to do, and that brings him "deep depression." Though he blames fate, Cummings can be faulted on elementary tactics. Taking routine intelligence reports at face value, he failed to assert his normal aggressive leadership. Energetic patrolling would have revealed the weaknesses in the Japanese lines, but Cummings had been preoccupied, thinking beyond this battle to his corps and army commands. Anxious to make his campaign a masterpiece he hedged, trying to get more men and matériel. As a result, Cummings already under sharp criticism for the delay in his area of responsibility. His superiors assume that he either did not know his enemy or lacked initiative. In either case he is caught.

In the pattern of Cummings's frantic contingency planning, Mailer adumbrates the force and scope of the threat from the Right. Having argued with Hearn that fascism would succeed rather than communism, because it is based on actual human nature, Cummings sees the need to go underground, trying to get into the State Department through his wife's family connections. Masquerading as a "liberal conservative," he will wait for the opportune time to initiate "the big step,

40. Ibid., p. 580.   41. Ibid.

the big leap," fanatically determined to make better use of it.[42]
use of it.[42]

Mailer uses Cummings's journal to introduce what has
become one of his most persistently developed themes, one
found in numerous succeeding war novels: "consider weapons
as being something more than machines, as having personalities, perhaps, likenesses to the human." The sexual attributes of weapons, particularly artillery pieces, weapons
as extensions of personal power, and the mechanization of
human beings are at the center of Cummings's speculations:
"Battle is an organization of thousands of man-machines who
dart with governing habits across a field, sweat like a radiator
in the sun, shiver and become stiff like a piece of metal
in the rain. We are not so discrete from the machine any
longer. . . ."[43] Croft and his machine gun at the riverline ex-
emplify Cummings's remark. These motifs of violence and
sexuality and their ramifications are examined in chapter 4,
particularly in John Hersey's *The War Lover, The End of It,*
by Mitchell Goodman, and Mailer's *Why Are We in Vietnam?*

The observation that men are interchangeable parts in
the modern technological society has become commonplace;
it is particularly applicable to war, where Erich Kahler's
theory that men have become "personalized functions" finds
rigidly ingrained application through military training. Cummings remarks to Hearn that "the majority of men must be
subservient to the machine and it's not a business they instinctively enjoy."[44] Cummings sees ironic proof of his assertion when Major Dalleson is coerced by the machine that is
the division into reluctant action. Dalleson bemoans his fate,
trying to coordinate a move against the enemy: "The machine
was coming apart, gears and springs and bolts were popping
out at every moment."[45] But the machine grinds on with
an infernal inevitability, and Cummings later realizes that
had he been there things would have gone largely the same
way.[46]

42. Ibid., pp. 321–22, 718.   45. Ibid., p. 653.
43. Ibid., p. 569.   46. Ibid., p. 716.
44. Ibid., p. 391.

"No matter what its horrors the twentieth century is a vastly exciting century for its tendency to reduce all of life to its ultimate alternatives."[47] Mailer wrote this line in 1959; his first novel sounds a clear call to arms against the forces of reaction, which can lure and seduce every man. Hearn was converted, and he was an exceptional specimen. During the final slaughter of the Japanese it becomes apparent that war can make of most men what Croft was by nature.

In his introduction to *The Naked and the Dead*, Chester E. Eisinger comments on Mailer's "terrifying appetite for violence" thereby accounting for Hearn's (i.e. Mailer's) conversion to the side of violence. But is Mailer working out his own psychoses, or is he expressing the spirit of the age in which he lives? *The Naked and the Dead* sounds a warning, amplified by *An American Dream* and *Why Are We in Vietnam?* These novels are his interpretations of a nation gone more than slightly mad with the interaction of violence and unlimited power. Not so much the simple confrontation of liberal versus reactionary, the danger now lies in the fundamental challenge to all authority. Mailer's inability to quell his tremors of revulsion and doubts about the protesters during the march on the Pentagon in October 1967 and the Chicago demonstrations of 1968 indicate at least his residual affinity for "the Establishment," to the extent that some framework must be perpetuated.

Several other novels address the danger implicit in general officers who covet political power, or in some way seek to transcend the precisely defined limits of their military authority. Stefan Heym's *The Crusaders* (published in 1948) features an armored commander, General Farrish, who is simply an embodiment of the will to power. Caught up in the very system he supervises, Farrish is metamorphosed, losing his humanity in the process: "His achievements in battle and the servility of the men with whom he had surrounded himself had strapped blinders on the general's eyes. . . ." Farrish is exuberant in combat, tragically simple and limited in

47. Norman Mailer, *Advertisements for Myself* (New York, 1959), p. 357.

his approach to the administration of military government
in his section of occupied Germany. Deceived about the political process, he longs for real power. But even the prospect
of a successful senatorial candidacy is insufficient: "And
what's a Senator, anyhow? One among ninety-six."

General Farrish is an outrider from the ominous strain
of "darker" command figures, who crop up in this fiction.
Simple-minded and willful, he gravitates toward power, and
his military successes make him attractive to politicians.
Heym's stark portrayal of the general represents him as a
malign force, but one susceptible to manipulation by subtler
men. Just three years later James Jones presented a razor-
sharp delineation of the threat, more fully developed, in a
brilliant cameo of Brigadier Sam Slater:

> "In the past," Sam Slater said carefully, "fear of authority was
> only the negative side of a positive moral code of 'Honor, Pa-
> triotism, and Service.' In the past, men sought to achieve the
> positives of the code, rather than simply avoid its negatives.
>
> . . . .
>
> "But the advent of materialism and the machine age changed
> all that, see? We have seen the world change . . . in our time.
> The machine had destroyed the meaning of the old positive code.
> Obviously you cannot make a man voluntarily chain himself
> to a machine because it's 'Honorable.' The man knows better.
> . . . "All that is left . . . is the standardized negative side of
> the code expressed in Law. The fear of authority which was
> once only a side issue but today is the main issue because it's the
> only issue left.
>
> . . . .
>
> "In the Civil War the machine won its first inevitable major
> victory over the individual. 'Honor' died. . . . And in our
> present time we must have complete control, because the majori-
> ty of men must be subservient to the machine, which is society.
>
> . . . .
>
> ". . . Modern Armies, like every other brand of modern society,
> must be governed and controlled by fear. The lot of modern man
> has become what I call 'perpetual apprehension.' It is his
> destiny for several centuries to come, until control can be
> stabilized."[48]

48. James Jones, *From Here to Eternity* (New York, 1951), pp.
340–42.

Cummings mentions "anxiety" as the natural state of mind for modern man; Slater now speaks of specific fears that must be inculcated into modern mass-man to insure the success of our technological society. Cummings thinks of himself as "lord of [his own] little Abbey," whereas Slater stresses the machine and materialism. This shift parallels the change from anxiety to fear, with a logic entirely consistent with the movement of the novels, although quite probably not intended by either author.

For Heidegger anxiety meant the unconscious yearning of the human soul for union with Being. Common to all men, anxiety signified a dim realization that human life is totally contingent; that the world is not its home. Occasionally, evanescent moments of insight enable man to discern the outlines of the truth.[49] Eighty years before Heidegger, Kierkegaard defined the same emotion as "a desire for what one dreads . . . an alien power, which captivates . . . with a sweet apprehension."[50] From a yearning for union with God to a dim feeling that the world of Becoming should lead to some state of permanence, this philosophical progression from the mid-nineteenth to the early twentieth century sets the stage for Sam Slater's talk about the supreme importance of fear.

Anxiety is general, an unresolved and unfocused feeling of apprehension. And it is predicated on a system of thought that is somehow dualistic, recognizing to a degree the probability of real existence beyond the phenomenal world, a matter of religious faith or secular philosophy. Fear, on the other hand, is quite specific. And in the materialistic world of technology, nothing abstract has meaning. Cummings's talk of a "fear-ladder" is fully developed in Slater's brief lecture to Captain Holmes. In a totally secularized society, with religion inanimate and philosophy incapable of convincing even itself of such a possibility as God or Being, only the fact of material existence is significant. The only true

49. Ernst Breisach, *Introduction to Modern Existentialism* (New York, 1962), pp. 82–92.
50. F. H. Heinemann, ed., *Existentialism and the Modern Predicament* (New York, 1958), pp. 34–37.

imperatives flow from force, and military power is the purest expression of force in this world. Jones puts into Slater's mouth the concept of the social megamachine, an obvious extension of technology's potential, as expressed by Lewis Mumford and Erich Kahler. (This is, of course, another example of the proleptic, anticipatory quality of *From Here to Eternity*.) Slater informs his fascinated listener that some men, because of their unique qualifications, "are forced to assume the responsibility of governing." In the society postulated above, "Only the military can consolidate . . . under one central control. . . . The war will take care of that."[51]

A strong undercurrent of concern runs through the command novels, but is often unspecific. *Seven Days in May* (published in 1962), although primarily an opportunistic exploitation of the generally ominous international situation, does provide an excellent expression of that concern. The book is an eminently readable mystery story; more importantly, it is completely credible. Given a society as open and unsuspecting as the United States in the early 1960s, operating the most colossal war-machine in history, the potential for a coup exists.

In 1968 Anton Myrer published his second novel, *Once an Eagle*. Having "done" his war novel, Myrer decided to write about the interaction of business, foreign policy, and national power. He first planned to place his central figure in the State Department, but shifted tentatively to an international news correspondent.[52] That his ultimate selection was a general officer is not without significance.

Once an Eagle captures brilliantly the essence of both extremes in literary portrayals of commanders, extending the characterizations best represented previously by Maj. Gen. Melville Goodwin and Mailer's General Cummings. In Sam Damon, Myrer produces a hero in the traditional mold, a man almost absolutely good (in the sense of Kant's "good will"), who opposes the flux of an imperfect world. Antagonist Courtney Massengale displays the "will to power," a twisted intellect and flawed personality that make him infinitely more

51. *Eternity*, p. 343.
52. Conversations with Mr. Myrer in April 1969.

formidable than Cummings. As individuals and as moral archetypes the two men compete over the span of a half-century.

Once an Eagle is the result of meticulous planning and detailed technical and historical research. The personal traits of the two major figures are central throughout the novel, although there is in the background a review of American wars since the revolution, with an implicit commentary on the reasons for American involvement in foreign wars. Damon and Massengale first meet during World War I, and the plot subsequently brings them together several times—each meeting a critical juncture in the philosophical and professional development of each man.

Myrer improved on the traditional opposition of coldly methodical intellectual staff manipulator versus limited, dynamic combat leader, though these elements are at the core of the issue. Courtney is the son of an illustrious general officer, from a vintage New York family. For a number of reasons, Court goes to West Point, where he is miserable but he does well, driven by his slightly masochistic iron will. His strategic marriage proves a domestic disaster but a professional boon. Like Cummings, Court has sexual problems, but they are more severe. Affected by *ejaculatio praecox*, he finds the demands of marital sex impossible; one of the final personal glimpses of Courtney finds him employing an exquisite *fellatrice*, luxuriating in the control of another human being.

In contrast to his antagonist's Eastern "establishment" breeding Sam Damon is a Nebraska farm boy. But like Courtney—and solidly within literary tradition—Sam loses his father early, forcing him to become a self-made man. In the vein of Melville Goodwin, he is almost too talented, but this is necessary for the later confrontations with Courtney. Married, Sam is a gentle, competent lover, whose regard for his wife does much to alleviate the hardships of a long service career. His education beyond high school is totally informal, but he possesses a keen, finely focused intellect that is not easily disoriented.

Sam Damon is reminiscent of Chaucer's "parfit, gentil knight." An idealized soldier, his life is a virtual catalogue of his nation's wars. *Once an Eagle* is organized in five sections, following Sam from boyhood through his death in the Asian nation of Khotiane. "Orchard" includes stories of the Civil War, Cuba, and the Philippines, which Sam listens to as his uncle and other old men relive their youth. In an early scene Sam reads an account of Benedict Arnold in action against Burgoyne. Like Arnold, Sam is a maverick, an individualist who insists that his concept of the right way must be followed.

In "Wheat," Sam fights in France, wins the Medal of Honor, a commission, and his wife. Massengale emerges as a GHQ staff officer, disturbed by the substandard cleanliness and discipline of Sam's company, until he learns who the commander is: "Anyone with a record like yours would have no disciplinary problem. That's axiomatic. . . . *Somebody's* got to be the monster from Staff . . . drive around with changes of orders. . . ." Listening, Sam hears a voice, "faintly metallic, disembodied . . . like a field order translated into sound. . . ."[53] This is Sam's first contact with Courtney Massengale, whose logical appraisal of the situation was exactly correct, and who, Sam realizes, wants the war to last forever.

"Chaparral" provides an exquisitely detailed picture of the bleak service years following World War I, along with glimpses into the situations in the Philippines and China, where Sam goes to observe resistance against the Japanese in North China. During the Philippine interlude the two men talk, one a staff major fresh from GHQ and now at MacArthur's elbow, the other a veteran company commander. History and military affairs are their inevitable topics. Courtney advocates the great-man theory of history; Sam inclines more to Tolstoi's philosophy. Testing himself on Sam's formidable intellect, Courtney argues with historical precedent, conveniently biased, by now an ominously familiar theme: the Renaissance was the last break-out of the individual "anarchistic tendency"; since then, Courtney argues, social forces have tamed the masses, who now look for leadership and a way out of the "chaos and uncertainty" that are part of the human condition. "The person who can act with

53. Anton Myrer, *Once an Eagle* (New York, 1968), pp. 196–98; hereafter cited as *Eagle*.

force and decision . . . turns the consciousness of his time. . . . People seek authority, they need it; they *want* to be told what to do . . . it's become instinctual. And in an authoritarian era the army is always the sharpest instrument of policy."[54] Like Cummings, Massengale trembled with the rage of murderous ambition at the sight of men moving forward to die, by command. It was his vision of divinity.[55] Certain that war is at hand, Massengale senses that Sam is no man to have as a direct competitor and tries to lure him with the prospect of power. Court charges that Sam is a "wild anachronism" who has forgotten the interests of his class and is guilty of a heinous intellectual sin, the "egalitarian fallacy."

In reply, Sam quotes Xenophon: "Each of you is a leader." Not simply stubborn, Sam will defend to the utmost limits of his physical and intellectual strength the position that his conscience and understanding identify as right. In his insistence on absolutes, he is medieval—even primeval. As a squad leader he ambushes and decimates with machine-gun fire two entire companies of German soldiers. During World War II he unhesitatingly uses gasoline to burn out Japanese who persisted in their resistance, living in caves overlooking American positions. Sam's career evokes the image of Emperor Carus or the warrior-princes of *The Iliad*. His simplistic ethics belong to Aristotle or *The Inferno*, radically out of place in the twentieth-century multiverse.

Illustrating Sam's moral position by example, Myrer depicts him during the lean years prior to World War II, reduced in grade, living in wretched quarters, and liberally tempted by a wealthy relative to leave the army. After proving himself in the civilian world merely as a personal test, Sam remains in the army, his motives totally inscrutable to his companions. But Sam senses a fundamental immorality in the irrational world of laissez-faire capitalism, which seems based on immoral disorder and caprice: "He was afraid of this world. He feared it . . . as a good seaman must fear a recklessly piloted ship. It was too ungoverned, too avaricious, too headlong: in a world where . . . bootblacks could make a killing in Alle-

54. Ibid., pp. 377–80.
55. Ibid., p. 382; cf. *Naked*, pp. 414–15.

gheny or Union Carbide, he did not want to enlist his services. It was . . . demeaning; his love of the tangible, of concrete and demonstrate values . . . was assaulted."[56] Sam sees
the military as a functioning meritocracy.

Myrer's antagonists both react strongly to the temper of
the modern age. Courtney's concept of human beings features a degraded Aristotelian faith in the efficacy of training
and conditioning. Sam Damon is the first of the "good" figures to cite the world's irrationality as a fault, and the only
one to subject himself to the world "outside" and prove
that he can surmount its challenges. With Courtney he shares
an inherent feeling for order, an affinity for a hierarchical
arrangement of all human affairs. It is significant that he sees
the military as a last refuge in a world gone astray. Both he
and Courtney scorn the scrambling race for material success
that typifies the world outside their sphere of enterprise. In
a world that respects fewer centers of institutionalized authority with each passing year, it is significant that both men,
superbly equipped for life in any age of man's history, should
gravitate to the military profession. Both are radically reactionary, but with a crucial difference, well sustained by
Myrer throughout the book.

"Liana" takes Sam through World War II. The final view
of Massengale here shows him suffused with rage at the
"filthy scientists" who have deprived him of his next professional showcase by destroying "the traditional forms of
victory" with the bomb. The truncated war, however, is only
a temporary setback.

"Delta" concludes Sam's tragedy. Myrer combines aspects of the Vietnam and Korean wars, producing a plot in
which American evangelical capitalism opposes communist
militarism in Indochina, on the verge of World War III. General Massengale personifies the "new warrior class" of which
Schlesinger warns. Leading, or led by, U.S. commercial interests, Massengale is ready to light the powder keg of
Khotiane, where Communist Chinese intervention has already
begun. World War III would merely help him solidify and improve his position. Observing Massengale's machinations

56. *Eagle*, p. 343.

Sam realizes that, as the British Empire historically proves, the standard adage of international relations should be revised to read: "The flag follows trade."[57]

Sam's death grows from his single-handed defeat of Massengale's great plan for an expanded war. Awaiting a plane that is to take him to a final meeting with a rebel leader, "Lt. Gen. Damon (ret.)" is killed by a "terrorist bomb." Dying, Sam articulates the precept that has been his guide: "the romantic spendthrift moral act is ultimately the practical one—the practical, expedient, cozy-dog move is the one that comes to grief. . . . If it comes to a choice between being a good soldier and being a good human being—try to be a good human being."[58]

Myrer leaves his readers with this cameo impression of Massengale. He needs a war to help him acquire position and leverage. American intervention, therefore, would be just fine. Under the influence of wine and the headier intoxicant of his own vision, Courtney's musings become words:

> It's hard to avoid the conclusion that we are drifting . . . into recession . . . into complacency, stagnation, timidity. The country lacks unity, cohesion, a sense of destiny. There's a very real question as to whether participation in an ideological conflict like this one here in Khotiane might not serve as a partial and much-needed mobilization of the nation's resources, as a focus for American concerns, economic and psychological, you know?

As Damon dies, preaching the categorical imperative to an uncomprehending combat soldier, the undersecretary asks for assurances about the Chinese Communists, indicating that a memorandum from Massengale on his new proposal for a modern version of John Hay's "splendid little war" might be received sympathetically. Massengale's life proves Acton's phrase, which court derogates as foolish: "Power corrupts; absolute power corrupts absolutely."[59]

Myrer's novel is a masterpiece of the genre. His control of characterization and plot is consistent and sure. The dialogue is not always credible as extemporaneous speech, but it does not detract seriously because Myrer's ideas are

57. Ibid., p. 783.   58. Ibid., p. 815.   59. Ibid., pp. 796–97.

supported by coherent intellectual development, allusion, and historical reference. Every page attests to scrupulous technical research and a strenuous attention to detail. This is particularly the case in battle scenes and descriptions of weaponry and tactics. Myrer creates an absorbing story of individual moral conflict while reviewing the trend of American foreign wars and examining the factors that influence, perhaps control, the quality of modern life.

Of all the novelists who have written on the subject, Myrer makes the strongest, most comprehensive statement about the confluence of military power and political coercion or influence. In addition, his conclusions are the most pessimistic. Damon's death and the dalliance between Massengale and the undersecretary, directly inspired by commercial and financial interests, emphasize that the ultimate culprit is neither militarism nor political power, but the profit motive, which Sam Damon had always viewed so apprehensively.

What is the dominant tendency in characterizations of flag-rank military officers? None "succeeds" without certain traits and abilities. All are strong-willed individualistic men who stand out in their ability to exert personal force sufficient to withstand jealous contemporaries, overcome the collective judgments of staffs, persuade reluctant superiors, or outlast intransigent enemies. Dennis, Beal, and Goodwin are presented as gifted warriors, lifted by dedication and a sense of mission beyond normal concerns, but severely limited in their capacity to cope with nonmilitary affairs. In General Logan and Admiral Torrey this stereotype begins to weaken, and in Sam Damon Myrer develops a character whose possible fault is altruism or a lack of objectivity.

The ominous command figures are joined by an obsession with power, and by their adherence to oversimplified theories concerning its optimum applications. Whereas men of the first group shun politics and only reluctantly submit to the influence that it exerts, this second category of flag officers court it avidly. In addition, they are all associated in some special way with the machine. Cummings's journal entries show his speculation on the interaction of man and machine in combat, and Slater's fascist catechism centers upon the necessary unity between man and machine. Farrish gleefully commands a division of armored weapons in battle, and Massengale, who talks about the cogs and wheels of war, is himself compared to a robot by Sam Damon on their first meeting. Their collective predilections indicate that a fundamental repudiation of human values, an alienation from the altruistic ideals that required a dozen major cultures and thousands of years to evolve. It is an intrinsic, collateral manifestation of the will to power, which is most obviously exercised through the machines of war.

Political influence irrupts into each of the novels about flag officers. Among the first group it begins with forthright, courageous General Dennis, opposing service politics and direct political influence in his resolution to prosecute the war in the best military fashion. An infinity of ethical rationalizations and strategic refinements separates his knock-out blow to Congressman Malcolm from General Massengale's Machiavellian gourmet dinner for the undersecretary, designed to negate Damon's mission and insure at least a "splendid little war" in Khotiane. Melville Goodwin is a prized knight in the army's gambit for more substantial budgetary considerations, and General Logan stoically accepts the political hobbles affixed to his command prerogatives, galling as they are. Admiral Torrey is opposed by Senator Owynn, Admiral Broderick's political arm of action. General Beal remains enigmatically unruffled by the presence of a political bomb in the racial problem within his command, apparently regarding such nonmilitary matters with Olympian detachment. "Judge" Ross and General Nichols are around to take care of things.

The darker figures court political influence avidly, seeing it first as another weapon in the general arsenal of power, and then as an end in itself. Farrish is easily persuaded by his sycophantic aide, seduced into military practices that are unethical, blaming subordinates unjustly and disregarding substantive issues for superficial gloss. He covets power greater than senatorial on his return. General Slater and Admiral Broderick envision personal aggrandizement through influence or conditions imposed by the war.

Generals Cummings and Massengale, separated by twenty years in conception, personify the worst possible strain of dynamic malignancy. A formidable intellect, fanatic sense of purpose, high military rank, and an insatiable hunger for power yoke the two solidly together. Their historical theories are similar; they hold other men in equal contempt; they are psycho-sexually disturbed; and they seek sublimative expression of their collected frustrated drives in the acquisition of power. Myrer extends Mailer's thesis logically: Massengale is in position to win everything, not even temporarily baffled by necessity like his predecessor. He is not haunted by phantoms of predestination; he believes in nothing but the ultimate desirability of absolute power. Not a romantic Faust, his major obstacle is merely human, and Damon dies vainly exhorting a soldier to lead the "examined life."

Generals who lead well in war but shy away from politics are—by novelistic consensus—valuable beyond price. Skelton remarks that the Goodwin "type" is handy to have "around" in wartime. A senior commander who understands, welcomes, and longs to manipulate political power is the Devil incarnate. As Admiral Torrey remarks, "Military power is the absolute power, that even money cannot buy."

The impact of commanders' professional actions on their families is consistently symbolic. General Logan's son returns to his father's sphere and accepts paternal judgment as his fate (1954); Jere Torrey follows his father into the navy and dies executing the admiral's battle plan (1962); and Donny Damon, true son of his anachronistic father, dies in a B-17 over Germany (1968). But as if written to make the specific point, Martin Dibner's *The Admiral* (published in 1967) describes the son's death by suicide, on the eve of the Battle of Midway, as he leaps from the hanger-deck of his father's carrier in silent expression of his deepest attitudes about war. These incidents demonstrate the price of success. Personifying their generation, the young men die, as is the case in war. For both Cummings and Massengale, marriage is disastrous; and neither Farrish nor Slater mentions a son. Afflicted by their common obsession, this group of officers fixes on power as the final, self-justifying end. The result is dehumanization, symbolized by their failure to establish social relationships except as instruments of power.

As previously indicated, several of the books covered in this chapter are among the best and most successful contemporary war novels. A natural expression of their age, they are based to some extent on identifiable events in the lives of historical characters, but their greater purpose is to examine the phenomenon of high command and the pressures challenging the men who achieve it. As society becomes more complex and polarized, the reality of power becomes increasingly apparent to potential readers and authors alike. The contemporary prominence of military men as ambassadors, special presidential advisers, members of the cabinet, and even as a president of the United States has not been without its effect.

These novels of command are largely dramatic in structure, style, and content. The action occurs primarily off-stage, so to speak, with dialogue, journals, notebooks, interior monologue (soliloquy), and letters usually advancing the novel's development. General Dennis's air war, Cummings's divisional campaign, and the Korean War are in the background; Melville Goodwin's numerous heroic acts, like Lear's fateful decision, are antecedent to the opening scene. Dalleson fights the final battle of Anopepei by means of a field phone. Except for *The Naked and the Dead*, *Command Decision*, and *Show Me a Hero*, the novels' plots are primarily episodic, depending on the developing character of the protagonist to sustain interest. Characteristically they follow Aristotle's dictum that drama should present the concluding phases of a longer action, beginning *in medias res*.

The most pervasive element of the novels of command recalls Mailer's comments about the twentieth century and its alternatives. Either by presenting two or more figures or by providing the protagonist with alternative choices of action, these authors impose the same restriction: Dennis can obey the mandates of direct military considerations or the subtler blandishments of long-term results and political influence; General Goodwin is temporarily lured from the steadying

influence of Muriel (Penelope) by Dottie Peal (Calypso), but
resumes his allotted destiny; Farrish can follow either Fascist
Willoughby or democratic DeWitt; General Logan has to
choose between allegiance to political restriction or sowing
the seeds of discontent within his command. Massengale-
Damon, Broderick-Torrey, Wouk's Tom and Roland Keefer,
and Beal-Ross are direct comparisons of alternative actions.
The ethical dilemma is always paramount, the central continuity of the novel at hand.

From *Command Decision* (1946) to *Once an Eagle*
(1968), the mood has darkened; there is no melioration of the
tragic possibilities. *Show Me a Hero* was the first to depict
the full implications of limited war, with civil constraints
constituting merely a minor component of the nemesis that
brings General Logan to defeat; *Once an Eagle* is a powerful
synthesis of the potentials outlined in earlier novels.

Of the books with command motifs the best are *Guard
of Honor*, *The Naked and the Dead*, and *Once an Eagle*. All
three are intricately plotted, with good characterizations and
absorbing action, but they share a defect common to the
rest: the author's intention is never far from the surface of the
novel, always pursuing the didactic goal. The nature of the
subject apparently makes objectivity difficult, creating an
atmosphere that tends to keep dominant ideas always close
at hand. Both Mailer and Myrer work to ambiguous, if ominous, conclusions, a strong point of *Guard of Honor*. But all
the nuances and possibilities suggested by the complex network of people and events in Cozzens's novel are suddenly
revealed as mere background, against which the intellectual
and moral perfection of "Judge" Ross stand in bright relief.
All of these novels show the author's predisposition to form
a tale that will best "point a moral." Neither slices of life
nor expositions of chaos in human events, these novels
are, like classical Greek drama, designed to instruct or to
memorialize.

The author who best expresses the composite impact of
these novels is Joseph Conrad. Learning the problems of
command first-hand, Tom Keefer baptises himself "Old
Swandive" and babbles to Willie about *Lord Jim*. Melville

Goodwin repeats lines from Tennyson's *Ulysses* and his life reminds the interviewer of Horatio Alger's, but both these allusions merely heighten the irony of Muriel's crotcheting. Her contemplative needlework evokes Conrad's symbolic knitters of black wool in *Heart of Darkness*. Firing the howitzer at the island's jungle, Cummings suggests Conrad's French warship, also in the *Heart of Darkness*: "Pop, would go one of the six-inch guns; a small flame would dart and vanish . . . a tiny projectile would give a feeble screech. . . ."[60]

The enigmatic, fatal quality of self-knowledge draws both Kurtz and Jim to death. Both Beal and Goodwin are characterized as possessing only slight knowledge of themselves; they progress blithely, upward and on. Cummings and Croft impinge only a little on the revelation, emerging dimly aware of some powerful impulse at work; Hearn's agonizing awareness makes his death a dramatic inevitability. Farrish, Slater, and Massengale, like Cummings, are fanatically devoted to externals and to the lure of power; they are similarly unaware. Torrey awakes after his disastrous battle, amazed to find that circumstances have made his losing battle a heroic delaying action of strategic dimensions. Logan is felled by a chain of "damnably" difficult circumstances. Sam Damon's futile death and Massengale's final delicate situation with the undersecretary indicate that perhaps Brand, the impulsive passionate Indian, best expressed the philosophy of *Once an Eagle*: "Life was a matter of luck. Luck and fate and chances—and reading the signs with wisdom, quickly."[61]

There is in these novels of command an explicit, consistent concern that military and political power must not be conferred upon one man. Aside from this, Conrad and perhaps *Beowulf* summarize the prevailing philosophy: defeat is probably inevitable for all men, but a man who does what he knows he must can shape the conditions of it.

60. Joseph Conrad, *Heart of Darkness*, ed. R. Kimbrough (New York, 1963), p. 14.
61. *Eagle*, p. 563.

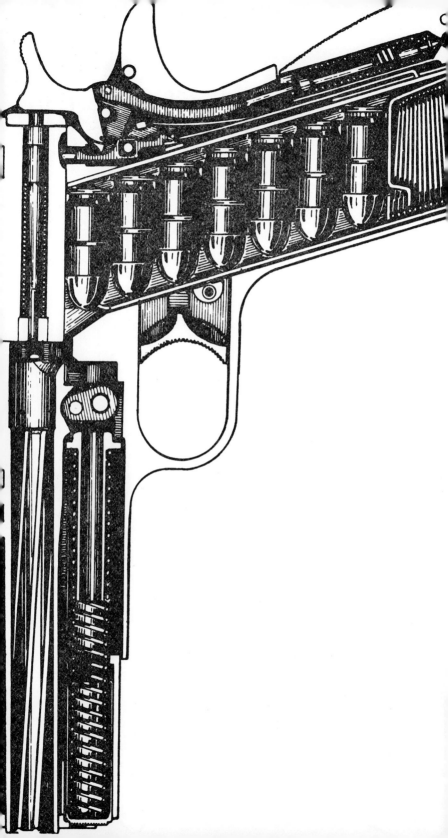

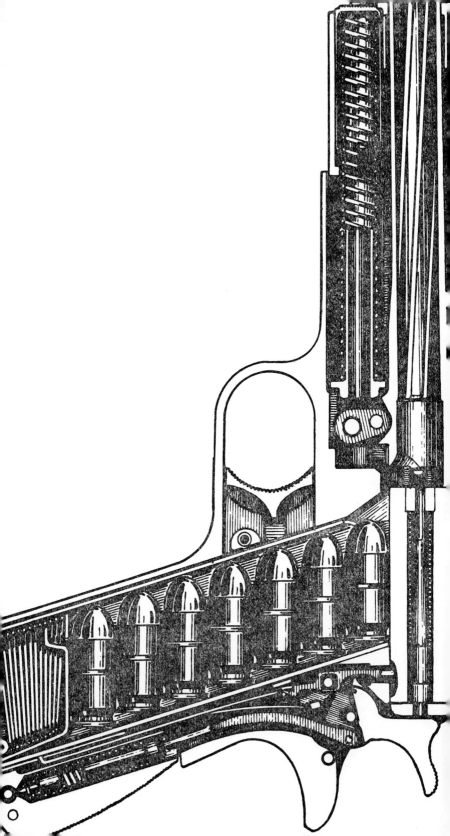

4.

SEXUALITY AND VIOLENCE
IN THE WAR NOVEL

The modern American war novel shows three primary facets of the relationship between sexuality and the violence of war. Though authors individually assume some consistent interaction between sex and violence, exact categorization of their work is not possible on that basis alone. The novels can be sorted into somewhat discrete groups, however, as they emphasize within the general environment of war these three themes: homosexuality and its implications; the correlation between sexuality and individual performance in combat or in reaction to violence; aberrant sexual response, perhaps aggravated by the violence of warfare, involving sexual identification with the machines and power of war.

In the novels examined as *Bildungsroman* and the literature of command, consistent organizational principles were evident. In both cases education is involved, a movement to a climactic point of revelation or realization. And, because of the need to provide a framework for the protagonist's development as he moves through education for life, or toward the moments of dramatic recognition, plot is almost as important as character. However, the novels discussed in this chapter are probably best described by W. M. Frohock's term—"novels of erosion." "Combining violence of action with a feeling of time as erosive," this type of novel stresses action over both character and plot.[1]

Alluding to the emergence of violence as a common theme in contemporary American fiction, Mr. Frohock notes that future historians and sociologists may someday ex-

---

1. W. M. Frohock, *The Novel of Violence in America* (Boston, 1957), pp. 21–22.

plain the development of the climate that fostered its culti-
vation, but he does not turn aside to discuss it. In the case
of these war novels, no explanation is necessary: war explains both violence and the "feeling of time as erosive."
Novels devoted to accounts of combat must cope with the fact
of death, and some elements of determinism or naturalistic decline are indigenous to such an environment.

Another useful guide in looking at this group of books
is Richard Chase's careful distinction between the "novel"
and the "romance." As he discusses these terms in *The American Novel and Its Traditions*, "novel" connotes the traditional English novel, and "romance" identifies the more
prevalent strain in American prose fiction, which also encompasses the works covered in this chapter. The "romance" is,
according to Chase, less tied to nominal reality than the "novel," stressing action and displaying flat characters who "may
become profoundly involved in some way, . . . a deep and
narrow, obsessive involvement." Characterizations tend toward abstractions, and the plot "may be highly colored." In
general the "romance" displays "mythic, allegorical, and sym-
bolistic forms."[2] The war novels at hand are intense, essentially humorless books, which emphasize the great pressure
of events on the protagonists, concentrating on their reactions
to those events. "Obsessive involvement" and an aura of
fated doom give to many of these novels an almost Gothic
quality, characters "drawn out of shape" like Sherwood Anderson's grotesques.

The triad of sex-machines-power is consistently manifest
in these novels, often explicitly associated with death or destruction. Primary sources for the section on homosexuality
are Ralph Leveridge's *Walk on the Water* (published in 1951),
Bentz Plagemann's *The Steel Cocoon* (published in 1958), and
Dennis Murphy's *The Sergeant* (published in 1958). Modern
war literature deals widely with homosexuality. To illustrate
"standard" attitudes toward the subject, I have included some
commentary and extracts from two of James Jones's novels,
From Here to Eternity (published in 1951) and *The Thin Red*

2. Richard Chase, *The American Novel and Its Traditions* (New
York, 1957), pp. 12–13.

Line (published in 1962), though the second will be discussed later in this chapter, and in more detail in the chapter devoted to the psychology of combat.

These novelists agree that the homosexual may be a good soldier, although his presence is divisive in a military unit. Homosexual characters tend to be intense, uncommunicative men, strong but brittle. Homosexuality is depicted as primarily a state of mind, not derivative of an organic condition. The social repercussions are uniformly disastrous.

The second section of this chapter—sexuality and combat performance—includes John Sires's *The Deathmakers* (published in 1960), a characterization from *The Thin Red Line*, and Irwin Shaw's *The Young Lions* (published in 1948). In these works sexual potency and polarity constitute a valid index to the whole man. The sexually agressive individual is a good fighter, but the natural fighter tends to be socially pathological as well. Also in evidence is the pairing noticed in the works on commanders, the dichotomy between "good-light" characters versus "bad-dark" characters, with conventional sexual morality the most important criterion. I include in this discussion a selection of incidents from other war novels to point up the prevalence of these paired characteristics throughout works of sexuality and violence.

Last, are the novels that delineate processes of evolution, or deterioration, whereby individuals exhibit sexual response to technological or purely destructive manifestations of power. War's violence exacerbates weakness, producing distorted accommodation to the environment of battle. These novels are Mitchell Goodman's *The End of It* (published in 1961), *The War Lover* (published in 1959), by John Hersey, and Myrer's *Once an Eagle* (published in 1968). I include *Why Are We In Vietnam?* (published in 1967) because Mailer develops a relationship between perverse or excessive sexuality and the general physical and moral pollution of the earth by the machine age.

Several thematic elements bind all three sections of sexuality and violence together. Combat may provide avenues for the sublimated dissipation of sexual energies, or it may be a direct sexual release, suggesting an occasional equivalency between the intensity of sexual experience and combat action. Caught in the fury of war, the characters evince only fragmented comprehension of their predicament, with an accompanying disintegration of the psyche. Their reactions are outwardly atypical, but the novels suggest that "normal" individuals may possess a similar potential. War inevitably pushes technology to new heights of ingenuity in the state's quest for geometrical increases in destructive power, which are necessary in the struggle for survival. Transfixed at the conjunction of that destructive power and the maelstrom of emotions that war produces, these figures undergo substantial alteration or "erosion." Their social inhibitions melt, and previously unsuspected weaknesses are forced into glaring prominence. Leslie Fiedler's *Love and Death in the American Novel* makes some contribution toward understanding these elements in American literature as a whole, though his frequent overstatements for whatever motives (for example, the alleged manifestations of homosexuality in *Huckleberry Finn* and *Moby Dick*) make his work as potentially dangerous to scholarship as it is fascinating for the general reader.

The authors of works discussed in this chapter parallel consistently the theories developed by Sigmund Freud in the area of individual accommodation to the modern world, set forth particularly in *Civilization and Its Discontents* and *Reflections on War and Death*, and the works of Erich Kahler concerning the influences on man of the industrialized society he has created, delineated in *Man the Measure* and *The Tower and the Abyss*. Whether unwittingly or by design, the writers weave into their novels a pattern analogous to the theses of both men. André Gide's commentary on society and homosexuality, and Carlyle's perceptive analysis of man and his machinery, Emerson on man and nature, and the general trend of romantic thought on the relationship of man and his environment, with which most of the preceding may be properly included—all contribute to an interpretation of the following novels.

In *The Seven Pillars of Wisdom*, T. E. Lawrence argues that Arabs resorted to homosexuality simply because women were either not available or, when they were to be found in the desert, were "raddled meat" unworthy of the desert warriors. Some, he concedes, might indulge to mortify the flesh for its appetites.[3] Gide's explanation of the heroism exhibited by the famed Sacred Battalion at Chaeronea is the strong bond of homosexual love that he alleges linked them. These two literary examples show the dominant theories of homosexuality. The first is that homosexuality is basically unnatural, the last resort of sexually deprived humans whose biological frustrations drive them to violate prohibitions of both man and nature. Second, there is the scheme set forth in Gide's *Corydon* dialogues, that homosexuality is part of nature's plan, as natural to man as to other animals, stifled by the false restraints of civilization.[4]

James Jones depicts a wide range of social attitudes on homosexuality in his two war novels. The later book, *The Thin Red Line*, includes two instances, one purely comic, that display the prevailing moral stance. Company clerk Corporal Fife, and his assistant Private Bead, who share a mutual antipathy, are brought by the circumstances of war to share a single task. But, "horny" after months away from women, they enter into a pact "to help each other out," involving either *fellatio* or mutual masturbation. It is plain in context that pragmatic expediency and urgent pressures from the proverbial "rusty load" are their motivation, that under normal circumstances neither would resort to homosexual practices.[5] Both are adequate soldiers: Bead is the first man in the company to kill a Japanese soldier; and Fife survives the campaign to become a competent squad leader.

The Thin Red Line's other instance of homosexuality is pure comedy. One day, in the process of diving for cover during a patrol, Private (later Sergeant) Doll happens to fall astride the posterior of Carrie Arbre, accidentally assuming the classic attitude of buggery. The sensation is not unpleasant, and Doll becomes obsessed with "that beautiful girl's ass" of Arbre's. He begins to protect Arbre from danger-

3. T. E. Lawrence, *The Seven Pillars of Wisdom* (New York, 1962), p. 29.

4. André Gide, *Corydon* (New York, 1967), pp. 23, 138–39.

5. James Jones, *The Thin Red Line* (New York, 1962), pp. 119–23.

ous jobs, trying to figure out a way to get Arbre to agree. During a wild orgy of drinking and fighting which follows the end of battle, Doll finds himself alone with Arbre. Drunkenly amorous, he puts his hand on Arbre's leg and murmurs about making love on nights like this at home. But Arbre understandably misinterprets the unspoken proposition and unbuttons his fly to accommodate Doll. "Coke sackers, cork soakers, and sock tuckers" were always around, and Carrie does not suspect that Doll wants him to accept buggery. Doll's rationale is that that way only Arbre would be "queer." But the chance fall and the accident of Carrie's anatomy casts a shadow over Doll that, in the mind of Carrie Arbre, Doll's prowess as a soldier cannot erase.

Jones's *From Here to Eternity*, which appeared several years earlier, handles the matter of homosexuality with greater seriousness and substantive attention to its implications. From the sequence and intensity of Bloom's final thoughts before his suicide, Jones makes it obvious that a single lapse into homosexuality is the unbearable factor in the boxer's guilty recapitulation of his failures. When news of his suicide filters to the stockade, both Prewitt and Maggio are astounded that Bloom would kill himself, but they agree that the reason was probably homosexuality. The reason for their conclusion is not obvious in the text, but the tenor if their thoughts is, as Prewitt muses, "If I ever saw a not-queer, it was Bloom."[6]

Bent on killing himself, Bloom lapses into uncharacteristic reflection, cradling the deadly '03 rifle in his lap, fondling with admiration the potent form of the bullet in his hand. He has sustained much: defeat at the hands of Prewitt, smaller but better than he; "busting out" of the NCO Academy; and being an unpopular Jew among hostile gentiles. But others have suffered as much, and other Jews get along in the army with minimal difficulty. Bloom recalls that once—just once—he had submitted to the blandishments of a queer named Tommy. Seeing Prewitt in a bar with Tommy, Bloom decided to square accounts with both of his conquerors, and called an anonymous tip to the Military Police. Ever anxious for evi-

6. James Jones, *From Here to Eternity* (New York, 1951), p. 584; hereafter cited as *Eternity*.

dence against homosexuals, the MP's rounded up all of "G" Company, and Tommy unexpectedly lets slip his affair with Bloom, or at least Bloom is convinced he does. Bloom's last thoughts, as his toe strains against the trigger, are: "You're a queer . . . a monster . . . and everybody knows you are a queer. You dont deserve to live."[7] In the hierarchy of his sins and shortcomings, Bloom places the lapse into homosexuality at the top. His phone call was actually responsible for the entire chain of calamitous events that began with Maggio's trip to the stockade. Both in Bloom's thoughts and in the action of the novel, the incident of homosexuality is a profound and pivotal disaster.

The other incident in *From Here to Eternity* impinges unexpectedly on one of André Gide's theories. Broke, Prewitt accompanies Angelo Maggio on a month-end "queer-chasing" episode. Jones makes no specific mention of explicit homosexual commerce during these ventures into Honolulu; presumably the "queers" are kept dangling by the prospect of success as the soldiers try their individual gambits to cadge free drinks. Also wary, the "queers" carry no cash: nobody gets rolled for a checkbook. Angelo, a pioneer in the field, complains, "Half the company hang out there at the Tavern anymore."[8] But he and Prewitt make contact with Hal and Tommy, have a few drinks and then accompany the two to their apartment, intent only on more drinking. As he usually does, Prewitt forces a crisis, insisting that the "queers" explain themselves, motives and genesis.

The discussion takes two directions. Hal theorizes that homosexuality is produced in "abortively respectable" societies by the general "frustration and disappointment in life." In a traditional vein, he explains that "homosexuality breeds freedom, and it is freedom that makes art," hence the fact that societies produce their best art in decadence.[9] Tommy is less sophisticated, insisting first that he was born "queer," then claiming that upperclassmen in military school forced him to "it." Prewitt bores in, saying that Tommy is queer because he wants to be evil, speculating that he probably wants to show hatred for the church, then citing Tommy's mother as the

7. Ibid., pp. 568–73.   8. Ibid., p. 369.   9. Ibid., p. 381.

probable source of his conviction that he is evil. Tommy agrees that he is evil but he defends his mother: "You dont understand. My mother was a saint."[10]

With his gratuitous allusions to religion and mother, Prewitt cites the source of his own problems, exactly. Moved to second thoughts by Prewitt's dialogue with Hal and Tommy, Maggio wanders off, feeling "tainted," howling guilty defiance to the world, until he is picked up, drunk and practically naked, by the MP's.

The confrontation between Prewitt and the artistic queers recalls some lines of argument adopted by Corydon. Citing an alleged remark of Goethe's to the effect that because it is as old as humanity, homosexuality is really natural, Corydon insists that culture's gain is worth any resultant "price of nature." Further, Corydon assures his interviewer, homosexuality occurs at a stable natural rate, but is more openly subscribed to during those "enlightened" eras when art flourishes —times not of decadence but of moral honesty. He concludes by insisting that "periods and countries without homosexuality are . . . without art," and that "periods of martial exaltation are essentially homosexual periods . . . belligerent peoples are particularly inclined to homosexuality."[11]

In staging the dialogue between Prewitt and the "queers," Jones effectively creates the same opposition of forces that exists in Corydon's rationalizing, which is based on an eclectic survey of history and a behaviorist psychology that equates human with animal responses. Jones's presentation supports the theory that labels homosexuality a social malaise, created by pressures from family, religion, and civilized sexual morality. But Bloom, the aggressive fighter who commits suicide because of feared homosexuality, evokes the lines from Gide that call "periods of martial exultation" and "belligerent peoples" natural spawning grounds for homosexuality. Both authors have linked artistic and martial energies, though in diametrically opposite configurations.

Walk on the Water, The Sergeant, and *The Steel Cocoon* all deal specifically with the relationships among men under

10. Ibid., p. 390.
11. Gide, *Corydon*, pp. 113, 142–43.

stress. In each novel a degree of unity is achieved by the simple fact that the military unit—a squad, a company, and a naval destroyer, respectively—forms the total social environment of its characters. In each case the plot is essentially episodic, opening with action and curving naturalistically to the deaths of major characters.

Walk on the Water (published in 1951) tells of an infantry squad fighting in the Pacific during World War II. Ralph Leveridge is primarily concerned with the bonds between men and the sanctity of the individual. This motif is heavily overlaid with religious and sexual guilt, the theme of the split psyche, intense accounts of combat, and the predicament of the creative sensibility caught in the midst of war.

The action recounts the decimation of a squad in combat. Charged with emotion from the first page, often out of control, the prose fuses war's violence, religious fervor, anxiety about death, and pure home-sickness—all in sexual experience or fantasy. Lorry Adams is a young homosexual who evokes Anderson's Wing Biddlebaum. Sublimating his sexual drives to music, he is a superb pianist, always tormented by the need to control himself. Ridden with guilt, he fights desperately, looking for death in combat, emerging as a superior soldier of heroic stature. But after being taunted and tormented into fellatio, Adams runs off, and is captured and killed by the Japanese. Tuthill, who ruined Adams, becomes a true Don Juan, unable to gain satisfaction from any sensation. He runs full circle and finally conceives a homosexual lust for his new tent-mate. Another soldier experiences orgasmic thrill when, during a moment of rage, he almost strangles his squadleader.

The relationship between squadleader Hervey and Cailini is the center of the novel. The literal savior of his men, Hervey is a perfect soldier, and an accomplished lover. Cailini is a writer. In Hervey's absence Cailini experiences a crisis, never clearly articulated in the novel. The elaborately metaphorical prose that Leveridge injects into Cailini's passages communicates great emotional pressure but is out of focus. There is a confused mysticism suggesting that Cailini is torn between Onanism and art. Having confided that he had once seen Christ in the palm of his hand, Cailini walks endlessly to tire

himself. Collapsing against a tree, he finds warts in the palm
of his hand and feels his soul waver between flesh and "the
great polar field itself." He experiences a vision of transcen-
dence:

> He was free at last. From the harvest of weakness he had gath-
> ered a monstrous strength. No more would he masturbate in
> Eden, that lost seed the pollen of warts. Never again would he
> beat himself to death with a rabbit's paw. Today he would start
> spending his fund of the mystical, the thing that is the ultimate
> in man. . . .[12]

In 1959, Mailer wrote in *Advertisements for Myself*:

> But to be with it is to have grace, is to be closer to the secrets of
> the inner unconscious life which will nourish you if you can
> hear it, for you are then nearer to that God which every Hipster
> believes is located in the senses of his body, that trapped, muti-
> lated and nonetheless megalomaniacal God who is It, who is
> energy, life, sex, force, the Yoga's *prana* . . . Lawrence's
> "blood," Hemingway's "good," . . . not the God of the churches
> but the unachievable whisper of mystery within the sex, the
> paradise of limitless energy and perception just beyond the next
> wave of the next orgasm.[13]

Mailer's exposition of hip grace expresses exactly the inchoate
turbulence of Cailini's vision, into which Leveridge appears to
have crammed every remotely relevant allusion. Mailer speci-
fies that the hipster is the American existentialist, born of the
Negro's accommodation to his condition: humiliated, exploited, always in the presence of death. That the existential
nature of life in combat can drive men back to religious resources long forgotten needs no further support. The "common denominator" for the mystic, atheist, psychopath, and
hipster is a "burning consciousness of the present, exactly
that incandescent consciousness which the possibilities for
death has opened up for them. . . ."[14] It is this that Cailini
encounters in war, complicated by the tangled expression

12. Ralph Leveridge, *Walk on the Water* (New York, 1951), pp.
249–50.
13. Norman Mailer, *Advertisements for Myself* (New York, 1959),
p. 351.
14. Ibid., p. 342.

of hope for some redemption through "art," never clearly delineated by Leveridge.

Walk on the Water is an honest attempt to analyze the emotions among men in combat. Despite the novel's lack of discrimination and several bathetic passages (such as one wherein a nurse worshipfully gazes at the pajama bottoms covering Hervey's "thighs," thinking "the beauty of its structure wanted to burst through . . . into observation," or the description of pajamas as "a shroud over a Michaelangelo [*sic*]"), some genuine insights are established. Men do regard each other as brothers, and deeply mourn the loss of friends. Sergeant Hervey is thoughtful and considerate of his men, but kills a prisoner in cold blood because he is an enemy and a potential threat to those same men. In Hervey's departure for the hospital, Leveridge exhibits the traditional Anglo-Saxon cloak of manliness that suppresses expressions of emotion between men. Hervey and Cailini stare into the mud, feeling uncertain of themselves, then both men softly mutter: "So long." Leveridge's intense involvement with his material produces a virtually private prose.

Dennis Murphy's *The Sergeant* (published in 1958) is the case history of a homosexual. Like machine-gunner Tuthill and Lorry Adams, Sergeant Callan is a noncommunicative man. Like Tuthill, too, Callan enjoys power and is a brave man. With both style and plot, Murphy comments on the relationship of military valor to potential homosexuality in certain personality combinations. Murphy's stylistic parallels reinforce the thrust of similiar actions to complete this analysis of interaction among personal courage, the instinct for death, and the imperatives of sex. Circular, the plot opens with an account of Sergeant Callan's heroism in World War II and closes with two instances narrated in a similar vein: one reveals his homosexuality, the other describes his suicide. Murphy's quiet objective prose tells the story of a strong man taken unaware by his obsession and transformed into a wretched supplicant, whose need outweighs his enormous sense of guilt. Like one of Sherwood Anderson's "Grotesques," Callan seizes on one value and it becomes his only defense in meeting life.

Callan's obsession, and the reason for his decline, is his passion for strength and self-sufficiency. In the beginning his attitude toward his company clerk, Swanson, is that of a solicitous father anxious to protect a son from women and wild life. But in their drinking sessions Callan reveals things about himself, and his own attitude changes significantly. At first he praises Swanson's brains and education, denigrating his own accomplishments. Callan's theme is "survival of the fittest": his examples are himself and the company commander whom he dominates absolutely. Married while he was drunk, Callan abandoned the woman, permanently. He confides to Swanson that it takes "something soft" to get involved with women. Callan raves about "guts" and the need for strength: "Christ how I hate weakness." Callan's eager innocence vanishes: "It went sly and unnoticed as the intensity of their times together grew."[15]

The breakdown comes rapidly. Callan follows Swanson to one of the bars they had frequented together recently, and where Swanson had gone alone, deliberately, to exorcise the memory of Callan. Swanson's rebuff enrages Callan and he grapples with the young man, making overtures that leave no question about his actual motives. Swanson is hospitalized as a result of the ensuing melee at the bar, and Callan goes berserk, appearing drunk at formation, humiliating Captain Loring, and taking up with a refugee woman whom he treats brutally. On the day of Swanson's release from the hospital, Callan appears nearby with a rifle. Brandishing it, he emulates the toreador's cry to get Swanson's attention then vanishes into the tree line, where he kills himself.

By using a similarity of style and incident, Murphy directs the novel's effective form into a circular pattern. Starting with the incident of the German ambush and Callan's heroism, Murphy leads back to that point in the tavern struggle and the suicide. He uses a passage of alliterative prose-poetry, with moving cesura, echoing syllables and consonants that suggest an Anglo-Saxon epic, appropriate to a recitation of heroic deeds. Like "a wild boy," Callan runs to outflank the

15. Dennis Murphy, *The Sergeant* (New York, 1958), p. 173.

German position, killing all the crewmen of the emplaced guns: ". . . in two huddled groups on each side of the road, the first group raked dead before the others had turned. He followed his firing, almost sorry they had not seen him sooner, wanting to plunge into them bodily. They were all hit but one who broke feeble and ran and the sergeant came on like a bull." Callan catches the German, strangles him in a bull-dogging wrestling hold, and then lies "terribly quiet, watching the silent blue sky."[16]

Meeting Swanson at the tavern Callan pleads with the boy, asking for understanding as he wrestles Swanson to the floor: "[Callan] held fast to the wrist and plunged his head into the crook of the boy's arm. The man was on [Swanson] then, one arm around his neck trying to pull him to the floor." In final desperation Callan claws at Swanson, "[and] the boy roared with lightning strength that came clean as a vision . . . shadows were gone forever and the strength ripped its way to the surface and coiled his neck into a muscled whip that cracked the man through the air. . . ."[17] This scene is a brutal reduction of the intricate potential suggested by the wrestling of Birkin and Gerald in D. H. Lawrence's *Women in Love*.

Then, in the final sequence, Callan returns to the woods to kill himself. He had waited on his knees in the treeline with his head "tilted, his neck bent nearly into his shoulder." Now he runs through the trees again, like the "wild boy" who had killed the enemy years before: "his rifle . . . light, part of his running self." Then, "faster through the trees he ran and the pain grew wonderfully and it had to go on, higher and higher, and his head leaned out to skip against the bark of trees and the blood came warm down his face. Through the trees there was a green clearing. . . . And so on the earth, beneath the blue sky, he became so quiet and so wickedly graceful . . . he rolled upon his back."[18]

The comparisons are obviously consistent. All his life Callan had waited for the moment of the ambush. "Not thinking at all," he rushes "like a bull" into deadly aggressive action against the enemy, "mad to touch one alive."[19] The

16. Ibid., pp. 10–12. 18. Ibid., pp. 251–53.
17. Ibid., pp. 235–38. 19. Ibid., p. 11.

compulsive rush is climaxed by the run-on verb, "fir-ing," that precedes his strangulation of the last German. In the tavern the bull imagery returns, but Callan is the voluntary sexual victim this time, placing his own head in the crook of Swanson's arm. After the whiplike reaction that throws him to the wall, Callan charges again "like a bull," before running out. Waiting in the woods, he bends his neck in submission—to death. With his final "Haaa . . . Haaaaaaa!" he waves the rifle like a toreador attracting the bull, then retreats to kill himself, again headed for a green meadow, as seven years before.

Other elements of Callan's attack on the German positions now appear in a somewhat different light. He had laughed, for he was sure he would be shot, but is then frightened in "a better way." He may be "sorry they had not seen him sooner," because his true goal was then, as now, death. In the final suicide scene the emotional rhythm of the passage is climaxed by the blood that flows from his head, which involuntarily "leaned out" to strike the trees as he ran past.

At this point it is helpful to consider Sigmund Freud's progressive deliberations on the identity of the two basic and apparently opposite forces at work in the psyche: the life instinct and the death instinct. In *Beyond the Pleasure Principle*, Freud neatly separated Ego and Sex, the ego growing out of animation, but allied with death and yearning primally for the original state of rest. Sex instincts, though somehow also devoted to that return, were at the same time dedicated to lengthening and complicating the path. But "the instinct toward perfection" and the evidence of some powerful "assimilatory force" working in the psyche clouded this picture. Freud admitted to the possibility of a mistaken thesis, and wrote: "A portion of the ego was . . . libidinal; sexual instincts operated in the ego." At this point the scientist deferred to the poet: citing the "Symposium," Freud began to redefine Eros. Sexuality moves in both camps, he concluded, emerging from the life instinct and the death instinct. Eros (much like Aristophanes' story of the prelapsarian hermaphroditic human) strives "to restore an earlier state of things."[20] But Freud, of course, pushes that "earlier state" back to inanimation, insisting that the goal of life is death.

In *The Anatomy of Human Destructiveness*, Erich Fromm examines Freud's contentions. Fromm contends that "destructiveness and cruelty are not instinctual drives, but passions rooted in the total existence of man. . . . They are not and could not be present in the animal, because they are by their very nature rooted in the 'human condition.' " Discussing the movement of Freud's theories, Fromm sees great significance in the final move from Ego-Sex to Eros-Death.

> In the Eros theory . . . man is no longer conceived as primarily isolated and egotistical, as *l'homme machine*, but as being primarily related to others, impelled by the life instincts which make him need union with others. Life, love, and growth are one and the same, more deeply rooted and fundamental than sexuality and "pleasure."[21]

So Freud retreated in the face of the mysteries of sex and the "economics of the libido" to a position that makes man less a behaviorist robot, more irreducible and complex. Indeed, in making this change, Freud announced the need for a wider definition of the "life" instincts, summoning poetry to his rescue, but remaining resolutely Mephistophelian.

The primary motif of *The Sergeant* is that some aspect of military valor is related to a condition that may produce homosexuality, accompanied by a strong morbid drive to death. Somehow, then, in the enigmatic "economics of the libido," Callan becomes pathological within the environment that he himself has selected. He personifies *l'homme machine*, out of adjustment, a brittle organic robot, and one of the most intriguing examples of the problem of homosexuality this literature presents. If psychologists have had trouble sorting out the components of the psyche and identifying their relationships, novelists experience the same disarray in attempt-

20. Sigmund Freud, *Beyond the Pleasure Principle*, trans. James Strachey (New York, 1967), pp. 68–110 passim; hereafter cited as *Beyond*.

21. Erich Fromm, *The Anatomy of Human Destructiveness* (New York, 1973), pp. 73, 446.

ing to portray the responses of psychological "types" to the pressures of combat.

The Sergeant shows that an exemplary combat soldier may be otherwise unfit by social standards. There is nothing startling in this. But in the broader context, novelists show that the whole, integrated individual will be as likely to fight well. Apparently Freud never did convince himself that the main thrust of human nature is toward self-preservation. Near the end of *Beyond the Pleasure Principle*, having cited sexual climax as the pinnacle of pleasure, he says that it results in a "momentary extinction of a highly intensified excitation." So, he announces, we are "concerned with the most universal endeavour of all living substance—namely to return to the quiescence of the inorganic world."[22] Assuming that Freud's Mephistophelian remark has some degree of validity, what sort of individual, then, is most representative of the "human condition"? And is the reaction in humans attributable to instincts or to conditioning? Fromm's comments on *l'homme machine* and individual isolation are certainly central to Callan's problem, virtually a Freudian construct. The question of how the sexual instinct acts to impel men towards life or death remains, intriguing and unresolved.

The third and last novel dealing with homosexuality is Bentz Plagemann's *The Steel Cocoon*, a story of men at war in a destroyer. A more perceptive version of the relationships among men under pressure than either of the preceding works, Plagemann's novel is sensitive to the subtle gradations and complexities of those relationships, and is less persistent in forcing conclusions. In plot, characterization, sequences of action, and tone of presentation, Plagemann shows the direct influence of Melville—particularly *Moby Dick* and *White Jacket*—on virtually every page. The narrator enters freely into the thoughts of the principal character, ex-Pharmacist's Mate Tyler Williams, an English teacher who went to war and acquired memories that drive him from his bed almost nightly. Why it happens remains an enigma to him. He echoes both pedagogue Williams of *White Jacket* and narrator Ishmael.

Tyler Williams is alien to naval society. Like Ishmael,

22. Freud, *Beyond*, pp. 107–8.

his thoughts frame the book. At the end, though he regards the navy and military service in general as a place of release from the "troubling responsibility of being an individual," he cannot escape the fact of his own guilt, and he wonders why it is that war is "agreeable to most men."[23] Like *White Jacket*, *The Steel Cocoon* is set aboard a warship, where Tyler Williams worries about the prevalent morality of "the world in a man-of-war." He cites no explicit instances of homosexuality among the crew, but speculates that their early knowledge of it probably explains the clowning "camp" mannerisms so much in evidence.

Women confuse and intimidate the younger men, who are often jolted by their early experiences with sex. When the destroyer *Ajax* hits port, the older men head for their accustomed whore-houses; the younger sailors settle for "moist gropings" in theatre balconies with equally young girls, or in desperation, for side-alley contacts with the ubiquitous "fairies." One sailor objects, "You have to fart around so much with women. . . . And then you never know until the last minute whether you're going to get in or not. . . . I just want to get my gun."[24] A young chief, holding court in a scene suggesting the "Mat Maker" and "A Squeeze of the Hand" from *Moby Dick*, expounds on a shallower but no less engrossing subject. As he and his younger charges sit sewing canvas, he relates one of his first adventures, a prostitute encountered after many months at sea, when he "was nineteen, and . . . had a rusty load." Relieved of the urgency, he realizes immediately that she is "an old hag," gray, spare, and toothless. Revolted, he vomits generously and decides on the spot that he can do without women for as long as he lives. That was four years ago. Soon after his recitation, pondering present complications with his wife, the desertion of his steady shack-job, and the sure knowledge that the next port will find him with the first whore he can hail, Chief McNulty wonders (by no means the first to do so) about the way things are: "Goddam the whole mess that made him need women."[25]

23. Bentz Plagemann, *The Steel Cocoon* (New York, 1958), pp. 37–38, 243–45; hereafter cited as *Cocoon*.

24. Ibid., pp. 63–64.   25. Ibid., pp. 207–10.

Cold feet, conscience, fear of disease, biological imperatives—the sailors are assailed by the entire spectrum of motives. Young men like McNulty would never turn homosexual; "fairies" are expedients of the last resort. Plagemann writes perceptively of the complex bonds between the older men and young sailors of the *Ajax*, recalling Leslie Fiedler's lines concerning Ishmael and Queequeg: "This is Platonism without sodomy, which is to say marriage without copulation; the vain dream of genteel ladies. . . ."[26] This is Plagemann's simple sociological explanation:

> Every old hand on the *Ajax* had his "boy," self-acknowledged, of whom he spoke with ribald affection. It was a satisfying relationship to the man and to the boy, a tribute to the one, a help to the other—the sort of relationship men fall into when their lives are lived apart from women. It must not be assumed that there was anything unnatural in this relationship. It was merely a normal expression of the capacity, or even the need, of all men for the love of one another. Simple, uncomplicated men found it much easier to give and receive this rough affection than did less spontaneous men, such as Tyler Williams. The nature of the relationship required that it remain un-selfconscious, that it not be defined or examined, but merely accepted with natural warmth, and implicit in the relationship was the knowledge that it was merely temporary, a pleasant and rather gratifying conjunction in the lives of two men, one somewhat older than the other, who are of mutual comfort and benefit to each other.[27]

These are natural affections, filial and paternal, similar to the relationship in civil trades between journeymen and apprentices, though in the enforced intimacy of a ship at sea stronger and more tangible.

A clearer expression of this theme appears in the work of D. H. Lawrence. Describing the implications of the relationship between Chingachgook and Natty Bumppo, he describes "a stark, stripped human relationship of two men, deeper than . . . sex. Deeper than property, deeper than fatherhood, deeper than marriage, deeper than love." These are men who have

26. Leslie Fiedler, *Love and Death in the American Novel* (New York, 1967), p. 375.
27. *Cocoon*, p. 20.

come "to the bottom of themselves."[28] Too educated and too self-conscious, Williams cannot begin to understand the relationships of the older men and their "boys"; it is an uncertain balance easily misrepresented. For adult men to establish similar bonds is infinitely more difficult, complicated both by cultural inhibitions and by psychological elements that defy definition.

A shipboard accident is the pivotal action of *The Steel Cocoon*. In varying degrees both Williams and his superior, Chief Pharmacist's Mate Bullitt, are culpable. Bullitt is without peer in his technical mastery, but he is aloof and disdainful, holding himself apart, rigidly alone in the society of the *Ajax*. The accident leads to the revelation of Bullitt's incompetent treatment of a sailor previously injured. His shield pierced, Bullitt declines into drunkeness and insanity.

Intent on absolving himself, Williams remembers the *Ajax* in terms of his sleeping compartment. With the red firelight glowing at night and the rhythmic pulsation of the engines, it was like a "classical return to the womb."[29] He recalls that he was reluctant to leave the navy, because it was a return to responsibility: "what waited inside the walls of military life was an incubus [intriguingly, *not* a succubus], to suck men out and destroy their souls."[30] He had failed to act responsibly in the matter of the injured sailor that ultimately caused the accidental explosion because, as he viewed it, his brief "military training" had imbued within him the axiom that he was never to act without a "superior's instructions."[31] Williams "escaped" from the navy to the walls of his study and the confines of the classroom, trading one womb for another. He cannot establish the direct connection between his reluctance to leave the navy and his own unexpiated sin of contributing to the fatal explosion.

In context, Bullitt appears to have been a tightly controlled homosexual, possibly not completely aware of his real problem. Professional excellence compensated for the

---

28. D. H. Lawrence, "Studies in Classic American Literature," in *The Shock of Recognition*, ed. Edmund Wilson (New York, 1955), pp. 956–57.

29. *Cocoon*, p. 86.   30. Ibid., p. 244.   31. Ibid., p. 169.

personal flaw, but when that failed him, he collapsed. Callan too was recognized before he knew himself, and Leveridge's Tuthill metamorphosed similarly. Bloom, Lorry Adams, and Callan all seek death because of homosexuality. Bloom was humiliated; Adams degraded and convinced of his hopelessness. Sergeant Callan killed himself rather than live with a weakness, though Murphy's presentation indicates a strong unconscious drive toward death operating in Callan.

There is a general agreement among contemporary war novels and much of American literature concerning the genesis of homosexuality: it is a psychological state, induced by the immediate social environment, not related to organic weaknesses. Introverted, intense, rigidly self-contained men are prime candidates. In none of the novels is homosexuality accepted as a normal pattern; it is a weakness, a despised and disruptive anomaly.

The changes from Leveridge's Gothic gloom of sex and mystery to Murphy's story of a "Grotesque" to Plagemann's embroidery on themes from Melville are considerable, but the emphasis on character and action, central to Chase's distinction between the "novel" and the "romance," is present in all three works. Any writer who undertakes to separate and analyze the intangibles of emotion that bind individual men together in small corporate bodies during the violent stresses of war risks both oversimplification and being misunderstood. The works just examined are serious and imaginative attempts to make the war novel something more than a mere I-was-there recitation.

Not only does Gide's Corydon equate belligerency with homosexual potential, he insists, in the "First Dialogue," that like heterosexual love, homosexuality is manifest in "all shades and degrees: from Platonic love to lust, from self-denial to sadism. . . ."[32] In *Civilization and Its Discontents*, Freud argues that the human, organic death instinct may be directed toward the external world, actually in the "service of Eros," working for the individual as an outward-directed aggressiveness and destructiveness. Any restriction of this outward focus of force, Freud emphasizes, "would be bound to

32. Gide, *Corydon*, p. 23.

increase the self-destruction."[33] Gide's proposal reflects back
to the previous works; both comments are germane to aspects
of the next group of war novels, which are concerned with the
relationship of sexuality and violence.

Most war novels work out some constant relationship
between sexuality and violent proclivities, which may be expressed as heroism, wanton butchery, or cowardice. A very
few, like *The Beardless Warriors*, are virtually untouched by
sex. The closest to a "standard" relationship is that a sexually
potent man is a good man in any situation. Mitchell Goodman has the hoary converse cliché come from the mouth of his
ranting Patton-analogue, General Batchelor, in *The End of It*:
"any man who can't fuck can't fight. . . ." Mailer's Sergeant
Croft, Danny Kantaylis and Sam Damon from Anton Myrer's
war novels, Jones's First Sergeant Warden, Sergeant Hervey
of *Walk on the Water*—are all positive examples of the prevalent comparison.

Glen Sire's *The Deathmakers* is a form of the psychological novel. It differs from the normal psychological novel,
however, in that Sire does not dwell on motives or subtleties
of thought, but creates instead characters whose actions
identify them. Each character is a construct, and the distortion
imposed upon characterization by the predetermined psychological goal weakens the book's mimetic credibility; it remains, however, a relatively superior war novel, a laudable
attempt to extract meaning from fiction. Sire acknowledges
the influence of a psychologist whose consultation influenced
"the creation of the characters" in this novel. With this explicit dedication to the study of motives, Sire delineates sexuality, aggression, and the death instinct—the "split psyche"
so prevalent in modern literature.

Emphasizing action, *The Deathmakers* begins in combat
during the final days of World War II, as an American
armored column penetrates Germany. The chief characters are
Captain Brandon, who commands the point element, and
his superior, named only once, known as "the colonel." The
colonel is a broad caricature of the Patton image, probably

33. Sigmund Freud, *Civilization and Its Discontents*, trans. and
ed. James Strachey (New York, 1962), p. 66.

designed to illustrate the drastic measures that must be taken
to get men to kill day after day. Brandon sickens of the war
when he kills another man in close combat. Admonished
by his superior, he replies: "Shoot me." Having killed, Brandon feels guilt; his own death is assured.

The column battles a stubborn rear-guard defense commanded by Captain Raeder, a personification of Junker military aristocracy. A soldier in the highest sense, Raeder is motivated by his loyalty to Hitler and to German nationalism. In
the sequence of battles he and Brandon become personal
antagonists. Sire maintains momentum by describing an action first from the attacker's point of view, then through
the reactions of Captain Raeder. Refusing surrender, Raeder
looks for death; he kills Brandon, whose dying effort, in turn,
wounds him. It is appropriate to the theme of the book that
Raeder is not granted the warrior's death he wants.

Sire's is not a subtle book; it is starkly realistic, overlaid
with symbolism that is perhaps too obtrusive. But his real
goal is a psychological exploration of the motives and emotions of men of war. This is best illustrated by Brandon's
conjecture about the word "fuck," which "was used to communicate the complete spectrum of human emotions all the
way from hate to love and back again to the flat, blank fear
of death." Brandon concludes, however, that "the war word,"
which says "everything and therefore nothing" does finally
convey a fundamental meaning: "No matter what a man was
saying, it seemed as if beneath the sense of his words he were
also communicating the idea that he was trying to hate the
idea of being alive."[34] Men who have resigned themselves in
despair to the fates of war thus conveniently free themselves
of the need to think beyond it. Sire reiterates the point in a
later scene. Like Vardaman reciting the names of his brothers
or touching Jewel's horse to establish the fact of his own being
after the death of his mother, Brandon, surrounded by death
in war, thinks of his wife: "Leslie, Leslie, Leslie. For Christ's
sake, don't think about her. Don't think. Fight. Fuck it. Fuck
them all. . . . And when you're dead you're fucked by the
fickle finger of fate. . . . It's too bad we aren't as ashamed of

34. Glen Sire, *The Deathmakers* (New York, 1960), pp. 34–35.

the word war as we are of the word fuck." Earlier, kissing her for the last time before going to war, Brandon had "sat unmoving, thinking to himself, 'This is Leslie, this is Leslie, this is Leslie.' "[35]

His shadow, Chico, is the spirit of war personified. Murderously aggressive, Chico is a squat, gnomelike killer, the point man for Brandon's advance element. The Browning automatic rifle Chico carries symbolizes both his prowess as a soldier and his superior sexual endowment. He repeatedly saves Brandon's life, appearing almost magically, always on hand to kill. Sexual intercourse is combat to Chico: "You got to take it out somewhere."[36] It is Chico who interrupts the advances of a German woman attempting to lure Brandon to her bed. Seizing her, he takes her to bed and is killed by an expert knife thrust.

The colonel is a bellicose man whose lurid speeches of gore and hatred inspire his men to fight: "Think of how they said they were going to kick the shit out of the world. . . . Think of how they would have fucked your mother and cut your heart out, and then thank God you've got a gun in your hands and you can kill the bastards." In the American tradition, the colonel's wife "was a bitch."[37] In compensation he has a French woman—his sexual plaything—in whom sex and violence mingle: her entire family was slaughtered by Germans, and she is a pathological killer. When the colonel strains against her and "gasps like a starved dog" during intercourse, she thinks of killing "Boche." On the same evening that Chico is murdered, the colonel realizes for the first time as he lies next to her that what he really wants from her is human understanding, something he has never experienced. About to force himself on her half-sleeping body he suddenly pauses: "But that's not why you want her, he thought. That's hardly it at all." For the first time during their relationship, he realized something of the real woman behind "the strange detachment that had always shielded her. . . ."[38]

Chico and the French woman represent the two faces of war. Chico is what Freud labeled the "primitive psyche,"

35. Ibid., pp. 234–35, 32. 37. Ibid., p. 92.
36. Ibid., p. 36. 38. Ibid., pp. 195–96.

freed and ready to destroy all whom war identifies as enemies.[39] Pure impulse, he is under tenuous control, apt to turn
on friends as well as enemies, motivated primarily by the
drive for impulse gratification in rape and murder. The
French woman is the finer, hard-won qualities of civilization,
perverted by the irresistible imperatives of war. Her hatred
and anguish metamorphose her, creating a monster that experiences sexual delight in slaughtering prisoners.[40] Chico's
death and the colonel's brief glimpse of the real woman he
had regarded as "meat" signal the effective end of the war.
So, both human aspects are necessary for war to disappear.
Bereft of their respective protective complements, Brandon
and the colonel die almost gratuitous deaths.

The human potential for war is placed in clear focus by
Sire's description of Chico raping a crazed young German
girl, having used his BAR to tear her father apart before her
eyes. He chokes her to accelerate her tardy responses, and he
finds "the stark female beast" that is his "counterpart." She
becomes a "wild, brown-haired little animal."[41] Sire's novel
illustrates strikingly an element of plot that has moved far
from its beginnings in the Leatherstocking series and *Huckleberry Finn*, according to Leslie Fiedler, prefigured in Poe's
tale of A. Gordon Pym and the relationship of Ishmael and
Queequeg. Numerous American war novels display a darker,
undisciplined adjunct to the hero, conventionally disposed of
when he has served his purpose.

Chico and Brandon clearly embody a variant of the
quality D. H. Lawrence saw woven into the fabric of American literature as he describes it throughout *Studies in Classic
American Literature*: American consciousness as a "torn, divided monster." Commenting on Deerslayer, Lawrence warns
that, although he says "hurt nothing unless you're forced to,"
Deerslayer has the essential American soul, "hard, isolate,
stoic, and a killer. . . . This is the very intrinsic-most American." The clearest statement of his thesis appears in the dis-

---

39. Sigmund Freud, *Reflections on War and Death*, trans. and ed.
A. A. Brill and A. B. Kuttner (New York, 1918), pp. 27–28, 31, 70.
40. *Deathmakers*, p. 169.   41. Ibid., p. 155.

cussion on Hawthorne: "Always the same. The deliberate consciousness of Americans so fair and smooth-spoken, and the under-consciousness so devilish. *Destroy! destroy! destroy!* hums the under-consciousness. *Love and produce! Love and produce!* cackles the upper consciousness." Lawrence mentions that the soul occasionally disintegrates, and when this "intrinsic-most American . . . breaks from his static isolation, and makes a new move, then look out, something will be happening."[42] Joe Christmas, at once murderous and penitent, is an example of the composite action in one figure.

Chico and Brandon personify a potential of the "under-consciousness" and "upper consciousness" in Lawrence's analysis. Chico with his BAR is a surrealistic distortion of La Longue Carabine, infinitely more ominous than Hemingway's Nick, who calmly plinks Germans off the garden wall in Mons. Chico's murderous impulse is almost impossible to channel. In an argument with his squad, he almost guns them down. His "blue-white" eyes glittering insanely, he relents when Brandon confronts him, presenting the only bond of kinship he recognizes.[43] Days after Chico's death Brandon deliberately sacrifices himself, walking with a white flag to the barricade concealing Raeder and the remnants of the rear-guard force. Risking his life to offer peace to the trapped Germans, Brandon no longer feels the "cold agony of the fear of his own death." Resigned, he wants to save lives, and "make up, somehow, for everything wrong he'd done in the war. . . ."[44] This feeling began the day he killed another man in close combat.

Brandon is the hero-as-victim figure, so prominent in American literature. Prewitt and Quentin Compson die for incompletely articulated reasons; Miss Lonelyhearts is fervent and compassionate but ignorant, rushing to meet the struggling cripple; and Robert Jordan is aided considerably by circumstances in formulating his sacrifice. Brandon is comparable to Ken Kesey's McMurphy, deliberately sacrificing

42. Lawrence, "Studies in Classic American Literature," pp. 955, 965–66, 985.
43. *Deathmakers*, p. 37.   44. Ibid., p. 269.

himself for the specific goal of saving others. Feeling compassion for the men of both sides, Brandon also has everything to live for. He offers his life out of conscience.

In this war literature, numerous "darker" figures are guilty of rape, murder, or similar violence. When the battle subsides, irrational force and unrestrained impulse cannot be tolerated, so the "dark" figures die or are diminished greatly. They die violently—if possible, heroically—but always conveniently. The rebellious, unruly character may aid or oppose the hero; he may be an equal, but more often is a subordinate. Not necessarily an Indian or a Negro, he is in these stories psychologically "dark" or menacing. To employ Leslie Fiedler's perceptive distinction, he represents not the "primitive world which lies beyond the margins of cities," but the unknown qualities "beneath the lintel of consciousness."[45]

The dialectic of opposing principles, the "torn, divided monster" noted by Lawrence as a fundamental element of American literature, runs through the pages of the contemporary American war novel as one of its most powerful currents. There can be little doubt that by the post-World War II period most of the polarity's manifestations have been consciously implanted by the authors. Sire was the first, however, to force the issue to an explicit synthesis of psychological theory and literary practice. That he did so indicates the compulsion to "point a moral," one of the most common characteristics of war novels as a group.

The notion that the emotional catharsis of physical violence, even of deadly combat, is somehow linked to sexual release is a theory to which there is wide subscription. Captain Wiley, Cozzens's hard-bitten fighter pilot in *Guard of Honor*, sums up fighter tactics against bombers with a savage, "Sock it to the bastards!" Twenty years later, that phrase resurfaces, equally ambivalent, as the refrain in Aretha Franklin's wildly successful song, "Respect": "Sock it to me, sock it to me, sock it to me!" In 1969 a veteran fighter pilot, back from more than one hundred missions over North Vietnam, challenging the deadliest concentrations of conventional air defense weapons in history, described his missile victory over

45. Fiedler, *Love and Death*, p. 366.

a MIG in air-to-air combat as "the most fun you can have with your pants on."[46] It is a cliché, and like many it may carry an essential germ of truth. In *Harm's Way*, as the attack on Pearl Harbor is announced, a delighted Paul Eddington mutters to his skipper: "Now we've got our *cojones* back, skipper. Now we're no longer the non-friggin' harem eunuchs."[47] And on the same day, James Jones's Chief Choate roars with joy over the rattle of his BAR, and Karen Holmes's most adept lover watches the tracers from his weapons stitch the canopy of a Zero, as the men of "G" Company vent the rage and frustration that Mrs. Kipfer's dedicated whores could only partially dissipate.[48]

Jones's *The Thin Red Line* is the most clinical of war novels, described by Mailer as the best of its kind. It too depicts the psychological states of men who fight, but is more concerned with a minute examination of their reactions and motivations, in the traditional sense of the psychological novel. Because its primary concern is combat, *The Thin Red Line* is discussed in more detail in the following chapter. But John Bell's unique problems with sex, guilt, fear, and violence make his case an appropriate one to discuss at this point.

Bell prefigures the evolution of Courtney Massengale, Anton Myrer's megalomaniacal general in *Once an Eagle*. In adolescence, while walking in the woods one day, Bell had come unaware upon a group of picnickers, isolated in the woods. Suddenly tumescent, he disrobed, crept dangerously close to the revelers, and masturbated furiously. Naked and far from his clothes, he surely would have been revealed if they had noticed him. This is a case of the simple titillation of guilt and the proximity of punishment, an association from bathroom adventures, as parodied in *Portnoy's Complaint*. Bell thinks of the incident years later, waiting for the order to attack: another time of excitement with a similar danger of discovery and punishment—death. When men die around him in battle Bell thinks of his wife's marvelous body; this

46. Briefing to students at U.S. Army CGSC, Ft. Leavenworth, Kansas (1970).

47. James Bassett, *Harm's Way* (New York, 1962), p. 39.

48. *Eternity*, p. 752.

is the reaction of a healthy subconscious, feeding images of life to the threatened organism.

Bell is a competent soldier, but he is motivated primarily by his overwhelming desire to return to his wife, Marty, for whose body he had resigned a commission rather than endure months of separation. Like him, she has an enormous capacity for physical love, and he knows that she must be "stepping out with, sleeping with, *fucking* somebody."

Jones's staging of Bell's crucial decision makes it obvious that a substitutive process has occurred. On the day that Bell gets a "Dear John" confirming his worst fears, he is also notified of his appointment by direct commission as first lieutenant. When he reads Marty's letter he is "shaken" and "as a professional soldier, quite ready to die." Enraged, he implores the company commander to help him. Losing the woman who is the index to his adjustment to life, he must forfeit the ever-present refuge of her life-giving breasts, where he would hide his face to forget the war. Captain Bosche hands Bell another letter: the commission. It confirms his decision to grant Marty the divorce.

Does Eros lose to Mars or Thanatos in the struggle for John Bell's allegiance? Or, has he passed through the mindless worship of sex to heed reason's blandishments, and now become worthy of leading men in battle? If losing Marty is symbolic emasculation and the loss of real power, Bell's commission represents acquisition of another power: a greater authority to direct the violence of war.

The final novel dealing with sexuality and performance is Irwin Shaw's *The Young Lions* (published in 1948). In "The Search for Values," John Aldridge complains that Noah Ackerman loses his humanity and becomes credible only as an allegorical figure.[49] Certainly allegory is one of the novel's two predominent aspects. The other is the theme that individual sexuality reflects, or prefigures, the sociological patterns that emerged after World War II in Europe. *The Young Lions* blends scenes of combat and allegory, distinctly modu-

49. John Aldridge, "The Search for Values," in *The American Novel since World War II*, ed. Marcus Klein (New York, 1969), pp. 53–54 (extracted from Aldridge's *After the Lost Generation*).

lated by the influence of Dos Passos. The novel's American contingent comprises the expected ethnic cross section, and the three protagonists move along paths that finally intersect halfway through the last chapter. In covering both sides of the conflict, Shaw provides the scope that the larger interpretation of his allegory requires.

Despite its numerous actions and multiple protagonists, *The Young Lions* is a tightly integrated book. The allegory shifts, but the action moves quickly along. In the opening chapter Christian lectures Peggy about ends and means. Frederick's sexual assault on her foreshadows Germany's attack on the world. At the end of the novel, Christian's fading mind questions his creed, and Peggy's personal knight-errant administers the coup de grace. Shaw's choice of names and patterns of action keep *Faust* and *The Faerie Queene* in the immediate background and in constant conflict with the actual "events" of the book.

Noah Ackerman and Michael Whitacre move on rising paths to a point of intersection with Christian's declining fortunes. Inspired by Hope, Noah learns to survive among his "friends," and becomes an almost perfect combat soldier. Michael becomes a fair soldier, supplying in dedication what is deficient by nature. Peggy Freemantle represents the source of his strength; she offers her glove as a token for him to wear into battle. Christian is the focus of variant forces. Frederick's amoral, gross sexuality, Gretchen Hardenberg's perverted brilliance and beauty, Lieutenant Hardenberg's sexual ecstasy at the spectacle of violence, and his cold-blooded assault on life—all are facets of the forces at work on Christian, working within Germany and, potentially, within every man. Shaw's characters are well opposed. Peggy balances Gretchen's diseased sensuality and Laura's crass materialistic ego. Joseph and Noah demonstrate two possible reactions to violence. Michael Whitacre is in no way exceptional, but he is intelligent and compassionate. Conscientiously he does what he must, persevering to the end.

The sexual impulse—excessive, ungoverned, and perverted—is analogous to the motives of war. Primitive Frederick and the exquisitely dissolute Hardenbergs cover the spectrum. The incestuous Hardenberg marriage illustrates the relationship of sex and violence; it also maintains the *Faust* motif in Gretchen's perverse beauty and her husband's megalomaniacal will. Peggy Freemantle and Gretchen are both fallen, diminished from the potential of Margaret ("Pearl"). To establish the fact firmly, Shaw has Christian tell his commander that he had an affair in Berlin with a girl named "Marguerite." Peggy is about as good as the world can tolerate, but Gretchen is truly "Margret-chen," fallen and lost. With her friend Eloise, Gretchen lusts indiscriminately after any "man or woman or beast of the field she can lay her hands on."[50] When Christian sees her later, she is, like Germany, in a state of advanced decay.

In Hardenberg a fanatic will dominates and distorts all other drives. Severely wounded, he struggles forward with a "crippled, animal-like gait," always able to subordinate every consideration to his will. War, "the most fascinating of all pursuits," is the "only real world," because it "completely fits the final nature of man, which is predatory and egotistic." Having sacrificed his face to war, Hardenberg feels that no one can accuse him of loving only the concept "safely from a distance."[51] Hardenberg, a student of Nietzsche, reminds Christian that Germany needs strong enemies to keep her strong. Later Hardenberg obligingly kills the man in the next bed, in an act of soldierly compassion for the quadruple amputee's agonized plea for death. The same will finally drives Hardenberg to kill himself, his morbid aggressions turning inward in frustration. Shaw draws the novel together with Christian's realization during the desert ambush that Hardenberg and his wife must be cousins. Hardenberg gasps, "abandoned, lost in pleasure," watching the British die, as Gretchen does making love.[52]

The allegory works like this. Frederick and Hardenberg are primal sexuality and will, aspects of the will to power, respectively. Christian, the rational, potentially better part of the German psyche, is a pilgrim in quest of an unrealized

50. Irwin Shaw, *The Young Lions* (New York, 1948), pp. 273, 160–61.

51. Ibid., p. 291.   52. Ibid., p. 206.

ideal. Together they comprise the demonic foe. Christian patiently explains to Peggy Freemantle that if the unification of Germany means extinction of the Jews, it is worth the price.[53] Peggy Freemantle is like Britomart, a personification of valor and of a national spirit. Battling Frederick, she stops him with the threat of death, then leaves both Joseph and Europe. Smitten by Peggy's charms, Michael (Artegal) forsakes Laura (Radigund) and takes up the true quest, sent on his way by Peggy, who offers her glove as a token. Phenomenally meritorious, Noah is the equivalent of Prince Arthur. The fact that he is killed indicates the nature of our age, in which the hero is also a victim. Entering the army at the portentous age of thirty-three, Michael represents his culture, both pragmatic and idealistic. He slays the tyrant and will return to Peggy to create a better world. Young Goodman Ackerman is perhaps better studied in his Biblical context. A literal savior, he fathers a son who will carry on after the deluge of world war. Though he does lapse into premarital sin with Hope, the sight of her, pregnant and tearful, gives him the strength to resume the fight. Noah is too good for his time.

Christian, too, retains a sense of honor. Killing the concentration-camp commander is both expedient for his escape and an act of expiation. Like Raeder of *The Deathmakers*, Christian wants to die under circumstances of his own choosing. He is a good man who dies in the service of a cause unworthy of him. His weakness is that the abstract concepts of order and (German) nationalism mean more to him than human lives.

The preceding novels sustain the theme that a sexually potent man is a good fighter; the man who rationally controls his appetites, however, is apt to be a better soldier for it. The psychic split noted among the works on commanders is evident here to a marked degree. In combat the "primitive psyche" must assert dominance if the individual is to survive. The theory that a good fighter may be a social misfit is also supported. Lawrence's comment about the dualism of American literature has long since been verified. It is logical that

53. Ibid., p. 19.

any such potential for psychological fracture should appear in novels of war.

The third and final section of this chapter covers works that explore General Cummings's comment that weapons are something more than machines, that there is an inevitable interplay between the machines of war and their operators. The books discussed are: *The End of It, The War Lover, Once an Eagle*, and *Why Are We in Vietnam?* In the literature of war, technology's geometric increase in power produces at last a figure so exquisitely attuned to destructive violence that he reacts sexually not to the sight of death and destruction, nor even to the weapons that produce it, but shudders orgasmically simply reading or issuing orders that will loose the power of the war machine, though he is several times removed from the action.

Writing of the Civil War, Crane describes a battle that sounds like "whirring and thumping of gigantic machinery."[54] Dos Passos carefully preserves the effect in his chapter titles for *Three Soldiers*. General Cummings talks of "man machines," saying "we are not so discrete from the machine any longer."[55] Private Willy of *The Barren Beaches of Hell* (published in 1959) thinks of himself as serial number "525271, a numbered mechanism activated by obscure necessity. . . ."[56] Captain Brandon of *The Deathmakers* observes as he emerges from the red haze of battle, "We're all less than the guns we've made."[57] The following novels demonstrate the process of evolution, or deterioration, whereby men react sexually to the work of their destructive machines, totally alienated from the reality of war and its human consequences. Norman Mailer's *Why Are We in Vietnam?*, capping the trend, places the discussion squarely in the stream of romantic thought that has opposed the concept of "progress" from the time of Emerson and Carlyle, as delineated in Leo Marx's absorbing

54. Stephen Crane, *The Red Badge of Courage*, ed. Sculley Bradley, et al. (New York, 1962), p. 100.
55. Norman Mailer, *The Naked and the Dead* (New York, 1948), p. 569.
56. Boyd Cochrell, *The Barren Beaches of Hell* (New York, 1959), p. 93.
57. *Deathmakers*, p. 145.

study of technology and the pastoral ideal in America, *The Machine in the Garden.*

The End of It is a story of death, and of a resurrection. Goodman's novel describes a process of vocational transference, as if extending the ethical potential of Max Weber's *The Protestant Ethic and the Spirit of Capitalism* to the conduct of war. Since the military unit involved is a heavy artillery unit, assigned either to corps or army, the men see nothing of the front lines, and have no idea of the results of their handiwork at trajectory's end. A battalion commander, whose civilian vocations included work on a Ford assembly line and selling cars for Chrysler, thinks of his current position as a "calling" in the holy cause of winning the war. The Fire Direction Center is "the brains of the factory," and a muzzle burst that kills several crewmen is "an industrial accident." Good spring weather brings a seasonal rush in business for his powerful machines, which fire only spasmodically in winter, a period of recession when, the narrator reminds us, "men died [only] one at a time or in small bunches." Control techniques that allow all batteries of all battalions to fire simultaneously on a single target represent "mass production."[58]

A forward observer, Lieutenant Freeman does well at his trade. Adjusting the distant, innocuous-looking puffs of smoke to the prescribed map coordinates, he is like a man creating something "with hammer and nails." An enthusiastic convert to military science, he writes to his friends at home about the complexity of artillery, something "like building a bridge, only in reverse." Haranguing the men to a killing pitch, General Batchelor delivers a Pattonesque litany of gory violence by alluding to their enterprise as a "holy war . . . a crusade."[59]

Lieutenant Freeman destroys his enemy from a distance by words whispered into a field telephone. Wielding such power, he begins to change. The complex balance of conscience, cultural inhibition, the anxiety endemic to war, and an

58. Mitchell Goodman, *The End of It* (New York, 1961), pp. 53, 55–56.
59. Ibid., pp. 240, 162, 111.

indefinable confusion of incipient guilt one day brings him to
the nadir of his humanity. Watching the shells of his battalion
tear apart an offending village, he experiences the "pure
pleasure of destruction," then a "transfiguration" of release,
like "a thunderstorm after a hot day. Release of all pressure."
He sees creation in reverse: "It is—then it is not. Something
moved, quivered in his groin, as if in response to a woman."
Watching in fascination he feels "an uprush of blood, as in a
man who has created something."[60]

Goodman uses several devices to maintain our awareness of the atmosphere surrounding Lieutenant Freeman, who
is abstractly attracted to the "terribly beautiful" spectacle of
his trade. Random bits and snatches of conversation in the
manner of Dos Passos, letters to and from "home" that portray the tragic innocence of noncombatants, cameo scenes
from rear-echelon areas where the corporate effort moves on
high levels—all are juxtaposed with vignettes of combat.
Then Freeman, who is for the first time within a few hundred
meters of a target, sees the obscene truth of his handiwork:
"One man at a time, each one a separate man running for his
life . . . they died in terror," the life "gouged out of them."
Dying to his former state, Freeman falls into unconsciousness.
Regaining consciousness, he takes up his binoculars and
scans the area again, his final sight "framed the stripped
branches of an olive tree that bore as its fruit half of a man's
body. . . ."[61]

The full realization of his guilt drives Freeman mad. He
is not cured until he can accept war's violation of the sanctity
of human life. His recovery is linked to the strong, vital
Mediterranean sun; he noticed, even during his shock in the
fatal barrage, that the "green life kept pushing up out of the
ground, glistening now as it met the on-coming sun." In a
literal purgatory, he rehearses nightly the vision that has become a sunrise over a bloody fountain from which half a human body moves upward. Closing his eyes in bright sunlight
he sees the same image, projected in the thin film of blood in
his lids. Always the persistent question of guilt: "Where does

60. Ibid., pp. 168–69.   61. Ibid., pp. 246, 251.

the machine end and the man begin?"[62] Momentarily in strong sun, he feels a release from guilt, "a being in the natural world," but that fades before his vision in which the truncated human corpse "rose higher than anything else." Remembering the speeches exhorting him in war and fragments of prayers from his religion, Freeman cannot resolve the guilt for his individual acts against other men.

Goodman apparently is attempting to express some awareness of what D. H. Lawrence would call the mystic "blood-consciousness" of Mediterranean peoples. Its intimate connection to the life force is somehow conveyed through the sun to Freeman, but he cannot accept absolution until the more conventional motivations have been explained and put into the perspective of his machine-dominated world. So Goodman calls on Walt Whitman. The sight of trucks filled with innocent, noisy replacements, headed north to the deadly mountains reminds Freeman of Whitman's allusion to war as *"the strong terrific game. . . ."* Whitman saw war, yet he sings about it like a "virgin" singing of ideal courtly love. How is that possible? Other phrases from "Drum Taps" occur to Freeman: "If need be a thousand shall sternly immolate themselves for one. . . . Those who love each other shall become invincible."

The blind inevitable surge of life that runs through Whitman's poetry brings the pattern of human experience into focus for Freeman. But the blend of patriotism, religious zeal, stark fear, and animal ferocity is alloyed with yet another component. "It begins as a mission: to save the world. It ends as another victory for the machine. The perversion of nature: the guns, the hermaphrodite killers, the castrating machines. The big gun: a blind eunuch, finally; like all machines, a neuter, emasculating all whom it touches."[63] Coerced into collusion with the machine, he can expiate his sin by helping the living. So Lieutenant Freeman's contact with the people whose soldiers he had killed cures him. He is saved, feeling alive again for the first time, "as if he were a corpse being warmed into life by the sun."

62. Ibid., pp. 247, 272.   63. Ibid., pp. 279–80.

Goodman expresses the general malaise of mass-produced machine warfare in passages that describe the "coupling of man and machine," as men whose trade is service to the machine are drawn by the strong thrust and recoil of the guns into a "kind of lovemaking; rhythmically, blindly. . . . Round and round, in rising excitement, until the barrels were almost too hot to touch." Elsewhere, "They were in heat and had not yet been satisfied."[64]

The End of It is a sustained attempt to isolate and identify the irresistible but intangible forces that operate on the mind and body of a man caught up in technological war. Goodman's intense involvement, however, causes him to push the analogy too far, as in calling the lieutenant's appearance to the people in the small village "a re-birth, the still-born god out of the machine," or in describing the rhythm of artillery firing as the "music of the machines, the music of a Black Mass in which men eat of each other's flesh and drink of each other's blood. . . ."[65] That "free-man" is undergoing a personal reenactment of the passion and resurrection soon becomes apparent, and is oppressively labored.

Goodman's success in delineating Freeman's initial, subtle metamorphosis calls attention to the insidiously alienating quality of war by machine, and it directs primary guilt back on a world that fails, short of war, to solve its problems.

In *The War Lover* (published in 1959), John Hersey created a twentieth-century version of Frankenstein's monster. Hersey's novel signals the fruition of a prophetic warning by Carlyle, duly noted and recorded by Leo Marx in *The Machine in the Garden*, and more recently discussed by Erich Kahler and Ihab Hassan. Commenting on "Signs of the Times," Marx says that Carlyle criticizes "an entire way of life." "Industrialism," opens an era when, in Carlyle's words, "the same habit regulates not our modes of action alone, but our modes of thought and feeling. Men are grown mechanical in head and heart, as well as in hand."[66]

64. Ibid., pp. 57, 246.
65. Ibid., pp. 279–82.
66. Leo Marx, *The Machine in the Garden* (New York, 1968), pp. 173–74.

What Carlyle saw, and called "hopelessly pernicious," says Marx, was the first shape of alienation. Furthermore, the idea "has dominated the criticism of industrial society ever since." The primary aspect of alienation is that, to an increasing degree, human behavior is determined externally, "by invisible, abstract, social forces unrelated to . . . inward impulse."[67] These words from the conclusion of "Characteristics" express succinctly both Carlyle's despair and his heroic refusal to surrender to it: "Here on Earth we are as Soldiers, fighting in a foreign land; that understand not the plan of the campaign, and have no need to understand it; seeing well what is at our hand to be done. Let us do it like Soldiers. . . ."

Studying the quality of modern life, Ihab Hassan remarks in *Radical Innocence* that a primary facet of life in this century is the paradox of "the unremitting organization of society and the unleashing of vast destructive energies against civilization."[68] This contest of powers produces what Erich Kahler describes in *The Tower and the Abyss* as "overcivilization and dehumanization." Modern society tends toward organization as "collectives . . . established by common ends" rather than as "communities . . . derive[d] from common origins."[69] Industrialization has brought specialization and the division of labor; it does not require that a man respond "as a whole, organic being," but only in terms of a peculiar function. Individual concerns are thus fragmented and human qualities "atrophy," and in some extremes, Kahler argues, specialists become *"personalized functions"* (emphasis added). As the individual works daily toward an externally directed end, "the collective, functional part of the personality grows at the expense of the individual and human part." Of crucial importance is the disappearance, or severe attenuation, of individual moral judgment, as "the concrete human particularity of the unique individual is displaced by the abstract particularity of the collectively specialized function."[70]

67. Ibid., p. 176.
68. Ihab Hassan, *Radical Innocence* (New York, 1966), p. 14.
69. Erich Kahler, *The Tower and the Abyss* (New York, 1967), pp. xiii, 9.
70. Ibid., pp. 22–23.

The "hero" of *The War Lover* is a flesh-and-blood an-
droid, a bionic centaur. Though the relationship varies, *The
Body* is never just a flying machine Marrow guides to and
from the air war over Germany. His decline and death form
an object lesson in human accommodation to technology and
to modern war, developing to its fullest the thesis central to
Goodman's novel.

Narrator Boman poses a problem from the beginning. His
story is dual: alternating chapters cover *The Body*'s last raid
and the action that precedes it, respectively. The first sequence
documents Marrow's terminal decline and the second establishes a case history. Hersey's use of the military twenty-
four-hour clock for "The Raid" and specific dates during "The
Tour" lends an aura of logbook veracity to Boman's taut
narrative. A small man with big problems, Boman has been
unsure of himself and overwhelmed by his massive, cocksure
pilot. He explicitly compares himself to Coleridge's Mariner,
and his story is a catharsis; the adventure tells at least as much
about him as it does about Marrow. As the dual strands of
Boman's narrative merge, the reader can easily visualize him,
crouched in the English crash boat, fixing a hapless crewman
with hypnotic eye, compulsively reciting his tale of an ill-fated
voyage.

The most striking aspect of Marrow's attachment to *The
Body* is the variety of his attitudes. Following Freud's suggestion that ships and vessels of all kinds are symbolic of "the
female organ," Marrow's comment that just looking at "her"
makes him feel "horny" is not unusual. But moments before
that remark he had postured like a strongman, remarking to
Boman, "It's part of me, kid." Boman says of Marrow that he
has a "centaur's chest"; in a dream he sees Marrow as "an
impressive organization of flesh and cloth and leather and fur
and rubber," with a chest that "could have been a generator,"
and with power literally flowing from his fingertips into the
aircraft.[71]

Flying and sex are always merged for Marrow, but the
relationship varies. He argues that he needs a "hoor house"

71. John Hersey, *The War Lover* (New York, 1959), pp. 5, 34, 43,
66–67.

or a mission every day. But he also theorizes that flying is like salt peter, killing the sex urge "in any guy whose got a lot of it." Marrow boasts that "fairies don't fly," but in the next breath says, "a flier can only go for himself." Three days before his final mission he brags to a woman, *"The Body . . . is my body. And when I fly I'm just pushing along with The Body sticking out in front of me."*[72]

But Boman learns that Marrow's famous war cry is really an orgasmic reaction to the proximity of death: he is a War Lover. Loving "fighting better than the things he's fighting for," Marrow "wants death. Not just for himself, but for everyone."[73] Unconsciously courting death, he feels happy only in aerial combat, eventually achieving sexual release at the sight of enemy fighters and the tremor in his own *Body* as the bombs fall and his own guns begin to fire. Boman theorizes that Marrow finally had experienced fear on that final flight, "not the clashes and killing but his enjoyment of them. For to enjoy, even to enjoy horror, was to live, and . . . Buzz had found life at the innermost heart of it, unbearable." When enemy fire tore open *The Body*, he "passively welcomed emasculation and disarmament" because of the "inner drive for death he did not know he had."[74] To demonstrate that all men have some of the same potential, Hersey has Boman point out that in flight they were all connected by oxygen-line umbilicals to the B-17, all part of the litter.[75]

In *The War Lover*, the most consciously "literary" of the straight war novels, Hersey deliberately cites tradition, often ironically. Most flagrantly, Boman mentions the squadron briefing officer, who has the impressive total of two missions and the prospect of no more, and who knows "miles of Conrad by heart." He's the only one among them who dares talk about " 'honor' and 'courage' and 'loyalty' and 'morale' out loud." The "Ancient Mariner" motif reappears in the final chapter of the novel. Marrow's decline is accompanied by the return of courage and vigor among the crew, heretofore bullied into sullen inanimation by their pilot. Like the Mari-

72. Ibid., pp. 140–42, 146–47, 314–15, 376.
73. Ibid., pp. 76, 381, 386–87.
74. Ibid., p. 396.   75. Ibid., p. 63.

ner, Boman blesses life, though unconsciously, when in the
midst of the fighter attack on the final raid he suddenly has a
vision of Daphne in "filtered sunlight." Unable to account for
it, he wonders why he thought of "the memory of desire,"
rather than of the "passage of fulfillment?" In the presence
of death he is sustained by the image of Life. When Marrow's
plane strikes the water, it miraculously breaks in half at precisely the right place so that the crew can simply "walk out"
and inflate their rafts.[76] Marrow sinks, clinging determinedly
to his *Body*.

"Mechanical in head and heart," Buzz Marrow becomes a
"personalized function," all his humanity distorted to aggressive lust. He and Kid Lynch (to whom Snowden of *Catch-22*
may owe some of his substance) are the extremes; some place
in between, Boman endures through a rational acceptance of
the need to endure life and persevere. A man of his time,
Boman submits to the collective that directs him toward its
goal of winning the war.

In 1967 Norman Mailer's *Why Are We in Vietnam?*
appeared, a psychological reader on the foundations of U.S.
involvement. It is an appraisal of the Garden savagely defiled.
Even more than *The End of It*, this book takes the special
curse off war as the particular culprit in loosing the beast of
technologically aberrant sexuality; it fixes the onus squarely
on industrial, "progressive" society. Given a society as Mailer
portrays it, the phenomenon of Vietnam is virtually inevitable.

Mailer gets quickly to the task of defining the American
sexual psyche. Dallas, that microcosmic manifestation of the
American mystique, is the home of red-blooded men, without
whose oil, money, and greed the wheels of industry could not
so felicitously spin. "Everyone of these bastards," Mailer
writes, "has the sexual peculiarities of red-blooded men, which
is to say that one of 'em can't come unless he's squinting down
a gun sight, and the other won't produce unless his wife
sticks a pistol up his ass—that man is of course a cop."[77]
Action in general, and violent action in particular, are inex-

76. Ibid., pp. 182, 403.
77. Norman Mailer, *Why Are We in Vietnam?* (New York, 1967),
p. 12; hereafter cited as *Why*.

tricably enmeshed with sexual response in America. Though
the sexual and scatological details of *Why* are too enthusi-
astically in evidence, they are germane and necessary for
emphasis.

Mailer extends the fundamental thesis of irreconcilability
—man and machine, father and son, technology and nature—
bound together in a matrix of questionable relationships and
violent sexual hyperbole, answering eloquently the "overwhelming question, 'Why. . . ?'" Still close to its violent
origins, America retains the frontiersman's love of the tall
story, his worship of the rugged individualist, and his awe of
guns and of mighty hunters: Daniel Boone, Billy the Kid,
Sgt. Alvin York, Pretty Boy Floyd, John Dillinger, Audie
Murphy, J. F. Cooper's prodigious hunter, Davey Crockett,
and the James Brothers all inhabit the same pantheon. That
prowess with a weapon equals sexual ability is an American
literary tradition as old as Rip van Winkle's rusted musket,
echoing through Ishmael Bush's warning shot to Abiram and
Asa, up through the work of Faulkner and Hemingway. The
theme of escape, both from society and from female presence,
also abounds in the same literature and has drawn more than
adequate comment. (The work of anthropologists in general,
along with Sir James George Frazer's *Golden Bough* and
Freud's *Totem and Taboo*, gives substantial evidence, however, that this is not an exclusively American tradition.)

Faulkner's hunting party in "The Bear" goes off into the
woods with minimum essentials; they live off their kills after
the first days. Contrast their wagon-bound pilgrimage with
Rusty's fixed-wing and helicopter radio-controlled assault on
the virgin North. Major de Spain may have believed in the
mythic efficacy of the hunt, but Rusty (a machine gone bad?)
proclaims his expedition a competition between him and
another denizen of the "CCCC-and-P" executive menagerie.
Not an escape, nor an excuse to commune with nature, the
hunting expedition is purely the occasion for another bout
of testing himself. His counterpart is suddenly called away
for an important negotiation, so Rusty must go without a
peer, reducing the trip's competitive nature. He is "dying inside for not being down there at the Canaveral table where

big power space decisions were being made by his opposite number. . . ." Rusty needs a bear to secure his corporate image: "He got a corporation mind. He don't believe in nature; he put his trust and distrust in man. 5% trust, 295% distrust."[78]

Stephen Rojack lives the updated American dream of success in *An American Dream*: he gets away literally with murder. *Why Are We in Vietnam?* is a similarly mangled extrapolation of ideas best presented earlier in "The Bear." A culture that operates basically on the profit motive encourages competition, which feeds hugely and becomes omnipotent; thus, the profit motive fosters and then manipulates "progress" through technology. All abstractions fade, and even the concept of guilt is altered, becoming simply the fear of being observably inadequate in the exercise of power. Only power and the possession of "things" retain significance. All drives are subordinated to the will to power. Just as Rojack's lovemaking with Deborah, Ruta, and Cherry are contests of will, so Rusty, the corporation "eggzek," is "full of will . . . strong as bulls these hide-ass Waspy mules . . . they go direction they want to go . . . their nose too long they sniff it up . . . they tie that nice dry-oiled West Point ramrod on their back just like they're a tomato plant on a stick."[79]

The Machine's assault on the Garden's last citadel is described by the guide: "Brooks Range no wilderness now. Airplane go over the head, animal no wild no more, now crazy." Just like man. Luke does not know for sure whether atom bombs or helicopters are the cause, but the cumulative effect is "general fission" of the psychomagnetic field, which is now a "mosaic" of fragments, "grizzer" has gone "ape," and "[helicopters] are exploding psychic ecology all over the place."[80] For Rusty, as for Chico, the pathological killer of Glen Sire's *The Deathmakers*, sublimation can accommodate only so much of the damned-up will-to-power, libido, killer-aggressor instinct, or whatever. Here, the energy that might have been spent constructively at Canaveral, putting the space program into a loftier orbit, is dissipated in spasms of killing

78. Ibid., pp. 48–49, 53.   80. Ibid., pp. 65, 113–14.
79. Ibid., pp. 31–32.

and despoliation. In Chico's words: "You gotta take it out somewhere."

"Grizzer," like Old Ben, represents the spirit of the land, perhaps here of earth itself. He is not, like Old Ben was, virtually invulnerable to human weapons; his nature is permanently altered by side-effects of the same poisonous technology that drives men to the wilderness seeking release from society's tensions, looking for a place to dissipate the aggressions of civilization. Mailer's allegory of Ruby Lil, the great whore of the Saskatchewan, supports the thesis. Ruined by "an auditor from Manitoba" whose sexual responses were so distorted that they could not be excited by any of her wiles, Ruby is herself perverted, "diminish[ing] to a dyke."[81]

The complex involvement between aggressive instincts and erotic instincts is obviously near the center of this book and many others more easily categorized as war novels. The notion that civilization somehow stifles and subtly alters the relationship and its manifestations is also implied, but it is difficult to articulate. Sigmund Freud's *Civilization and Its Discontents* provides a clue. In his earlier *Reflections On War and Death* (published in 1918), Freud simply asserted that "inhibited impulses" cause "remarkable reactions," but that the primitive psyche is always ready to reassert itself, as the ubiquity of warfare indicates. Sexuality, says Freud, is the most difficult of the instinctual energies to suppress. In his later work, unable to distinguish between "aggressive instincts" and "erotic demands," Freud simply states that they are closely related, and "hardly ever appear in pure form, isolated from each other. . . ." "Libido" is Freud's term for the manifestations of the power of Eros. Operating from its "home" in the ego, it is significant in the struggle between the individual and society in the problem of its distribution between "ego" and "objects." Constant petitioning from internal and external sources for distribution of sexual and aggressive energies explains, to his own satisfaction at least, Freud's famous conclusion that "possibly the whole of mankind—have become neurotic."[82]

81. Ibid., pp. 115–16.
82. Freud, *Civilization*, pp. 65, 68–69, 85–86, 88, 91.

In 1930 Freud wrote that much human anxiety was derived from man's knowledge that he has the power to exterminate himself; the world of D.J. and Rusty is dominated by the prospect of instantaneous mass incineration, as predicted, "next time." Barely nosed out and running a strong second in the pack of contenders threatening civilization is the profit-oriented commercial foundation of world society, represented by "CCCC-and-P," specifically compared to the U.S.S.R. To avoid onerous comparisons and mistaken identity, Rusty's corporation adds the fourth "C" as a discriminator.[83]

Mailer depicts D.J.'s parents as possessors of an awesome mythic sexuality, gigantic and violent in its exercise. But when duty calls, financial fervor overcomes all, and Rusty "zips the corporation fly." Virility, business acumen, a predilection to violence, and the ceaseless need to prove himself in competition are Rusty's traits; he is the personification of success in a world that worships it.

In Alaska, as in Faulkner's Mississippi woods, inhibitions can be relaxed. But in Mailer's Alaska there is no communion with nature; high-tension sexual energies and throttled aggressions boil and blast. Even Alaska is an insufficient sink; the psychological maladies of an entire super "syphilization" erupt beyond, so it's "Vietnam, hot damn."

Ike McCaslin refuses his tainted inheritance. Fully initiated into the diabolical mysteries, D.J. and Tex, "killer brothers, owned by something," freely renounce humanity. In full possession of their faculties, they are irrevocably pledged to the "deep beast" that sends them to "go forth and kill." As Mailer sees it, technology has utterly destroyed nature, and has progressed far in the final assault on man.

Another grim forecast is issued from the closing pages of *Once an Eagle* (published in 1968). As Sam Damon dies with his cherished credo on his lips, General Massengale looks confidently to the next peak in his assault on ultimate power. Afflicted by *ejaculatio praecox* from his youth, always sadistic, and as a mature adult incapable of normal sexuality, Massengale enjoys the services of a beautiful *fellatrice*, primarily for the "sense of power over her . . . the control of another

83. *Why*, p. 29.

being." In an argument with Sam over the morality of rule, he insisted that "there's nothing essentially corrupting about power if it's used wisely, for the objective in view."[84]

Massengale is an extension of Mailer's obsessed General Cummings, with the advantage of being totally free of medieval forebodings about "necessity." His traits are markedly similar, even to a pleasurable shudder at the sight of a line of men and matériel moving forward to death and destruction at a given time and place.[85] But Massengale's susceptibility to the magnetic attraction of power is infinitely more subtle than that of any other character in war fiction. Myrer shows him, midway through World War II, dreaming of the perfect battle of "annihilation" and of a postwar world ripe for the sure actions of "a military junta" controlling the "subservient citizenry."[86]

Courtney serves in the general headquarters of the army in Washington, never far from the seat of power. His keen intelligence and exquisite imagination enable him to envision the consequences on ships' bridges, crowded operations rooms, and fields of battle around the world as he issues orders, "draw[s] out maps or secret documents . . . [and] attend[s] conferences" that result in the movement of masses of men toward "some distant, furious, rendezvous." At certain crucial moments in his life, while performing these preparatory acts, "he [is] . . . visited by a tremor not unlike those fugitive, precarious seconds before the onset of orgasm— but without the ensuing sense of loss, the depletion, the all-consuming chagrin."[87] And in 19— he waits exultantly, vibrantly ready to "risk" World War III in Asia to enhance his career.

In *Man the Measure* (published in 1942), Erich Kahler discusses Ernst Juenger, "the intellectual spokesman of Nazi youth," citing him as an oracle of the modern *Zeitgeist*. Kahler explains that Juenger regarded the war primarily "as a revelation of the new world power, which is technology." The

84. Anton Myrer, *Once an Eagle* (New York, 1968), pp. 799, 383; hereafter cited as *Eagle*.
85. Ibid., pp. 381–82; cf. *The Naked and the Dead*, pp. 414–15.
86. *Eagle*, p. 537.   87. Ibid., pp. 528–29.

ultimate culprit is not militarism per se, but an age that prostrates itself adoringly before the manifestations of technology, worshiping power. Man, warns Kahler, becomes
"assimilated to the machine."[88] On a par with the machine or
even subservient to it, man loses his human perspective.
Juenger saw and understood. The authors of the four novels
just discussed also see and also understand. Their novels are
warnings, alarms that announce the assimilation and subservience Kahler saw in 1942. In *Why Are We in Vietnam?*
Mailer announces a vision of the end, accurately citing war
as a symptom rather than a cause.

As stories of individuals whose humanity is perverted by
war, the novels examined in this chapter tend finally to
support the conclusion of Mailer's work, which continues the
general thrust of romantic criticism of the industrial age, as
described by Leo Marx: Man must control technology or be
incidentally exterminated by the accumulated flux of its byproducts—war, physical pollution, and psychological dislocation.

Not surprisingly, these books, more than any other collection of war novels, are near the center of contemporary
literature, where sexuality, the final human citadel, confronts
the power of technology and the dehumanization inherent in
rigidly organized, mass social bodies. So it is that the characteristics of the "romance," as delineated by Richard Chase,
emerge consistently, asserting the primacy of unique human
values. The accumulated body of allusion and analogue bears
this out. The works of Lawrence, Whitman, Melville, Freud
and his associates or disciples—these constitute the literary
tradition on which the novels are founded. And because war is
becoming an increasingly appropriate parallel for the general
quality of civilized life, the war novel has become almost a
novel of manners, representative of the age.

Writing of "The Modern Self in Recoil," Ihab Hassan
quotes Lionel Trilling's reminder, in *Freud and the Crisis of
Our Culture*, that literature is essentially "concerned with the
self" and during the past two hundred years has been particularly focused upon the "self in its standing quarrel with cul-

88. Erich Kahler, *Man the Measure* (New York, 1967), pp. 594–95.

ture."[89] Among the most prevalent patterns to emerge from contemporary literature are two that dominate the war novels of sexuality and violence: first, the persistent portrayal of the hero-as-victim, and second, an almost inevitable rendition in some form of the fragmentation, or splitting, of the psyche. Captain Brandon, Sergeant Hervey, Lieutenant Freeman, Noah Ackerman, Sergeant Callan, Buzz Marrow, and the laconic, cheerfully murderous blood-brothers of *Why Are We in Vietnam?* are all victims of elements that overwhelm them. Their attitudes range from deliberate sacrifice to saving others or atoning for guilt, through unconscious submission, to a chilling, premeditated surrender of individual humanity to the coercion of external forces. But they are victims, deprived of tragic stature in a world that has witnessed the decay of the intellectual, moral, and social frameworks that make tragedy and dignity possible.

The second element is spelled out by Bellow's Dangling Man, Joseph, who writes, "Great pressure is brought to bear to make us undervalue ourselves. On the other hand, civilization teaches that each of us is an inestimable prize." That ideal could be supported in 1944, but now "civilization" is itself the primary source of the "great pressure." Between Joseph's final "Long live regimentation!" and "Vietnam, hot damn," lies the crucial, desolating realization that to move from civilian society into a war is not, after all, to change the milieu significantly.[90] The distinction is not even one of degree rather than kind, it merely involves variant modes, which are equally destructive of the self.

But the fracture, at least the pull of opposing forces, that Joseph acknowledges is rife in contemporary war novels, especially those discussed in this chapter. Dos Passos's use of multiple protagonists is an explicit sign of the forces at work on the individual in what Henry Adams rightly calls the "multiverse"; various human responses to a given situation are much more easily delineated with separate characters. Accordingly, and in virtually every case, these novels show the

89. Hassan, *Radical Innocence*, pp. 20–21.
90. Saul Bellow, *The Dangling Man* (New York, 1960), pp. 119, 191.

disintegration of the moral entity by depicting various aspects of the protagonist. Hervey-Cailini, Brandon-Chico, Boman-Marrow, and the triad of *The Young Lions* all support this assertion, as do many of the characters in the novels of command and, of course, as does *Why Are We in Vietnam?*. It is interesting to note that although Mailer makes a great point of stressing the Jekyll-Hyde pun in his work, and in pointing out their manifest differences, the two are essentially the same, probably by design. In their world there is no light, only varying shades of "darkness visible."

In an age that appears bent on annihilating individuality, the impact of moral distintegration on introspection and individual analysis is self-evident. Left, perhaps, with nothing in common but their status of victims and their essential humanity, readers of the modern novel are increasingly challenged by proposals such as Ralph Ellison's in *The Invisible Man*: all men are becoming faceless and invisible. The narrator recognizes his own hopeless anonymity in the face of blind white society, admitting it "frightens me." He closes with a reminder that the question of identity may not be confined to specific categories of men: "Who knows but that, on the lower frequencies, I speak for you?"[91] D.J. also hints directly at this: "For every Spade is the Shade of the White Man. . . ."[92]

By now, it should be obvious that the term "war novel" provides a rather general term of reference, almost as broad in scope as the word "novel" itself. The genre has grown far beyond a simple narrative of experiences to become a flexible vehicle well suited to exploring a wide range of human situations. The novels covered in this chapter are primarily directed inward. *The Young Lions* might be cited as an exception, but its figures are as easily applied to the motif of the fragmented psyche as to the more immediately apparent external allegories. (Indeed, this is also the case with *The Faerie Queene*, which *The Young Lions* often parallels in its general theme.) In *The Deathmakers*, Glen Sire is compelled to add in his acknowledgments a caveat regarding the basic psychological

91. Ralph Ellison, *The Invisible Man* (New York, 1952), p. 503.
92. *Why*, p. 26.

pattern of his novel, indicative of the sociological commitment evident in many other war novels. Like Leveridge and, to a lesser extent, Murphy and Mitchell Goodman, Sire allows the moral orientation of his book to overpower purely literary considerations. The individual authors reveal a strong inward bias. The narrative voice of *The Steel Cocoon* discusses Tyler's problem, in which the navy is a virtual womb, apart from the responsibilities of the outside world. In *The Sergeant*, young private Swanson battles the cocoon-like attraction of the evening barracks to sally forth amid the dangers of French taverns and French girls. And John Hersey, a major author with a Pulitzer prize to his credit, is similarly involved, drawn closely into his adumbration of *The War Lover*, which details Buzz Marrow's malignancy to a point beyond simple redundance.

The quintessential spirit of our age is best expressed in *Why Are We in Vietnam?*. Discussing the genesis of American existentialism in "The White Negro," Mailer says that it grew from the Negro's awareness "in the cells of his existence that life was war, nothing but war. . . ."[93] So, the hipster's anxieties stem from life lived on the brink of death. It is therefore natural that D.J's recitative of a later decade should reflect those factors now operating on the whole society. The bomb and the whole spectrum of anxieties spawned from technological progress have displaced the problems of a simpler age: "Mr. Anxiety . . . in place of Herr Dread."[94] Now everybody is in the emotional pressure-cooker.

Even nature is tainted by "progress." D.J. observes that a caribou in the process of being butchered by high velocity bullets moves away deliberately, "each step a pure phase of the blues. . . ." Another animal tumbles down a mountainside like "an old Negro heel-and-toe tap man falling down stairs. . . ." So D.J.'s insistent racial ambivalence takes on specifically hip philosophical overtones, and his ties are extended beyond "Spades" and "Eenyens" to Earth—just another victim of progress.[95]

93. Mailer, *Advertisements*, p. 341.
94. *Why*, p. 92.   95. Ibid., pp. 97, 99.

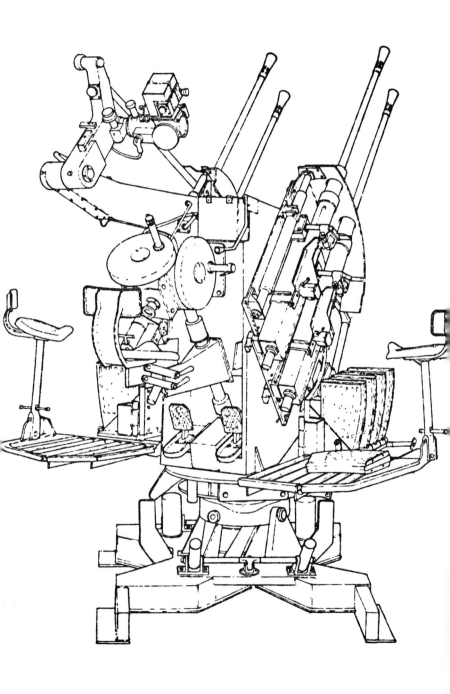

5.

THE PSYCHOLOGY OF COMBAT

So far this study has only skirted the primary distinguishing aspect of war novels: accounts of combat. Fighting, the memory of it, or the prospect of it impinges on all the works previously considered. But the books examined in this chapter are explicitly devoted to combat. These novels are fictional representations of action. Though they may be based in varying degrees on actual experience, they are not simply debriefings of fighting men. Other than fear, there are no standard reactions to combat. The elements that emerge from these attempts to extract meaning from combat constitute a body of mimetic expression which extends the reach of contemporary literature deeper into the realm of human experience, furthering the quest for the meaning of experience.

Two primary issues surface in the books discussed in this chapter: one is the question of guilt; the other, of the motives that animate men who fight. A third issue, implicit throughout, is technology's impact on men in battle.

Guilt appears in three palpably different forms. The most prevalent is guilt for killing another human being—the absolute fact of murder, regardless of motive. Another manifestation is the religious-sexual guilt that has been endemic to contemporary American literature. Finally, there is social guilt, caused by the failure to perform well in combat or by feelings of responsibility for the deaths of others. Glen Sire's *The Deathmakers*, Edward Loomis's *End of a War*, and James Jones's *The Thin Red Line* are the primary novels used to explore guilt.

The second set of novels deals with the motives that make men kill. Predictably, the emotional climate of combat varies. The enemy is sometimes an apocalyptic evil made the object of a crusade. He may be reduced by terminology to subhuman status (e.g., Hun, Gook, Wog, Chink). Or he may be considered merely another hostile facet of war, like the weather or the terrain. In some representations the simple fact that an armed foe, unknown and perhaps unseen, is prepared to kill him, produces enough anger to motivate a man to kill. Simple prudence dictates that if somebody is trying to kill you, it is best to get him first. This straightforward motivation is almost always linked with guilt: can a "normal" man be so accustomed to killing that it produces no psychological counteraction?

This second group of novels demonstrates a break from, or a metamorphic change in, the issue of guilt. Discernible in some of the later books about World War II, the change becomes pronounced in novels of Korea and Vietnam. As in Richard Matheson's Hackermeyer of *The Beardless Warriors*, the personal guilt is gone, but in its place is a growing conviction that there is something absolutely wrong with war, and particularly with this war—that it lacks justification. The desire to serve one's nation, the lust for reputation or place, the aura of intrinsic merit that has traditionally been attached to military service—all of these motives are enormously vitiated in the more recent books, reflecting accurately a mood of the times.

The Korean War novels focus on the American combat soldier's ordeal and devotion, on his newly acquired "professionalism." The two best novels of the Vietnam War go beyond the issues of personal guilt and motivation to conjecture about the overall stance of this nation in its wars. There is, in this examination, a curious sense of alienation, reflected in the mode of presentation: David Halberstam's *One Very Hot Day* (published in 1967) is an allegory; and John Sack's *M* (published in 1966) is a book of the absurd, linked genetically to *Catch-22*.

In addition to the novels by Halberstam and Sack, I include Tom Chamales's *Never So Few* (published in 1957) and Ernest Frankel's *Band of Brothers* (published in 1958), with brief allusion to other novels of the Korean War. One of the best World War II novels, Harry Brown's *A Walk in the Sun* (published in 1944), manifests the feeling of chaos in war that is attributable to the combat experience of infantry soldiers, but a feeling which also precedes the development of an attitude more generally characteristic of novels of Vietnam.

Most of the books cited in this chapter show the influence of technology on the individual soldier's reaction to combat. Some novelists offer support for Erich Kahler's thesis that machines produce a schizoid alienation from the fact of killing, although several concentrate on the inexorable effect of conscience upon men who fly planes in combat. Characteristically, though, the accounts that concern close combat are more deeply involved with problems of guilt and the adequacy of motivation or justification than those novels focused on problems of command. Technology is, of course, an inextricable element in the growing expression of alienation that is endemic to modern literature. I cite its influence here because it is particularly important to this study. Black humor and the absurd are well established modes of dealing with the problem of horror or with questions that are not susceptible to treatment by rational discourse. So it is not surprising that this chapter begins with a study in traumatic shock over an individual combat death, and concludes with Yossarian's nephew, John Sack's Demirgian, gazing contemplatively at the devastation of a foreign countryside and finding the American army "good."

The total reaction to combat is too complex to be reduced to specific states or emotions. Among the war novels, there is support for Freud's statements about the interaction of aggressive and erotic instincts, but individual authors weight particular aspects according to their own experience or artistic prejudices. Following the thrust of major emphasis in given books, I discuss the novels in relatively arbitrary divisions, with several references to works examined in previous chapters.

The "hero" of *The Deathmakers*, Captain Brandon, undergoes an experience that constitutes a superb statement of the paradox involved in war. Pursuing a sniper through the woods, Brandon brings him to bay, and the German charges.

With the heightened perceptions of a predator, Brandon sees "the eyes, wild, terrified, crazy, and the long, stringy, blond hair waving violently. . . ." Guns empty, the antagonists grapple.

> . . . the German was on him with clawing hands and the tremendous strength of a wild animal. Brandon could smell the man's sweat as he locked with him and they rolled on the ground, fighting for each other's throats. . . .
>
> . . . .
>
> Brandon saw the white blur of the man's throat and he reached for the knife in his boot and slid it into the flesh of the throat. . . . The thing underneath him twisted and turned and clawed at his face . . . and was quickly still, but Brandon didn't know this, and he was still . . . working the knife in the throat when Chico ran up and pulled him off.
>
> The Captain didn't know Chico and he crouched and slashed at him. It took four of them to hold him, until he finally realized where he was and what had happened.[1]

Brandon had killed men before, but with the cannon and machine guns of his tank. And at long range, "they're not people, they're ducks." Wrestling the German, Brandon is an animal, fighting instinctively, intellect extinguished by the flood of fury that brings him victory. A superior instinct for the jugular keeps him alive, and when the tide subsides Brandon almost giggles hysterically as he stands beside his victim. He walks away, but turns abruptly and returns. Strangely compelled to remain, Brandon tries to think of some word or act of expiation that will release him. Twice he turns away, and twice he returns, "as if the body of the dead German were forcing him back . . . as if it were calling him back with its voiceless voice, sudden, stinging, sharp as a whip. 'Jesus Christ,' he whispered aloud, to the body of the dead German. He looked up through the high trees, pointing at the ashen sky."[2] Sire recalls Henry Fleming's "Gawd! Jim Conklin!" in Brandon's recognition and return to humanity.[3] Talking to his commander about the incident, Brandon says,

1. Glen Sire, *The Deathmakers* (New York, 1960), pp. 15–16.
2. Ibid., pp. 17–18.
3. Stephen Crane, *The Red Badge of Courage*, ed. Sculley Bradley, et al. (New York, 1962), p. 47.

"Sometimes I think it's worse to kill a man than dying yourself. I think they've almost succeeded in breeding that into us. I don't know. I don't know."[4] The antecedent for "that"— what they have bred into us—remains ambiguous. From the moment he returns to his senses beside the dead man, Brandon begins to lose his instinct for life, literally pursuing death at the head of his column.

Like Myrer's Alan Newcombe, looking down at the body of the Japanese major whom he had bayoneted during a night attack, like Lt. Loggins, lying in the hospital after calling fire on his own position, like George Leggett of *The End of a War*, Brandon has crossed the boundary: "Something wrong has happened and nothing will ever make it right."[5]

A writer who depicts human nature reacting to the stresses of war must decide on, and then present consistently, his own conception of that human nature. Sire's version reflects an essentially behavioristic creature, whose instincts have been repressed or somehow altered by civilization. Brandon kills, but is immediately assailed by powerful surges of conscience. Freud might say that Brandon's "primitive psyche" lapses into a dormant state, allowing the learned inhibitions of society to rule his subsequent conduct. Several war novels depict strong conflict when the imperatives of duty and social obligation encounter a deeply ingrained individual disinclination to kill: it is not the fear of being killed, but a fear or subconscious revulsion of killing.

This fundamental trauma is depicted as the result of a public duty that conflicts with human nature or with strongly operative social imperatives—a qualitative evaluation as various as the men who write of it. But whether a writer believes that man is essentially noble and altruistic or a brute who enjoys combat, the presentation of that trauma always includes some fracture within the individual's reaction to his predicament. This predicament is always a dilemma: the op-

4. *Deathmakers*, p. 20.

5. Ibid., p. 18; cf. Anton Myrer, *The Big War* (New York, 1957), p. 284, Joe David Brown, *Kings Go Forth* (New York, 1956), pp. 253–56, Edward Loomis, *The End of a War* (New York, 1958), pp. 219, 243–44 (hereafter cited as *End*).

position of social imperatives and the mandate of human
conscience, the dictates of individual reason opposing external
events.

In 1961 Robert Ardrey's *African Genesis* was published.
This most persuasive "personal investigation into the animal
origins and nature of man" is based on the thesis that man
evolved from a "missing link" species of predatory, flesh-
eating apes, creatures who mastered the use of weapons
before *homo sapiens* appeared on the scene and who passed
along to him their genius. "Man," writes Ardrey, "is a predator whose natural instinct is to kill with a weapon." Like
Ardrey many novelists conclude that it is probably natural
for man to fight, but just as natural for him to regret it, a
peculiarity of human nature. Ardrey calls civilization a reflection of the "command of the kind," for some sort of order,
logically extended from animal beginnings, "a necessary inhibition and sublimation of predatory energies" without
which man's increasing capacity to kill would have long since
removed him from earth. "Civilization is a compensatory consequence of our killing imperative; the one could not exist
without the other."[6] The theory of weapon-wielding mam-
mals aside, this sounds familiar. Here, human nature possesses the paradoxical elements of creation and destruction noted
by Freud and detected by D. H. Lawrence in American literature. According to Ardrey, civilization is the manifestation
of a collective race-wisdom that transcends the individual
ability to defeat it.

In *The Modern Temper* (published in 1929), Joseph
Wood Krutch sounds a far bleaker warning about the basic
opposition of forces at work in the human psyche. Animal
vigor, Krutch argues, propels entire peoples along the path to
civilization, and new cultures are born. At a certain point,
detachment from nature reaches the stage at which human
intellect looks about for the purpose of life, something beyond
life itself. Finding none, the intellect wearies, vitality and
natural virtues decline, and its collapse follows, quickly.
Ardrey sees human history as a magnificant victory over a

6. Robert Ardrey, *African Genesis* (New York, 1969), pp. 322,
354-55.

savage beginning, finding hope for the future in civilization, an outgrowth of "nature's most ancient law," which commands "order." Krutch's 1929 prognosis is grimly pessimistic: "The antithesis between human and natural ends is . . . ultimately irreconcilable, and the most that man can hope for is current defiance recurrently subdued. He can deviate so far but no farther from the animal norm."[7] These two appraisals of man are typical of the positions assumed by writers of modern war novels. *The Deathmakers* is nearer Ardrey's optimistic thesis. In *End of a War*, Edward Loomis places his protagonist nearer to Krutch, showing that man is most truly human when guided by reason, but that he is trapped between irreconcilable forces.

End of a War describes the problems of a young man who adjusts to war's dilemma by assuming that "a man has got to do his public duty and take the private consequences. . . . That is, if he believes a duty when he sees it."[8] George Leggett's monologues, however, are not merely impressionistic reactions to random external events. The author clearly uses them to show in detail the rationalizing process by which Leggett arrives at his decisions.

Leggett learns that war is a series of moral compromises and unpleasant discoveries about himself. More astute than Henry Fleming, he reasons pragmatically, like Hackermeyer, choosing means that will bring the desired or necessary end. His final sorrow grows from the realization that "ends and means on earth are so entangled / That changing one you change the other too; / Each different path brings different ends in view."[9] Like Koestler's Rubashov, Leggett struggles to understand and then accept personal responsibility for his individual acts.

Leggett undergoes experiences common to young men in war. He is shocked to discover the "personal malevolence" of war, realizing that the rifle bullets crackling overhead are

7. Joseph Wood Krutch, *The Modern Temper* (New York, 1956), p. 36.

8. *End*, p. 218.

9. Ferdinand LaSalle, "Franz Von Sickengen," quoted in Arthur Koestler, *Darkness at Noon*, trans. Daphne Hardy (New York, 1961), p. 203.

fired at him, personally. The question of motivation appears during his first combat, when a comrade rages that a man "with a rifle," who actually sees him, wants to "shoot [my] head off," in contrast to the mortarman, who "cannot see" the consequences of his firing. After the first skirmish Leggett feels that he has "done his duty . . . that no more duties should be put upon him."[10]

But Leggett struggles daily to balance his "public duty" with the quiet nagging of his own conscience. The crucial point is his first decision to kill. On guard, protecting the members of his own squad, he sees an enemy sentry who does not see him, who is in fact dozing harmlessly in the moonlight several yards from Leggett's position. Preceded by intense rationalization, his decision is based on loyalty to his friends—"the same way they'd kill him for me." Repeating the necessary sequence with trained percision, Leggett kills the unsuspecting sentry, who is nonetheless an armed enemy. "He fired as he had been taught to fire, squeezing the trigger slowly and gradually so that the rifle fired at the right moment as if by itself."[11]

Leggett's efforts to delay or prevent the decision and then his cool execution of the necessary act demonstrate the basic paradox of human nature: the ability both to decide to kill and to regret the killing. Later Leggett feels the impact of conscience: no rifle fires "by itself." Loomis depicts him heroically rescuing one of his own wounded men from danger, not quite sure why he thinks at that moment of the German he had killed, unaware that he is acting out a rite of expiation, literally trading one life for another. Leggett allows his men to execute a youthful, unarmed sniper, having captured him only minutes after he had killed a member of their squad. On the evening that Leggett enjoys his first German woman, several men of the battalion are killed in a bitter fire-fight.

But in Leggett's case, the sexual guilt is a minor aspect of his larger crime: a sin of omission involving the death of friends. Young as he is, he is fully aware of his predicament.

10. *End*, pp. 22–21.   11. *Ibid.*, p. 96.

Conscience is "something from outside [him]self," but he has no faith, no guide. Though he mocks his own "heavy language," its truth remains with him: "It's up to me. . . . though of course I'll probably never feel really well again." He had once thought that a man could fight wars as necessary if he kept his ends in view.[12] The novel concludes with Leggett's musing that though tired, he has "no right to sleep."

Loomis's young hero is rational, convinced that the universe he inhabits is also rational. He thinks of conscience as something outside himself—a greater power which attends his acts—and may be responsible for what he does. With reason failing to quiet his conscience, it is loyalty to his friends that primarily governs Leggett. "Kill a German to keep a friend" becomes his byword. Having decided in wartime to subordinate all other considerations to the need for unity in his squad, Leggett is appalled later to realize the humanity of those who had been "the enemy." He finds that the responsibility is his.

The incidents in Loomis's novel are like the beads on a rosary. Each is emblematic of a meaning; together they should be the basis for understanding, acceptance, or consolation. Loomis's prose communicates the obvious conclusion that Leggett's dilemma remains unresolved. This is a superior example of a war novel written as catharsis, almost a spiritual exercise. Loomis is so intent on resolving the issue that his book is a virtual ledger or account book of personal moral philosophy.

Like *End of a War*, James Jones's *The Thin Red Line* (published in 1962) is the story of a completed combat action, with unresolved consequences. As the adventures of Robert E. Lee Prewitt indicated, Jones has a special affinity for guilt, and a unique ability to delineate its subtle variants. Commenting generously and at length on an author who is no longer "the worst writer of prose," Norman Mailer concedes in *Cannibals and Christians* that Jones's third war novel is a technical masterpiece, suitable for use "as a textbook at the Infantry School." The thrust of Mailer's comments is that

12. Ibid., pp. 216–19.

Jones lacks the guts to plunge into new areas, and has resolved to be among the best in a limited field. Momentarily carried away by his own generosity in praising another's work, Mailer goes to familiar excess in calling *The Thin Red Line* a military text; but it is, as he says later with intuitive accuracy, a thorough study of the psychology of combat. The clinical detail in Jones's dissection of each character and action accounts for Mailer's complaint that the novel is too technical. Nevertheless, "Jones has a strong sense of a man's psychology, and it carries quietly through his pages."[13] Nobody is more keenly aware of each man's individuality than is James Jones. His novel is an imaginative sequence of combat actions, staged with great competence; it is, however, his startlingly various insights into the possibilities of individual motivation that give *The Thin Red Line* its psychological veracity. As a fictional account of combat it is unsurpassed.

Like Mailer in *The Naked and the Dead*, Jones achieves unity of time and space by making his novel an account of island combat. The center of the action is "C" Company, its men and their problems in war. Clearly, the company is an organism that survives the deaths of individuals, retaining its identity. The action, initiated by the plans of higher echelons, develops as logical extensions of the psychological patterns of the individuals who make up Charlie Company.

Jones is unrelenting in his portrayal of officers. None of the lieutenants makes a substantive contribution to the combat of the company; they all die stupidly. Tall uses the company as a rung on the ladder of his career. "Bugger" Stein, still reeling from the "six months of astonishment" that marked his introduction to active duty, is virtually useless. A lawyer, he tries to explain the war in rational terms, but his concept breaks down in a vision of an infinity of hilltops across the universe, each part of the universal war. Captain Stein tries to explain to a wretched private that he was totally justified in killing the Japanese soldier who was the company's first combat victim: "I'm not saying whether this is right or wrong. But we really have no choice. We have to do as society

13. Norman Mailer, *Cannibals and Christians* (New York, 1966), p. 112.

demands."[14] Stein argues for a purely teleological morality, which does not recognize right and wrong, and hence cannot be troubled with sin or conscience. This is situational ethics, concerned only with good and bad, in context.

The complex subject of guilt is treated in many ways in *The Thin Red Line*. Private Bell's massive sexual complications gradually subside when power, in the form of a direct commission, is substituted for his unfaithful wife. Private Bead's guilt, like the insane fury of his attack on the Japanese soldier, is compounded—at least in part—of elements of sexual complications. Squatting over a cat-hole to relieve himself, Bead is surprised by the Japanese. Unwiped, weaponless, and with trousers at half-mast, Bead fights fanatically. He wrests the rifle away, then shoots, bayonets, and beats his man to a bloody mess. Looking in the soldier's pockets he finds family pictures, and is filled with emotions similar to Brandon's, although not articulated. He wants to hide his "graceless" killing, and when questioners pursue the issue of blood and his general condition too far, Bead breaks out in mad frustration: "Why! Why! How the fuck do I know why! . . . Maybe my mother beat me up too many times for jerking off when I was a kid."[15] Jones describes this as "a sudden half-flashing of miserable insight." After Captain Stein's lecture on social obligations Bead is temporarily reconciled, to the extent that he feels able to "survive the killing of many men." Mad Welsh beats the idea of guilt by abstracting himself completely. Objective to the extreme, he can laugh at the logic that though he enlisted to beat the depression and lived in comfort "on the Army" for several years, he is now required to make full restitution in the terrors of combat.

The central figure of this novel is Don Doll. He rises from private to sergeant and platoon guide. His development follows exactly the plot's action and movement. Jones merges in his own observations with those of the characters, "helping" articulate otherwise unavailable thoughts, much as

14. James Jones, *The Thin Red Line* (New York, 1962), pp. 174–75; hereafter cited as *Line*.
15. Ibid., p. 173.

Faulkner does in *As I Lay Dying*. Doll possesses a "secret weapon" of sorts: the belief that each man lives a kind of private fiction about himself. Thus armed, Doll is able to drive himself to do just a little bit more when the occasion presents itself. He believes that most people probably learn the same thing; the difficult part is to pretend that it has not happened. Accordingly, Doll begins calling everybody's bluff, taking nothing at face value. During air raids he practices his private fiction, standing up despite "eviscerating, ballshrinking" terror (Jones's modifiers are physiologically perfect). To his astonishment he finds that he can convince others that he is without fear: another lesson learned.

Part 4 depicts Doll's most crucial stage: his first kills, his humiliation of a rival, his brash challenge of Stein's judgment. A good soldier, Doll does things as he has been taught, adjusting his sights for the range, leading his man, and squeezing the trigger:

> So Doll had killed his first Japanese. For that matter, his first human being of any kind. Doll had hunted quite a lot, and he could remember his first deer. But this was an experience which required extra tasting. Like getting screwed for the first time, it was too complex to be classed solely as pride of accomplishment. Shooting well, at anything, was always a pleasure. And Doll hated the Japanese, dirty little yellow Jap bastards, and would gladly have killed personally everyone of them alive if the US Army and Navy would only arrange him a safe opportunity and supply him the ammo. But beyond these two pleasures there was another. It had to do with guilt. Doll felt guilty. He couldn't help it. He had killed a human being, a man. He had done the most horrible thing a human could do, worse than rape, even. And nobody in the whole damned world could say anything to him about it. That was where the pleasure came. Nobody could do anything to him for it. He had gotten by with murder. . . . Doll felt an impulse to grin a silly grin and to giggle. He felt stupid and cruel and mean and vastly superior. It certainly had helped his confidence anyway, that was for sure.[16]

Jones merely snags the surface of that tangle of emotions and instincts embracing sexual ambiguity, the hunter-killer instincts, heterogeneous love, masculine camaraderie, the Eros-Thanatos snarl—persistently a part of American literature

16. Ibid., pp. 197–98.

from Rip van Winkle through the Leatherstocking Saga, Hemingway and Faulkner, to Mailer's explication of the hipster in *Why Are We in Vietnam?*. Wisely, Jones does not attempt a full exegesis of Doll's state of mind. The new, infinitely complex factor—guilt—tightens the knot perhaps beyond unraveling. And Freud is not more helpful than Apeneck Sweeney: Eros, death instincts, sexual instincts, or, "That's all the facts when you come to brass tacks: / Birth, and copulation, and death."[17] Several bow-shots ahead of the field in *The Thin Red Line*, Doll, too, realizes some of the complexity of the situation.

Of all Jones's characters only Witt, at the bottom of the social scale, evinces signs of loyalty as a motivation. In Doll's random inventory of his own feelings only hatred of the enemy might possibly be attributable to patriotic or altruistic origins; the rest are selfish, a series of small instinctual triumphs over inhibitions acquired during his lifetime. The "pleasure" of guilt makes Doll credibly complex. He does not understand himself, but he is intensely aware of the myriad emotional and moral components of his reaction.

The consistently successful soldiers of *The Thin Red Line* have in common some interest that overrides the immediate fact of daily combat. Welsh is fueled by gin and his endless contempt for everybody around him, smugly sure that they react individually about the same way for women or for "fuckin' property" as they perform in combat. Witt's dumb desire to help out, and his animal loyalty to Charlie Company keep him from worrying about personal danger. Charley Dale's ignorant, vicious, and inarticulate ambition fills his horizon completely. Sergeant Doll is in the best position because he knows the secret of private fears, and has mastered his own.

Freud's analysis of human nature and warfare, *Reflections on War and Death* (published in 1918), remains the most consistent nonfictional correlative to novelistic accounts of combat. "Our unconscious . . . does not believe in its own death," he asserts, "it acts as though it were immortal. This

17. T. S. Eliot, "Fragments of an Agon," *The Complete Poems and Plays* (New York, 1962), pp. 80–81.

is perhaps the real secret of heroism. The rational basis of
heroism is dependent upon the decision that one's life cannot
be worth as much as certain abstract common ideals."[18] The
men of *The Thin Red Line* are ever conscious of the immediate
peril that surrounds them, but Jones alludes to "numbness"
as the emotional vehicle that transports them at crucial points.
He describes with clinical exactitude the chemical and physio-
logical changes of adrenaline on the systems of the men in
Gaff's assault party. Amid the roar of their grenades exploding among the Japanese, their bodies having made the
decision to fight, "Numbly, they [do] the necessary." When
the brief, savage encounter is ended, "Numbly they stared at
each other. Each had believed devoutly that he would be the
only one alive." Later Jones describes what an uninvolved
bystander would call "vicious" or "vile atrocity" during a
mopping-up operation: "two or three . . . were shot out of
hand by tensefaced, nervewracked men who wanted no fucking nonsense."[19] In combat, instinctive reaction must preempt
conscious decision. And during their rest-and-recuperation
break the men of "C" Company adjust, remembering with
"awed wonder" their own vanished dead. And, "As the
blessed numbness receded, the unbelievability of each man's
death to himself returned to ridicule and plague each one
who had ever thought that."[20] The only man who tries to
reconcile his actions with his ethical precepts is "Bugger"
Stein, who is intelligent but hopelessly ineffective in action.

In contrast to the painfully rational Leggett of *End of a
War*, the characters of *The Thin Red Line* rely on instinct.
Their reactions are determined primarily by strong biases
over which they have little control, but each individual is
governed by a different set of reactions, which accounts for
the book's success. Jones demonstrates this by the various
shadings of guilt in his characters and by the "numbness"
that eventually prepares each man for the ordeal of combat.

As Jones's comprehensive treatment in *The Thin Red
Line* indicates, motivation is an area of considerable specula-

---

18. Sigmund Freud, *Reflections on War and Death*, trans. and ed.
A. A. Brill and A. B. Kuttner (New York, 1918), p. 62.
    19. *Line*, pp. 296, 298, 439.   20. Ibid., p. 343.

tion and variety of treatment in novels that deal with individual combat. In many cases the answer is simply fury: battle rage such as that of Crane's Henry Fleming and evinced
to some degree by Hackermeyer and Myrer's Alan Newcombe in *The Big War*. It is compounded, like the fury of
Homer's Achilles, from the knowledge of death, fear, instinct,
and bodily chemistry. In *Do Not Go Gentle*, David MacCuish
portrays a youthful hero who fails at a critical moment of
battle because the man he could have saved from death
strongly resembles his hated, dead father. Warped by life,
he finds in combat, and in the bonds that it engenders, a truer
representation of humanity than he can establish outside the
arena of war. Sire's Captain Brandon and Leggett show opposite extremes of guilt. In *The Thin Red Line* more subtle
shadings appear, and in *The Beardless Warriors*, Matheson
shows a young man who has "come through" the shadows of
conventional guilt—sex and religion. For him, guilt comes
from inadequate performance; killing his enemy is a sign
of a job well done.

The following novels of combat are dominated by the
concept of motivation. There is action but almost without exception they eventually explore the question "Why?" These
books, therefore, cannot be separated from the milieu in
which they were written. Former resistance leader Jean-Paul
Sartre discusses the problem in *What Is Literature?*, clearly
reflecting the pressures of the recent world war: "When the
enemy is separated from you by a barrier of fire, you have to
judge him whole, as the incarnation of evil; all war is
Manicheism. . . . But vice-versa, the conquered and occupied
populations, who mingled with their conquerors, relearned
by familiarization and the effects of clever propaganda to
consider them as men. Good men and bad men; good *and*
bad at the same time."[21] Sartre's comment implies the consistent supremacy of reason. Even while it yields to other
drives and allows the "Manicheism" to predominate during
the fight, reason carries throughout the knowledge that this
is a temporarily necessary fiction, a means to a pragmatic

21. Jean-Paul Sartre, *What is Literature?*, trans. B. Frechtman
(New York, 1965), p. 66.

end. Another appraisal of motivation comes from Samuel P. Huntington's startling attempt to synthesize a theory for a workable balance of power between the military and civilian elements of society, *The Soldier and the State* (published in 1957). His comment that the Korean War was the first occasion when American soldiers "fought a major war solely and simply because [they] were ordered to fight it," is relevant here. Huntington asserts that far from identifying with the political goals of the conflict, the American soldier in Korea "developed a supreme indifference to the political goals of the war—the traditional hallmark of the professional. And 'professional' was the one term seized upon by newsmen and observers to describe the peculiar psychology of the Korean fighting man as distinguished from his World War II counterpart."[22]

Two points should be established here. One is that novels of World War II, the great bulk of them written during the 1950s and early 1960s, do not deal with politics and national issues unless the specific character of the protagonist dictates such concerns, as in the novels of commanders. These stories of combat dwell upon individual accommodation to war and the continuing issue of guilt, eventually getting around to the issue of motivation. Secondly, novels of the Korean War display the "professionalism"—the air of detachment—to which Huntington alludes, and the two significant novels of Vietnam to appear thus far reflect contemporary disillusionment and existential despair.

Never So Few is the story of Con Reynolds and his achievement in organizing resistance against the Japanese in Burma during World War II. It is an exceptional blend of historical fact, fictional narrative, and philosophical synthesis, tracing Con's development as a leader while describing his struggles to formulate a personal moral code. Though the novel provides action, the emphasis is on ideas. Starting from a datum of guilt over shortcomings in his past life, Con labors to establish the proper relationships among competing loyalties: the pragmatic imperatives of his military

22. Samuel P. Huntington, *The Soldier and the State* (New York, 1967), p. 389.

mission and the absolute dictates of his own conscience.

Con begins as a relatively uncomplicated young man who, though often revolted by his duties, reasons that the "end" of victory completely justifies the "means" in his guerrilla offensive against the Japanese. He caps a series of professionally sound but personally odious acts by executing piecemeal a trusted lieutenant who is a traitor. His unit will profit by such stern discipline. Con, however, finds the war a moral quagmire; his standards are assaulted from the beginning, both by the decisions he is required to make and by the challenges thrust at him from all sides. Chamales's use of the locale lends credibility to the confluence of philosophies and cultures in the jungles of Burma, where East and West both can be accommodated. This, combined with his narrative skill and plot development, saves the book from tediousness.

Con's missions bring him into contact with numerous people and diverse ideas. The thoughts of Melville and Emerson, along with Hindu concepts that predate Plato, are introduced early in the novel. A Hindu elder tells Con that men are like spiders, weaving their own fate, and that "a spider . . . afraid [cannot] weave a web of quality." Danny, renegade cousin to the English king, muses, "A man twists the strands of his own rope."[23] Both incidents evoke the Mat-Maker episode of *Moby Dick*, when Ishmael observes that "chance, free will, and necessity—no wise incompatible . . ." work together in a man's destiny.[24] A Hindu, dying slowly of painful injuries, demonstrates the efficacy of his beliefs by calmly accepting death. Teaching Con, he says, "Whatever form a man continually contemplates . . . that same form he remembers in the hour of his death, and to that very form he goes."[25] During a later convalescence, Con reads Emerson, where he might well have come across these lines from "May Day": "A subtle chain of countless rings / The next unto the farthest brings, / And, striving to be man, the worm / Mounts through all the spires of form."

23. Tom Chamales, *Never So Few* (New York, 1957), pp. 8, 29; hereafter cited as *Never*.

24. Herman Melville, *Moby Dick* (New York, 1950), p. 214.

25. *Never*, p. 295.

From his commander, Con hears variations on an old theme. While deploring his nation's lack of moral unity or sophistication, the colonel acknowledges the resourcefulness and courage of Americans, but insists that no idea sustains them in combat: "... it is negative ... born of his environment, of his social fear; his shame of fear. A don't-let-your-buddy-down sort of thing."[26] Commenting on men in general and on their tendency to choose leaders unworthy of them, Burman Nautang says that if men would recognize their own worth rather than insisting on recognition from others, there would be no problem; they would ridicule their leaders' attempts to incite them, for "they would have too much respect for humanity because of their own humanity."[27]

But Con's crisis grows out of a conflict between simple loyalty and the complex pragmatism of war:

> Now Mao is fighting Chiang whose basic weapon is the Springfield rifle also. And Chiang and Mao are fighting the Japanese whose basic weapon is American steel. And the English whose basic money and supplies are American are fighting the Japanese. And the Russians, who are basically supplied by the Americans, besides being against the Japanese are on the side of Mao fighting Kai Shek because Mao is a Commie. So the Russians who are fighting with you are also fighting against you. And the Chinese you are fighting with are fighting not only with each other but with the Japanese whom you are fighting against. . . .[28]

Chamales's novel is permeated with the philosophy that character is fate, illustrated by Con's death. To the woman who would have been his wife had he lived, he confides, "We die for recognition, we kill others for it . . . and find it's not what we thought it would be, then we're afraid to admit our error, to change, so we drown ourselves in recognition, finding in it only a numb insensitivity. . . ."[29] Here Chamales shows the direct influence of James Jones, to whom he expresses dedicatory gratitude for inspiration and help in writing *Never So Few*. Ishmael's declaration that "with my own hand I ply my

---

26. Ibid., p. 77.   28. Ibid., p. 432.
27. Ibid., p. 344.   29. Ibid., pp. 344–45.

own shuttle and weave my own destiny" applies to Con, also.[30] He dies, stupidly, in a routine action, having decided before it began that life was really not worth the price he must pay. Weary of living, he violates a fundamental rule of urban combat, and trips a fatal booby trap.[31] Suddenly, as he stands there, Con realizes he has come not out of conscience, but out of regard for his increasing reputation. The impact of self-knowledge and his disillusionment register on his consciousness only after his subconscious has already decided on death. In a sense, Con develops as does a tragic hero, and he finally concludes that to survive in war men must abandon the values that give human life real significance. His condition at the end parallels the proposal advanced by Joseph Wood Krutch, that at that stage when the intellect looks about for the purpose of life, the human organism and the society that spawned him are ready for dissolution, having progressed beyond the bounds established for simple animal vitality.

When writing of combat, Chamales concentrates on consequences, not on scenes of action. Con finds his friend Danny after an ambush: "Flies flew in and out of the Englishman's half-opened mouth, dead Japs lay all around him. . . . Cowered in the corner of the hole was the other Kachin. . . . His eyeballs were round and white and glazed."[32]

The motives for which fictional characters act are determined largely by the writer's point of view. When the subject is war, it is without question difficult to sustain objectivity. But it is not an immutable principle that the souls of a poet and a warrior are incompatible. History preserves the image of squat Socrates, fighting for Athens as a durable hoplite, and the surprising epitaph that crowned Aeschylus' prodigious career demonstrates, in Edith Hamilton's view, that "he merited honor so lofty, no mention of his poetry could find place beside it." That honor was the recognition of his courage. A veteran of Salamis, he was also a "Marathon-warrior." The epitaph concludes: "His glorious courage the hallowed field of Marathon could tell, and the long-haired

30. *Moby Dick*, p. 214.   31. *Never*, p. 492.   32. Ibid., p. 458.

Mede had knowledge of it."[33] He would say, with Plato, that "only the dead have seen the last of war."

With the exception of a small group of novels about World War II that emphasize the chaos and futility of the war, the books discussed in this section were written later than the other studies of combat, and are about Korea and Vietnam. These novels stress the element of motivation. *Never So Few* shows a man in the attempt to reconcile what is with what ought to be. From this point, the novels shift to what might be called the "professionalism" (to which Huntington alludes) and then beyond to a new objectivity, born of despair or frustration.

Two incidents from the literature will set the stage for a discussion of motivation. The first is from *The Naked and the Dead*: Martinez and the Japanese sentry. Although terrified, Martinez stalks the unsuspecting machine gunner, siezes him from behind, and knifes him. Afterward Martinez feels like weeping, but not because of guilt. He is reacting to the danger that he has just passed through. The dead man is merely loathesome; Mailer explains that the revulsion Martinez feels is like that "a man feels after chasing a cockroach across the wall and finally squashing him. It affected him exactly that way and not much more intensely. He shuddered because of the drying blood on his hands, but he would have shuddered as much from the roach's pulp."[34] The guilt is gone. Martinez is a professional with a job to do. The job includes killing a man with a knife, dangerous but rather like tackling a giant bug, with no human complications involved.

The second incident comes from Ernest Frankel's *Band of Brothers*, a book that memorializes the first Marines in Korea, and their fight out of the Chosin Reservoir in early 1951. Private Dorn watches, pertrified by fear, as a Chinese officer contemptuously approaches him, spits on him, and prepares to kill him, leisurely drawing his pistol. Dorn suddenly acts:

33. Edith Hamilton, *The Greek Way* (New York, 1964), p. 145.
34. Norman Mailer, *The Naked and the Dead* (New York, 1948), pp. 595–96.

All the humiliations, all the fear and anger he had known in all of his life, rose in Dorn and choked him, impelling him to fight. He lashed out at his adversary, caught him off balance, threw him down, rolled him over, grasped his head by the hair, and smashed it against the rocks. . . . Dorn's hands were on his throat. The Chinese gurgled, pushed desperately at the bleeding face, arched his back, trying to unseat him. Dorn felt the pressure of a scabbard against his knee, grasped it, pulled the knife from the man's belt. Then he drove it again and again into the twitching body beneath him.

When there was no more movement, he leaned back, looking unbelievingly at the contorted face, staring at his weapon and at his bloody hands, grunting with the effort of drawing breath. He felt as if he had murdered his past.[35]

This struggle resembles Captain Brandon's battle, but the difference is significant: Dorn knows throughout exactly what is happening to him. He is aware. Still astride the dead man, he recalls a childhood battle with a larger boy, a victory that proved him to his father; once again he has "come through." Henry Fleming and Hackermeyer, like Brandon and Private Bead of *The Thin Red Line*, passed into an unconscious rage, with reason suspended by overwhelming fury, but Dorn, though terrified, retains a sense of perspective. Personifying Americans in Korea, Dorn evolves from a soft, unsure youngster to a competent fighting man, motivated by the need to hold his own among his comrades. The issue is resolved entirely within the scope of human relationships. Killing the Chinese, Dorn saves his friend, and survives a severe passage into manhood.

Martinez and Dorn have in common the absence of guilt for killing. Mailer's perceptive description of alienation shows that Martinez is truly concerned only about himself and is not interested in the humanity of others. Martinez is cut off from other people by the depth of his hatreds. Dorn understands that he had done "murder," but he knows it is justified by the circumstances. Both men demonstrate a suspension of the Freudian cycle that is so pervasive in the literature of war. Dorn illustrates the operation of Sartre's assertion that "all war is Manicheism." Private Dorn's experience demonstrates his hierarchy of values.

35. Ernest Frankel, *Band of Brothers* (New York, 1958), pp 184–85.

Thematically typical of these novels, *Band of Brothers* shows men totally engaged by the action war requires. Introspection is rare. Personifying the traditional concept of a hard-nosed, ruthless natural warrior, the company executive-officer, Lieutenant Anderson is disintegrated by enemy fire immediately after an argument in which he struck his superior over the issue of obedience. Anderson was cruel and impulsive, a fearless "natural" warrior who also shot prisoners without compunction. Whereas Company Commander Patrick gropes for the right way to do things, Anderson knows instinctively what is required, as long as sheer aggressive spirit is sufficient. Such motivation is dangerous in a modern limited war. Gradually the men realize that although he feels fear acutely and often is unsure, Captain Patrick is a superior human being, sensitive to his responsibilities in a way that Anderson could never comprehend. The ultimate "truth" that Patrick finally grasps is simply "something that had to be learned, part of becoming a whole man. . . . *Somebody's got to do it.* Always, somewhere, somebody has to take the ridge, has to struggle and fight and maybe die for all the rest, for weak and the fearful and the selfish and the ignorant and the unaware."[36]

"Somebody's got to do it." This simple truth that enables a man to do what must be done is not general but specific, unique in every case. In Curt Anders's *The Price of Courage* (published in 1957), a young officer advances from the disastrous gaucheries of eager ignorance to become a superb combat leader, having learned that the essence of winning lies in moving that frightened, grimy soldier at the point: "It's just a matter of getting one man around one rock. If he don't make it, nobody else can, either."[37] Pat Frank's *Hold Back the Night* is another fictionalized version of the Marine withdrawal from Chosin, reflecting the same attitude of stoic resignation toward the enemy and the weather. The enemy come "in waves . . . it was like trying to stop the sea, for they flowed and eddied around the mounds of their own fallen." Friendly aircraft drop napalm, leaving "a wave of men . . .

36. Ibid., p. 360.
37. Curt Anders, *The Price of Courage* (New York, 1957), p. 308.

burning."[38] The Marines survive because they fight as a team; and the incinerated enemy on the frozen hills are no more human than the cold.

The final image of *Band of Brothers* is Jesus Sanchez, killed, frozen in a spread-eagle position, and lashed to the tube of a howitzer. In battle men forget the generalities that may have unleashed the war, dealing only in the specifics of the relationships that bind them together in fighting units. They fight on command, but they die for each other, not for causes.

The novels of Korea affirm that the inarticulate, "Don't let your buddy down" attitude that typified American fighting men and their code to Chamales's Colonel Pearson is their dominant motivation. These books also emphasize the totality of an alien environment in which the human enemy is simply one more factor, suggesting the conditions of human existence conceived by Sartre and Camus: man alone in a hostile universe. Men fight not merely one another, but the very world they inhabit.

The literature of the Korean War is slight in both volume and quality, a situation probably explained to a large degree by the absence of a national commitment to that war. Mr. Huntington attributes the "professional" attitude of the men who fought in Korea to the rotation policy, whereby every man could look forward to a specific date when, if he survived, his war duty would be over, in sharp contrast with the accumulated years spent overseas by men during World War II. The "professional" detachment from larger issues, manifested in the attitude that fighting the war was an unpleasant but necessary job that had to be done, reflects a new detachment, a resignation to events, also present in the few novels that the war produced. Many of the more thoughtful books of World War II appeared more than a decade after its conclusion, but no such phenomenon followed the Korean "police action." Only *Show Me a Hero*, Melvin Voorhees's novel of an American commander in Korea frustrated by politics and fate, introduces substantial issues beyond factual accounts and memorializations.

38. Pat Frank, *Hold Back the Night* (New York, 1952), p. 172.

Some of the World War II novels manifest an atmosphere of chaos, or a feeling that events are quite out of control, bearing a strong resemblance to the emotional and intellectual environment of the two significant novels to emerge during the late 1960s from the American involvement in Vietnam. Because of its length and the degree to which all Americans have been compelled to assume moral attitudes toward it, there is a strong probability that the Vietnam War will eventually produce a novel of intellectual and artistic scope sufficient to place the experience in perspective. It will take some time, however, before the largely emotional impressionism that characterizes most of the novels which have appeared thus far can be controlled and subordinated appropriately.

Harry Brown's *A Walk in the Sun* (published first in 1944) evinces a spirit materially akin to novels from the Vietnam War, but it incorporates an artistic unity and a moral objectivity not found in the later books. It is one of the finest novels about war. Less than two hundred pages, Brown's novel is nonetheless the detailed account of a completed action. Stressing the isolation of combat, Brown tells the story of a platoon in action after landing on the Italian coast. The novel presents subtle surrealistic overtones as the platoon moves through a series of individual catastrophes in which the members of its chain of command and all who represent links with the world beyond the platoon are destroyed or removed from the scene.

The central consciousness is that of Corporal Tyne, upon whom responsibility for the platoon's mission finally devolves. As men disappear an aura of fated disaster seems to brood over the patrol. On the landing craft's approach to the beach Lieutenant Rand examines the landing area through his binoculars. He is killed almost immediately by a shell fragment. Later, another soldier in the platoon uses the fatal binoculars to scan the beach from a ridgeline; he is cut down by randomly cruising German fighter planes. One sergeant who leaves to find the company commander is riddled by a machine gun, and a man who later volunteers to act as runner simply disappears. The ranking squad leader cracks under the accumulated strain of several campaigns, and a motorcyclist who volunteers to scout ahead for the platoon vanishes from sight forever.

Brown's descriptions of actions and equipment are all credible with a single glaring exception: there is no communications equipment in the platoon. No radios link them to the company commander or to adjacent units. No telephones or wiremen are mentioned. The platoon moves tentatively through the countryside like a small circle of light through uncertain shadows. Symbolizing their vulnerability, the platoon's sole source of information is a pair of deserting Italian soldiers, whose intentions and veracity are impossible to appraise.

Fate closes in on Corporal Tyne, insidiously. When Lieutenant Rand was killed, he became custodian of Rand's map and binoculars. The binoculars now lie with dead McWilliams along the strafed ridgeline. The platoon has only the map and a sketch, no orders, no specific mission. Next, Sergeant Porter collapses just as a German armored car approaches, leaving Tyne suddenly in command. An *ad hoc* plan disposes of the armored car, and the men move to their objective, where Tyne rapidly sketches out another scheme, using basic fire-and-maneuver tactics to distract the Germans and suppress their counter-fire.

Brown paces his short novel adroitly; the action it describes covers time and infantry distance equal to a leisurely reading of the book. In moments or relaxation the corporal's companions discuss typically irrelevant subjects, such as the respective merits of photography and painting as art, or the manifold joys of camping. In reality they are diverting themselves from the fact of their predicament, momentarily "escaping" from it. Until the final pages both time and distance are vague, but as Tyne reveals his plan to move against the objectives, a farmhouse and a bridge, each man becomes intent on the ebbing seconds that separate him from the inevitable confrontation with his fate. It all comes down to the moment when a soldier must defy his common sense, his instinct for survival, his humanitarian feelings, and all the painfully learned manners of civilization—standing up in a strange field in the face of death, to kill or be killed.

The human mind's capacity for accommodation is incredible. How, indeed, do men reach the state of Tyne and his companions? In *Fire Mission*, William Mulvihill describes one theory:

> It was different for the riflemen. They had always been in the infantry from their first days in the Army. They had been trained, maneuvered and remaneuvered for this very act; they knew what to expect and were ready for it. . . . The idea of walking towards the next town with the Germans shooting at them was imbued in their collective minds as a normal act: it had lost all aspects of being a fantastic, unreal and dangerous thing to do. They expected to do it for it was part of their life, their reason for being where they were and what they were: infantrymen.[39]

But as trainers from Baron von Steuben in the colonies during the American Revolution to those of the present day have found, training a man to move forward in the face of fire is one thing, getting him to return that fire is often a totally different, and more difficult, problem. Mulvihill's passage is a behavioristic explanation of motivation. Brown's novel implies another factor, possibly Freud's "primitive psyche," the "numbness" experienced by Jones's fighters, the emergence of the unconscious, or perhaps simple surrender to the idea of death—anything to end the tension and suspense that has led to the moment when living men must carry out, on the ground, instructions devised by other men looking at maps.

The conclusion of *A Walk in the Sun* resembles Private Hicks's surreal adventure in Thomas Boyd's *Through the Wheat*. At Tyne's signal the action begins, and he runs, leading the platoon across an open field to "the mysterious farmhouse, the farmhouse that was waiting to gather him in and hide him from the world. . . . The farmhouse loomed up, and it was waiting." The irrevocable act usurps all prerogatives; it alone has meaning. All who had questioned the situation or peered beyond are eradicated. Tyne hears the supporting machine gun, firing from "the next world," and to his sharpened perceptions all present action seems static. "His mind became clear as polished glass. Everything in his life

39. William Mulvihill, *Fire Mission* (New York, 1957), p. 89.

had led up to this moment. It was his. Nothing could take it away from him"—or save him from it. Released from anxiety, Tyne runs toward death: "It is so terribly easy."[40]

Brown's novel is tightly unified in time, place, and action. The action is credible, growing from contingencies that would befall any plan carried out in the chaos of small-unit tactics. The plot unfolds naturally, like that of Jones's *The Thin Red Line*. The realities of combat—that leaders will be carried away by attrition, that men are suddenly thrust into unexpected situations of responsibility—are also truly represented. Brown's soldiers are primarily intent on their own narrow interests, eager to work well among the men with whom they share the life of a combat soldier. Brown extracts sustained suspense from a brief platoon action that a regimental operations officer later would acknowledge as part of a battalion action, lost on the flank of the larger, divisional objective. In practice, as Brown's novel demonstrates, operations often precede the printed orders and plans that are reflected in later records, compiled and issued after the fact.

A Walk in the Sun succeeds because it captures the unique atmosphere of a group of men moving toward possible death, in the process of preparing themselves to meet that potential. Talking on oblique subjects, understating their situation, the men gradually reach the point at which each is capable of an act of bravery that is almost incomprehensible to an observer not involved in their situation. On signal they all act as a single man, utterly dependent on each other. It is not the characterizations, plot, or action that makes this novel "work"; it is Brown's success in depicting the development of a situation that makes cooperative action the only salvation. Individually the men have no consequence, but as a platoon they have an assignment to carry out. Unless they execute that assignment there is no justification for their existence within the context of the war. Therefore, each man subordinates himself to that end, for there is no rational alternative, no other way to esablish an order amid the greater chaos of war. Thus, the objective farmhouse becomes a temporarily sufficient end.

40. Harry Brown, *A Walk in the Sun* (New York, 1967), p. 187.

To date, two significant novels can be attributed to the Vietnam War, David Halberstam's *One Very Hot Day* and John Sack's *M.* Amid the spate of opportunistic potboilers that have erupted on the subject, these two books stand out as serious literary attempts to comment on the situation. Vietnam was a political issue the way World War II never was, the way Korea could have been. Accordingly, the fiction carries a strong emotional bias. Halberstam won a Pulitzer prize in 1964 for his reportage on Vietnam, and his novel (published in 1967) covers the same early period, before large-scale commitments of American men and money had been made.

One Very Hot Day portrays realistic action with caricature figures, like a morality play. Individually, each major character might be encountered over the course of several years, but that such a monumental collection should be assembled in the scope of one slight action makes the book function as an allegory. The novel is otherwise too forced, totally lacking in credibility.

Halberstam's plot is simple, following the conception and execution of a three-part military operation involving South Vietnamese units and their American advisers. During the single day of the operation all three units are ambushed by the Viet Cong, obviously the result of methodical treachery. As the first ambushes are reported it becomes increasingly obvious to the Americans with the third segment of the force that they, too, are among the Viet Cong's targets for the day. Using a point of view that fluctuates from apparent omniscience to informal interior monologues, Halberstam fills in the background of each central character with flashbacks and conversation. The third ambush occurs with the inevitability of a thunderstorm after a hot, humid summer's day, but with some variation in the expected pattern.

The characters of *One Very Hot Day* are personified clichés, a weakness that seriously undermines the novel. There is a "new-style" West Point graduate: judiciously ambitious, conscientious in the extreme, immoderately faithful to his equally faithful wife. Lieutenant Anderson, the big, strong, blond, intelligent Midwesterner, who is fluent in Vietnamese, eager to please, and determined to do his duty,

is totally predictable. Capt. "Big William" Redfern is a lib-
erated black officer, whose dark skin, enormous size, insatiable appetites, and agreeable disposition make him a figure of
almost mythic proportions among the slight Asians in the
Ranger unit he advises. Captain Beaupre is an over-age-in-
grade retread from the Second World War and Korea. "Once
he had been a tiger, a good killer," but now, in his third
war, fat and old age have reduced him to timorous reticence.
"By chance someone, perhaps an IBM machine" found out
that Beaupre had had some experience in guerrilla operations
in Korea, so he was extracted from the comfortable, anonymous haven of a prep-school ROTC assignment, labeled
counter-guerrilla expert, and sent to Vietnam, with less than
two years before the completion of his twenty.[41]

The other characterizations are logical extrapolations
from that beginning. The Vietnamese battalion commander
smiles, listens to American intelligence estimates, and then
conducts his operations in known safe areas, free of Viet
Cong. The single Vietnamese officer to make a good account
of himself is Lieutenant Thuong, a transplanted northern
Buddhist among southern Catholics in the army. For emphasis, the only other Vietnamese singled out as good soldiers
are another northerner and a common soldier who is, by
birth, a Cambodian. The American commander is a sardonic,
slight colonel who knows that the fact he will never be a
general accounts for his assignment in Vietnam. Closely integrated into both the South Vietnamese and American or-
ganizations is an anonymous, efficient Viet Cong intelligence
ring.

A curious morality emerges from this novel. Big William,
terror (and part-owner) of a few Saigon brothels, and the
tenaciously celibate Lieutenant Anderson are both killed.
Beaupre's excursions into the Saigon stews are uniformly
disastrous: although he is willing, the captain is haunted by
some potent inhibition that consistently renders him impotent in his half-hearted forays. At the end of One Very Hot
Day, it is Beaupre, "a short hulk of a man carrying an im-

41. David Halberstam, One Very Hot Day (Boston, 1967), pp.
90–91.

mense load," who bears the body of Lieutenant Anderson away from the site of the third ambush, which, except for Beaupre's courage and initiative, would have been disaster unmitigated by even the slightest vestige of success.

Beaupre, *l'homme moyen sensuel* in uniform, is the real center of the novel. Long a soldier and never a thinker, Beaupre's personality had been submerged in alcohol, fat, and frustration. But he not only survives, he rallies the remnants of the force from the verge of annihilation and gets the reluctant Vietnamese to repel the ambushers, aggressively. Beaupre is obviously speaking for Halberstam when he reviews the differences among the three wars he has seen. World War II was "simpler . . . even in Germany . . . you were not ambushed or tricked or betrayed. The distrust had begun in Korea when suddenly it was a matter of more than fighting and killing, instead it was a matter of wondering where you were going and whose intelligence had set it up and who was paying. . . ." In Korea, Beaupre had dealt with double agents and line crossers for the first time. Now, in Vietnam, it was again different. "Compared to this country, Korea was simple: here you began with distrust, you assumed it about everything, even things you thought you knew. *Even the Americans seemed different to him now, and he trusted them less; in order to survive in this new world and this new Army, they had changed.* Yes was no longer exactly yes, no was no longer exactly no, maybe was more certainly maybe" (emphasis added).[42] Beaupre's own change from fighting in an infantry regiment in Europe, to dealing with double agents in Korea, and now to giving formal advice to an inscrutable man who wants none—illustrates Halberstam's point eloquently. Finally Beaupre has to convince himself that the small man he loathes really is a "good man," after all, so that he can maintain the humiliating pretense of courteous supplication, trying to get a proud fool to exercise the fundamental intelligence that can prevent disaster.

As an advisor Beaupre had been unimpressive, but not ineffectual. He saw the pattern of the ambushes long before Anderson, and began to work on his Vietnamese counterpart,

42. Ibid., pp. 126–27.

who finally relented and changed his plan, sending a confirmation of the old plan "in the clear" back to both the American and Vietnamese headquarters, confident that the Viet Cong monitoring their radio net would accept the bait. In contrast, Lieutenant Anderson, enraged by his frustrating efforts to flush a hidden sniper, loses his composure most uncharacteristically and stands in the open brandishing his rifle, shouting: "Come out, you sonofabitch, come on, come on out. I'm waiting, I'm here."[43] The incident is emphatic but it overloads an already unbalanced presentation.

In sum, Halberstam's novel praises the average American soldier while denouncing the government that sends him into such complex situations unprepared. Ostensibly the worst soldier of the lot, Beaupre rallies the Vietnamese, heroically crawls to get a grenade launcher from one body, uses it to suppress enemy fire, secures the radio from the dead operator, and calls for support. Residual professional pride keeps Beaupre going. A soldier's instinct had kept him near the point of the column. In contrast, battalion commander Dang was in the middle, cut down instantly with his radio operator, and Anderson was killed outright. With Lieutenant Thuong to help him, Beaupre makes the most of the second chance.

One Very Hot Day is an honest, well-executed representation of an incident which, except for the exaggerated characterizations, rings true. Halberstam handles sex with discretion and does not resort to the four-letter lexicon or indulge himself in direct editorial exhortation. He emphasizes the military and psychological aspects of a complex human situation. Beaupre is not an impressive hero, nor is he presented as particularly altered or affected by the day's action. Exuding fear and sweat, he does what must be done. He is terrified and hyper-sensitive about his own morality, but nonetheless he moves under fire, aggressive and effective. His heroism is not an instinctive reaction during a split-second of danger. It is a victory of reason over fear and the instinct for self-preservation.

Several tangential points buttress the book's effect considerably. As Beaupre uses the radio to request air support

43. Ibid., p. 120.

and other help, the operator on the other end, safe in the main compound, spouts specious drivel in sports metaphors, promising help and telling him to "stay put, ole buddy." The crackling, buzzing radio could well symbolize the uncomprehending government that sent Beaupre into the field. Even while bearing Anderson's body across his shoulders, Beaupre thinks about the clean sheets back at the main compound and about the eighteen months that separate him from the completion of his allotted twenty years in the army. He notices resentfully that the Vietnamese are already bunching up again, "laughing and talking, even ones carrying the dead." His professional eye is never relaxed; his sense of duty prevails virtually despite his clearly articulated disillusionment and open disgust.

Halberstam calls attention to sharp changes in Americans' attitudes and moral perspective. Deeply alarmed, he is pessimistic about the future. John Sack's *M* (published in 1967) describes the absurdity that encompasses a modern, vast, bureaucratic government and the wars it wages. In 1955 Sack wrote a frothy lampoon of war called *From Here to Shimbashi*, based on his own experiences in Korea. His book on Vietnam, however, reflects careful invocation of several venerable war-novel traditions, all of them used in a way that makes *M* an obvious descendent of *Catch-22*. In the established pattern Sack follows an infantry company, M (Mighty Mike, phonetically), from basic training through a half-year of duty in Vietnam.

Demirgian is perhaps, the nephew of Yossarian, his resolve appropriately vitiated by the times. He was conceived more than one-hundred years after Petya Rostov's youthful élan and nationalistic fervor sent him galloping "whence came the sounds of firing and where the smoke was thickest" to his death. Demirgian could never become so enthralled. But even though he knows with perfect acuity what is going on around him, he surrenders to his environment, shamefully. Like Petya, Demirgian wonders at the first sound of bullets passing him; unlike Yossarian he ultimately knuckles under. Six months after entering Vietnam, "he had seen no communists neither had he met a Vietnamese who cared a fig about communists or a feather about his fighting them." Therefore, halfway through his tour, in a minor position of authority, Demirgian looked about him, and "he found the American army good."[44]

Sack's book is an example of the "non-fiction novel." He includes at the end a list of real men whose actions and/or names he has used. Technology intrudes upon Demirgian's life in strange ways. Symbolizing military efficiency in action, a bumbling officer at the Pentagon using paper clips carefully matches crisp, green IBM computer cards with personnel requirements all over the world, one at a time. Because the westbound plane flies fast, the men of M eat nothing but breakfast; the stewardesses' protocol carefully states that "lunchtime" is "noontime, an hour which never caught up with M's upholstered plane. . . ."[45] The company's first casualty is an accidentally self-inflicted wound. Reported by radio to headquarters thence to Saigon's master personnel computer by data-link, the action inspires the computer to award the young stalwart his Purple Heart, by order of the president, literally before the medical evacuation helicopter has landed.

Numerous other instances link this book to Heller's. Sack's hospital features a patient similar to the Soldier in White, into whom one bottle drips a clear liquid as another accepts a slightly colored liquid that drips from his body, while a PFC is "sucking things out of him with a vacuum machine. . . ."[46] A soldier whose sole ambition was to become an MP and avoid combat is frustrated by a chance ink smudge on his records, and is last recorded as AWOL on his first leave, the object of an intensive manhunt by those same MP's. Prochaska yearned mightily to get to Vietnam and fight the yellow hordes. He winds up on the Riviera, working his will on bikini-clad female occidentals. In basic training a "veteran" lieutenant gets to the heart of the matter during his instruction on the art of digging a foxhole. Foxholes should be deep enough so that when it is occupied there will be "nothing above it, only your head."[47]

M falls far short of Catch-22 in every area, but it does

44. John Sack, M (New York, 1967), p. 168.
45. Ibid., p. 77.   46. Ibid., p. 164.   47. Ibid., p. 32.

occasionally succeed in reemphasizing the absurdity of war and in underlining the shift in attitude indicated by Captain Beaupre's speculations on changes within the army during his own career. The most striking example is this rendition of Demirgian and the rest of "M" Company at reveille during their training:

> Now a bugle sounded, issuing from a drab signal corps MX-39A/TIQ-2 record player at the adjutant's office a half-mile away. . . . Somewhere in the night an American flag was rising, but M saw only its desolate barracks lights and above them in the south the cold constellaions of Sagittarius, Scorpio, and Libra.[48]

Every modifier is depressing, and each line asserts the impersonal, tenuous link that only vaguely suggests the true potential of the ceremony. The focus is ever farther from the ostensible subject, beyond the formation, the flag, the record player and beyond the earth itself, a mote in another "cold constellation." This description is sandwiched between two sharply contrasting glimpses into the nature of things as they are. In the scene immediately preceding, two equally ignorant soldiers, one white and one black, are seen energetically quoting scriptural passages at each other, each searching for some reassurance that a personal God looks after him. And then, as the notes of the recorded bugle call fade away, a sergeant reads the list of overseas orders, an inscrutable permutation of indicated perferences and the only vaguely logical, slightly malicious whims of the officer who had wielded the IBM cards and the paper clips in the basement of the Pentagon.[49]

Sack compares the Americans in Vietnam to firefighters trapped in the attic of a "gingerbread mansion . . . fighting to save it (and themselves) from annihilation."[50] In the manner of Vonnegut, Sack randomly employs allusions to Coleridge, a line from *The Anatomy of Melancholy*, a captain whose mission is to earn "his freedom and existence" by conquering them "anew" each day, references to Swift, and Brecht, and Dante. But these contrasts or parallels are never

48. Ibid., p. 65.   49. Ibid., pp. 62–67.   50. Ibid., p. 132.

developed. Always near the surface is the feeling that finally erupts from Demirgian as, half-way through his tour, he thoughtfully intones: "I'd like to burn the whole country down and start again with Americans."[51]

The process of depersonalization is clearly drawn in a chilling change of the moral climate. Private Bead of *The Thin Red Line* reacted strongly to the guilt that attached to his killing of the Japanese soldier who interrupted him, and Sergeant Fife can look back and realize clearly how much he has changed. Thus, even among the emotionally overcharged men of "C" Company, there are lingering doubts. Private Dorn and Captain Patrick of *Band of Brothers* learn to accept the killing as part of the overall process involved in war, the war itself as part of life. Their desperate affection for their fellows binds the men of Korea together as a functioning body of men, joined together for mutual survival and in resignation to the idea that it must be done. But in the novels by Halberstam and Sack those bonds are immeasurably weakened, replaced by the knowledge that survival until the magical date of rotation will bring departure from war, back to the Land of the Big PX. Halberstam shows Captain Beaupre standing a few feet from a badly wounded Viet Cong soldier who was in the party that just ambushed his unit. Pausing only slightly, he again raises his rifle and empties the magazine into the enemy. The men of *M* burn and shoot entire communities, where enemy action is not confined to men in uniforms carrying weapons, but can come, literally, from "babes in arms" and the mothers who carry them. These incidents contrast sharply with Sergeant Leggett's agonized rationalization over the morality of killing an armed enemy soldier who happened to be temporarily in repose on guard duty, but an armed enemy soldier nonetheless. Earlier, the strong imperative of duty was sufficient to propel Corporal Tyne and the rest of the platoon of *A Walk in the Sun* through several miles of hostile countryside and enemy action up to the stone walls and ominously beckoning windows of the "mysterious" Italian farmhouse. Demirgian and his cohorts

51. Ibid., p. 168.

of *M* ride in helicopters over a land that is almost magical from the air, to land and destroy shacks that may have housed the enemy at one time.

Except for the characters of *The Deathmakers* and *The Thin Red Line*, where specific sexual complications were involved, the novels discussed in this chapter show combat to be less an emotional wringer, more a test of the reason and motivational convictions of the individual soldier. Furthermore, as the group of novels from the World War II period suggest, the phenomenon of alienation or a negative reaction to the sheer chaos of combat is keenly ingrained. A minority voice in the earlier novels, it has become the dominant strain in the later ones.

The collective thrust of the war novels tends toward one final point: war is part of the normal intercourse among nations in a technological civilization. Individual combat, the accounts of it presented by novelists, often accords with various psychological appraisals of human aggressiveness, most notably the theories of Sigmund Freud. But above the combat of individuals is the fact of war itself.

In *The Anatomy of Human Destructiveness*, Erich Fromm concludes from his studies that "major wars in modern times and most wars in antiquity were not caused by damned-up aggression, *but by instrumental aggression of the military and political elites*" (emphasis added). He also refers to another characteristic, common to populations of powerful nation-states: "awe of and respect for power." Thus, he writes, it is not surprising that "the number and intensity of wars has risen with the development of technical civilization." Only with the advent of some unimaginable utopia, where individuals have "full freedom" exercised in the absence of "all forms of exploitive control" by "dominant classes," could the rate and incidence of wars be expected to diminish.[52] Since Fromm's solution involves reversing mankind's journey along what Rousseau calls "the lost and forgotten road, by which man must have passed from a state of nature to a state of society," the prognosis is grim indeed. Thus, says Rousseau,

52. Erich Fromm, *The Anatomy of Human Destructiveness* (New York, 1973), pp. 214–15.

humanity entered an iniquitous period wherein the natural in-
equality among individuals, exaggerated and distorted, became an institutionalized perversion of nature. Anxious over
property, men required protection, best provided by some sort
of social organization, which has developed into Fromm's
"technical civilization."[53] Clausewitz, who gave war to the
masses and formally directed it against the enemy state
rather than merely against the enemy's armed forces, was
right. Ahead of his time, he saw that "war *is* a continuation of
policy by other means." A proleptic genius, he prepared the
way for total technological war. Not its armed forces but the
entire population of the opposing nation-state—that is the
enemy.

The progress of Myrer's Sam Damon, the modern analogue to Chaucer's "parfit gentil knight," expresses this literature's most coherent response to Clausewitz's formulation. As
a World War I sergeant, he used stealth and ruthless application of the rules of war to decimate a large force of the
enemy: "The object of war is to kill, right? Destroy the enemy
—by the use of mass, economy of force, movement, surprise.
That's the name of the game. We used surprise, right?"[54]
For this, a battlefield commission. Almost a half-century later
in a place much like Vietnam, Damon is again challenged
about his principles, about his reluctance to enmesh his country in another war, in the face of his reputation as an absolutely ruthless combat soldier. He replies that war is the
last resort, used only when all alternatives have failed. Then,
and only then, naked force must answer, and in its own
limited way.

> Yes: once you are in the battle all means are at hand. Who is
> going to debate niceties of design, degrees of ferocity, then?
> Flame-throwers, napalm, phosphorous, crossbows, poisoned
> stakes, shumines—don't expect men caught in the desperate
> straits of war, crushed with a thousand hellish decisions,
> to resort to Marquis of Queensbury tactics then. . . . Once the

53. Jean-Jacques Rousseau, "The Social Contract," in *The Political Philosopher*, edited by Saxe Commins and Robert M. Linscott (New
York, 1947), pp. 271–93.

54. Anton Myrer, *Once an Eagle* (New York, 1968), p. 108.

word is said—that one final, utterly irrevocable word—then there is no turning back: the wraps are off, the game is on, all manner of deviltry is unleashed.[55]

War looses all the dark potential of the human soul. To win may require suspension of the otherwise indispensable rule of laws and reason. The absolute worth of pure motive has always redeemed any combat action necessitated by it. When logical reason fails, war supplies the deficiency, providing the ultimate means to the desired end. But as he feels life leaving him, Sam, for some reason, finds himself adrift between Kant and Sartre's Manicheism. Perhaps it is the blank lack of comprehension in the soldier to whom he addresses his last words. He cites the specifically Kantian definition of "practical" and advises that when the occasion demands choice between military expediency in the interest of national goals and the dictates of the human heart, a man must try to be the best human being he can. No motive can justify killing, but to live in the world is to compromise.

Once an Eagle is the most ambitious and most successful attempt by any novelist to handle war in American life. Recognizing it as a timeless and universal phenomenon, Myrer brings to this work great literary talent, meticulous research, and scholarly objectivity. Because he asserts the possibility of a hero in this age, Myrer is in the minority in some respects, but he joins the other novelists in concluding that the soldier who cannot devise some sustaining rationale for killing other men just like himself—killing for no other reason than that he has been told to do so—faces enormous problems, though society seems to have lost sight of the issue. War can be a vendetta, a crusade, a break in the monotony of life, a "job." But the matter of guilt is never far from the center of these books dealing with combat. It is true, as Halberstam's reluctant hero dimly realizes, that attitudes have changed between wars, but the majority of these novelists agree that the problem of guilt is still there and still potent.

55. Ibid., pp. 787–88.

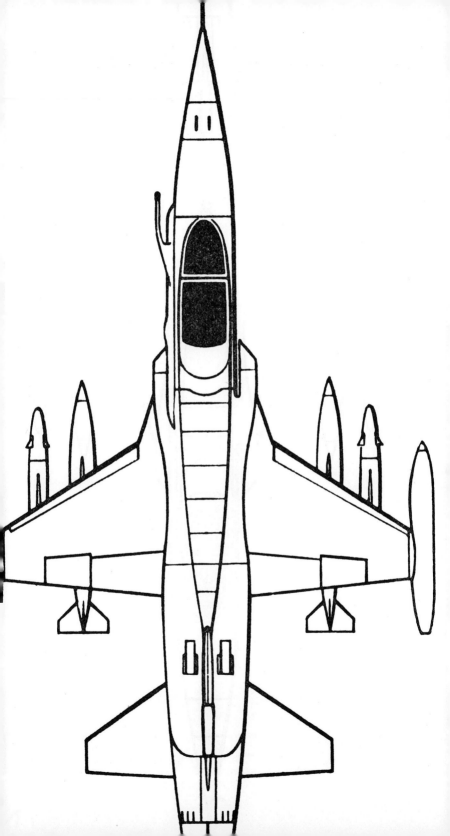

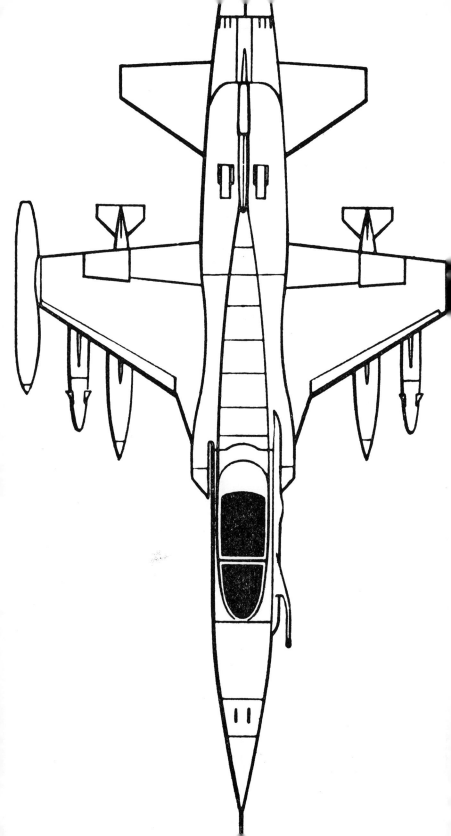

6.

AT WAR WITH TECHNOLOGY: KURT VONNEGUT, JR.

Kurt Vonnegut's work displays uniquely the thematic fusion of technology (or science) and war. Both elements dominate: war consistently demands spectacular new achievements from science; and technology flourishes in the hothouse of conflict. In addition, war provides an immediate focus for all the ingenuity that science and "progerse" can muster. Finally, in a special way synonymous with science and the idea of progress, war provides a milieu particularly suited to Vonnegut's depictions of modern life.

Several common denominators link his novels. Vonnegut sneers at the concept of free will, a delusion found in all the universe only among the dominant fauna of the planet Earth, according to the observations of Tralfamadorian passers-by. He bemoans the "stupidity and viciousness" of humanity, delineates the infinite variety of human duplicity—and, for the record, refuses to take anything seriously. Identity-enigmas proliferate almost as freely as his intentional misquotations and fractured allusions. And there is a consistent inconsistency in details from book to book: a Heraclitean flux alters the perspective, characters, and historical incidents with each retelling. Vonnegut's first novel raises the theme basic to the rest: in the last battle, man will fight his own technology for survival. *Player Piano* (published in 1952) is a clear call to arms, sounded early in the campaign. By the 1970s American fiction and nonfiction alike reflected a similar, growing dissatisfaction with rationalism. The player piano that figures in the novel demonstrates the uneasy alliance of art and science, showing technology's fatal influence on the human spirit. The player piano is but another facet of the same science that replaces men with computers to make Earth "an engineer's paradise."

Paul Proteus and his father prefigure Dr. Hoenikker, who brings the final blessing of science in *Cat's Cradle*. Hoenikker's stray Laborador and Paul's cat represent links with the vital natural world: both are destroyed. The dog is Ice-Nine's first victim; the cat is incinerated by the automated janitorial and security systems of Proteus's engineering works, located in that part of New York where Proteus Steinmetz worked earlier, shaping the twentieth century. Paul's father has organized and automated the science of his country in its defense. Now Paul is heir apparent, with emotions like those that fill Julian Castle of *Cat's Cradle* when first presented with his father's legacy of corpses.

A full generation before the space age forced science to yield the full bounty of technological miracles, Vonnegut fired this warning salvo. Paul Proteus is tried for betraying his trust, for plotting to limit the scope of machines in the lives of the American people. To do so, he insists, is right: "A step backward, after making a wrong turn, is a step in the right direction." Earlier he had dared ask whether it might be possible to do something wrong in the name of progress. With Priest Lasher and latter-day Sinn Fein Finnerty, he recklessly tries to turn the nation around. Their movement is called the Ghost Shirts, echoing an earlier similarly futile attempt by the American Indians to resist "progerse." All people except the managers are, in Vonnegut's vision, like the beleaguered and betrayed Indians of *Bury My Heart at Wounded Knee*.

Though *Slaughterhouse-Five* is Vonnegut's most widely known work, *Cat's Cradle* is in many respects more intriguing. It is an independent work, whereas *Slaughterhouse-Five* draws heavily on *Sirens of Titan; God Bless You, Mr. Rosewater;* and *Mother Night*. These form a preliminary triptych, providing collectively a seedbed for the characterizations and ideas of *Slaughterhouse-Five*.

Sirens of Titan (published in 1959) shows that creation, as Genesis describes it, was merely an intricate process for providing a critical spare part for Salo, the errant Tral-

famadorian messenger, stranded on Titan. Destined to spend
millennia there, Salo cannot continue his appointed rounds
until Space Wanderer, formerly Unk, born Malachi Constant,
"happens" along. Married now to the former wife of god-like
Rumfoord and father to a semiwild son, the Wanderer unwittingly supplies the vital piece for Salo's C+ inter-galactic
space-phaeton (as in E=MC²).

Deism is a strong and early theme in Vonnegut's novels.
Eons since, machines gladly replaced the moribund verte-
brates of Tralfamadore and now continue the mission of
greeting the far corners of the universe. Later, in *Cat's Cradle*,
Bokonian Genesis records the moment when Adam, still grog-
gily half-baked, sits up, stares about in puzzlement, and
wonders about the purpose of "all this." God asks, "Everything must have a purpose?"—and departs, a bit confused
himself. He leaves his great machine, in Conrad's phrase,
"to knit when it should embroider."

As in the short stories, even this early novel segues
firmly away from science fiction as a sufficient theme, to
fiction that uses science mainly for immediate background.
Frustration, problems of identity, and a dominant Vonnegut
theme—that people are continually used for ends they themselves know nothing of—these weave the pattern of *Sirens*.
Ultimately God toys with all of humanity, and to no particular end. This God is remarkably like Professor Hoenikker
of *Cat's Cradle*. He is a technician so fascinated by the infinite possibilities of process that he cares nothing for consequences. This realization brings Bokonon to the point of
freezing himself with Ice-Nine, creating a recumbent statue,
eternally thumbing his nose at "You Know Who."

In *Sirens*, Malachi Constant is the playboy of Earth. Out-
rageously rich and equally immoral, he is lobotomized by
Niles Rumfoord and sent on his special mission. Rumfoord's
"chance" venture into the interstitial labyrinth of the space
warp's "chrono-synclastically infundibulated" Never-Never
Land places him in a position directly analogous to Constant's, but at a higher level. Like Billy Pilgrim of *Slaughterhouse-Five*, Niles is an inveterate time traveler. Unlike Billy
he has some vague idea of the general purpose and a schedule

of sorts, an arrangement which allows him to materialize for brief periods at his home on Earth. Also Niles Rumfoord has a sense of mission; unfortunately, the wrong mission. God is to Rumfoord as Rumfoord is to Constant. And so it goes. In *Cat's Cradle* Hoenikkers's elder son, Frank, places various combinations of bugs in a bottle and watches them fight. Then, just as on that day near Alamagordo and on the day Hiroshima died, Hoenikker, too, thought he knew what he was doing—thought himself the master of a process whose ultimate end is totally beyond him.

Niles uses Malachi in his great invasion of Earth, a later elaboration on the tempestuous family reunion staged at Hastings in 1066. The "Martians" are in fact Earth people who have been kidnapped to Mars, conditioned, and launched homeward in suicidal disarray with hopelessly antiquated weapons to bring to fruition Rumfoord's grand design for Earth. Because he moves with relative freedom in time Niles thinks himself a veritable god. But though he knows the future, he still thinks it possible to change events. He capitalizes on the invasion to establish a new religion and to make of this particular war something truly useful and therefore memorable. Setting the stage for the new religion, this war will be cost-effective. A "magnificently led few will . . . die for a great deal," rather than allowing millions to pass beneath the "quick lid" of Earth for Mom, apple pie, and Vaterland. Like others before him, however, Mr. Rumfoord is deceived. A dupe, he tries to improve things through war.

The rule of necessity is unsubtly present. Malachi Constant (constant messenger) seems invulnerable in his wealth and overwhelming immorality. But he becomes an automaton, dumbly bound by the destiny once recited for his edification. Earth to Mars to Mercury to Earth to Titan—and he is done. No. Unknown to him, the final stop is Earth. The immediate director of Mars's demise, Rumfoord thinks that because he knows some he knows all. But near the novel's end, on Titan, as his faithful dog fades into a fissure in the continuum of Time, and he himself slides helplessly elsewhere, Niles is forced to the realization that is but another dupe, of Whom? Earlier he explained for Chrono (and the reader) the meaning of human history, and the meaning of the Constant family motto: "The messenger awaits." Even mechanical Salo revolted, committing suicide after revealing his message to Rumfoord. But "as it was supposed to happen," Malachi reassembled him, and Salo's sense of mission returns.

Sirens of Titan introduces the first of Vonnegut's long series of womb images—here, the Cave of Harmoniums on Mercury. Feeding on the music of their sphere, the Harmoniums are exquisite parasites, displaying at once the beauty, utter harmlessness, and essential futility of art. The failures of art incite the rage of Eliot Rosewater in *God Bless You, Mr. Rosewater*. Similarly in *Cat's Cradle* art somehow fails to redeem the world from the curse of science, despite Angela's noble suicide and Newt's enigmatic paintings. In *Mother Night* Howard Campbell and his Russian friend are practicing artists (playwright and painter, respectively) whose work ornaments their lives but does not deter its ultimately negative course. Art fails because this universe is the grand design of a bumbling mechanic. It has no purpose but to run, and it makes no provision for esthetics.

Niles Rumfoord is the presiding vicar of destiny in *Sirens*. Another Rumfoord appears in *Slaughterhouse-Five*. Sharing Billy Pilgrim's hospital room, this "Harvard history professor, Brigadier General in the Air Force Reserve, official Air Force historian, author of twenty-six books, and a multimillionaire since birth," represents, as Niles does in *Titan*, the worst possible elements of applied "progerse." Whereas Niles Rumfoord is "chrono-synclastically infundibulated," Billy P. is merely unstuck in time. Rumfoord appears to know what is going on, although that appearance is deceptive; Billy is simply dumbfounded by events. The change to a simpler terminology and to a less complex protagonist in this later book points up Vonnegut's altered focus. Perhaps convinced that issues are more complicated than he thought, Vonnegut presents a more open plot, not closed out, as in the earlier novels, with the neatness of suicidal vow, satirical mimicry of biblical injunction, smugly neat death of exploited messenger, or impending martyrdom of mod messiah. *Slaughterhouse-Five* ends only twenty-three years after it began, more than twenty years before the wavering cross-hairs on the sights of Lazzaro's laser come to rest on the expectant speaker in Chicago. Here, time really is out of joint, and perhaps not even He Who started it all can make it right. Vonnegut might be demonstrating that though death comes to all, it may not solve anything. The author no longer flaunts his mastery of events; the center of attention is beleaguered Man, Billy Pilgrim.

As the author generously explains in a later edition, the title of his novel, *Mother Night*, is taken from a speech by Mephistopheles in *Faust*, wherein Goethe's devil proclaims the primacy of Darkness and the inevitability of its triumph. So it is in this novel. As Mephisto is used and toyed with by God, so Howard Campbell is exploited. Young Campbell is recently married to a German beauty, launched upon a life of fulfillment as poet and playwright. But an unprepossessing agent of his government recruits Campbell on the eve of World War II. A combination of Lord Haw Haw and Ezra Pound, Campbell broadcasts nightly vituperation of the U.S.A. as he is bid by the Nazi regime. His efforts earn him the hate of his homeland, grateful admiration from the Nazis, and dutiful respect from the officer who hired him and from President Roosevelt—the only two persons aware of his role. Campbell's nocturnal blasts carry coded information through the ether. After the war he is captured by a zealous young American officer and tried, then released on a technicality. The official gratitude of his nation does not include recognition, so he is literally smuggled back home and allowed to live in seclusion.

Campbell is sought out for various reasons by diverse elements of his public. The Israelis classify him with Eichmann. When he finally surrenders to their agents, he winds up in a cell next to that worthy. Here the story begins—and ends. These edited memoirs, complete with the editor's protestations, reveal the harsh and crabbed course that destiny allotted for Campbell. The Russians want Campbell as an exhibit to show the world what kind of reprehensible beings the U.S. shelters from justice. Ex-Lieutenant O'Hare, who captured Campbell, wants to finish the job that was interrupted before at the scaffold steps. To the American Nazi party in its sick mutations, Campbell is a hero, sought out as patron saint and cosmic celebrity. And the FBI is interested because of the weird human congeries that swirl about him.

Mother Night (published in 1961) sets the moral and philosophical tone for the rest of Vonnegut's novels (with the exception of Eliot Rosewater's benign "... be fruitful and multiply," which concludes that book). It's all here: Mother Night is the presiding power, and with some humor. The blatant Russian plagiarist who finds the trunk concealing Campbell's literary masterpieces proves to be smashingly successful with the poems and plays, until the regime finds that he has unleashed a deadly intellectual virus: he is shot for displaying originality. Identities slip and slide: Campbell himself was a double agent; a genial middle-aged artist who is Campbell's neighbor during his years of hiding proves to be a Russian spy (shades of Colonel Abel); when Campbell's dead German wife miraculously reappears, she proves to be the woman's younger sister, also a Russian spy; and Colonel Frank Wirtanen, who recruited Campbell for his wartime role surfaces in a letter to the imprisoned Campbell. Now named Sparrow, he offers to testify at Campbell's impending trial. Campbell refers to Wirtanen as his "Blue Fairy God-mother," a term carried over into *Slaughterhouse-Five* and applied to a particularly efficient and compassionate British prisoner of war. O'Hare also appears in *Slaughterhouse-Five*, as the anonymous narrator's wartime companion.

Suicide appears prominently in Vonnegut's books. Whether this is stoicism, existentialism, or merely an un-conscious device, he uses it consistently. Beginning here in *Mother Night*, it is a topic always near at hand. When Resi Noth, masquerading as the lost wife, Helga, dabs her lips to deposit cyanide there, the reader sees the planting of an idea that blooms into glorious harvest in *Cat's Cradle*, where the Ice-Nine statue-making business claims tens of thousands. In particular, Resi prefaces the mocking suicide of Mona. Eliot Rosewater wanders along the brink of suicide, trying to forget the young firemen he killed in the war. One of the Rosewater uncles hangs himself to solve a financial dilemma.

And in *Cat's Cradle* the theme is fully developed. Suicide is indeed the single irreversible and catastrophic act that a man can perform totally of his own will, defying even God. As the Bokonian rules for the game specify, the act is preceded by the triumphant incantation: "Now I will destroy the whole world."

In *Mother Night* war is everywhere. Campbell is able to sustain himself for a generation on war surplus items. Racism, espionage, and political chicanery all reflect the temper of these times. Campbell recounts war's minor horrors, including the death by hanging of his father-in-law, recalls anecdotes accumulated during his acquaintance with the Eichmann syndrome in captivity, and the passionate pronouncements of the American Nazis. He offers this analogy for the condition of the soul "in a man at war": it is like "the stink, diseased twilight, humid resonance, and vile privacy of a stall in a public lavatory."

The narrator of *Mother Night* looks for death as a relief from a world in which "a human being might as well look for diamond tiaras in the gutter as for rewards and punishments that [are] fair." Self-taught about God, Campbell expects nothing from "Him." Tired of attempting to solve the complexities of causes and effects that do not match, Campbell surrenders to the Israelis and looks forward to the suicide that will soon end his problems, foiling Colonel Wirtanen's generous gesture.

The problem with Eliot Rosewater of *God Bless You, Mr. Rosewater* (published in 1965) is that while fighting in World War II with his infantry unit and exhibiting his usual exemplary military prowess, he inadvertently kills some German firemen, mistaking their uniforms for those of soldiers. After the war he becomes an alcoholic, marries a beautiful woman, inherits the staggering wealth of the Rosewater foundation, starts a life-long career of underwriting firemen and fire-fighting units, and becomes an authentic practicing philanthropist.

After wandering for years, he realizes that his conscience cannot be outdistanced, so he settles down in the Rosewater Vaterland (Indiana) to do good among the people. Howard

Campbell had his "ratty attic" in Greenwich Village. In *Cat's Cradle* the oubliette that the narrator and the other survivors of Ice-Nine share is more tomb than womb: an underground hide-away that could easily become their final resting place. Eliot's refuge is a smaller cubicle, though complete with toilet and telephone. As is typical of Vonnegut, this image is evoked in the mangled Freudianism of Dr. Brown's treatise on civilization and conscience. With the population at large, the battle between enlightened self-interest and conscience has reached such proportions that "a normal person, functioning well on the upper levels of a prosperous, industrialized society, can hardly hear his conscience at all." From the remainder of the treatise, the reader quickly learns that Eliot's disease is not alcoholism, but simply the obsessive, persistent desire to love and to want to help others. Eliot is virtually unique in his affliction. Wife Sylvia is more nearly normal. Reacting to his unstinting compassion toward the great unwashed, she lapses into "samaritrophia," which is "hysterical indifference to the troubles of those less fortunate than oneself." The special "oubliette" of *God Bless You, Mr. Rosewater* is psychological, the hole into "the tyrannous conscience" is pitched by "the rest of the mind" in the final development of maturing samaritrophia. Precisely because he is so humanely involved with other people, Eliot has, according to the learned Dr. Brown, a terrible potential for the disease. But Eliot prevails, a personification of that overwhelmed but undaunted conscience.

Norman Mushari is sick with envy of Rosewater, and determined to help a feckless cousin disinherit Eliot. Norman's adolescent trivium was building model airplanes, masturbating, and admiring the power of Senator Joe Mc-Carthy. His psyche suggests the later statue, created on the plains of Titan by Salo, of the genius who discovered atomic power, displayed in the mechanical Tralfamadorian's stone impression "with a shocking erection." Eliot is a gentle man, mad with love for others. As in *Slaughterhouse-Five*, he is fond of William Blake, whose poetry expresses Eliot's feelings and adorns the otherwise unmemorable interior of his cell. Mushari's conniving comes to naught when Eliot recovers his "sanity" and is able to take control of the Rosewater fortunes.

Into *God Bless You, Mr. Rosewater* Vonnegut crams most of the traditional devices of the novel, dating from the epistolary tradition onward through the myriad recognitions, mysterious documents, and unusual events that unfold during the course of an English novel. A key element is Dr. Brown's report on the Rosewaters—one source of Mushari's scheme. In addition, there are Eliot's mad-Hamlet letters to Sylvia, Senator Rosewater's speeches on the merits of free enterprise, Harvey Ulm's paranoid fugitive poetry and his novel, the famous Rosewater family history, and the philosophy of Kilgore Trout. But, whereas John Barth uses such traditional material to reproduce the aura of the learned eighteenth-century author, as in *The Sot Weed Factor*, and to create an intricately wrought plot, as in *Giles Goat Boy*, Vonnegut strews his building blocks with apparent abandon, perhaps striving for the hidden architectonic of Dos Passos's *Manhattan Transfer* or of James Joyce's *Ulysses*. Perhaps.

But among jumbled shards such as Ulm's Mailer-esque celebration of the "old avenger," the Rosewater genealogy, and Eliot's poetic madness, the Vonnegut themes come through insistently. An example is Eliot's version of Plato's myth of Er from the *Republic*. Plato explains that souls waiting to be reborn must return to Earth as a matter of expiation. They do not choose wisely because they are, after all, fallibly human. In Eliot's version, "Heaven is an utter bore." Souls famished for the experience of space and time take whatever life is offered them by the Master Cynic, God. The narrator notes, however, that something in the quality of twentieth-century life is causing newly eligible souls to swear off reincarnation. Somehow, life now is worse than during periods when inquisitions and other consequences of superstitions made earthly life a truly active hell.

Kilgore Trout emerges as something of a philosopher, an adviser to Senator Rosewater. Prolific with ideas but totally without promise as a writer, Trout earlier elicits Eliot's anguished lament that his ideas go unacknowledged because nobody will wade through the unforgivable prose that drowns

them. Trout explains the Protestant ethic, as further elabo-
rated by Emerson, to the senator: "Americans have long been
taught to hate all people who will not or cannot work, to hate
even themselves for that." Eliot's work in Rosewater country
was a noble experiment in "how to love people who have no
use." In time, Trout reasons, progress will make all people
useless—a notion that explains the indifference of the deistic
God who inhabits Vonnegut's pages. Trout also points out
the non-Freudian explanation for Eliot's obsession with firefighters and their departments. The volunteer fire department
represents the only consistent practice of "enthusiastic un-
selfishness" in contemporary American life. So neither the insanity that Mushari hoped to reveal nor the massive guilt
complex that to the unsubtle reader seems obvious is, in fact,
the true explanation.

God Bless You, Mr. Rosewater is a prime example of the
time-warp, kitchen-midden school of writing. In anticipation
of Slaughterhouse-Five, God Bless You introduces a book
about the bombing of Dresden. Reading it, Eliot is visited by
a vision of the world's demise, made real to him by a vision
of Indianapolis, fire-bombed. There is also this image of myth
and history, art and carnality, interleaved: the picture of the
Sheltland pony and two whores, one of whom is about to
try an "impossible sexual congress." The Rosewater family
tree is joined to that of the Rumfoords, and a small bird utters
in explication: "Poo-tee-weet?" as Eliot emerges from the
dark night of his apocalyptic vision. Strongly attracted by it,
Eliot explores the dry fountain in Dr. Brown's garden, suggesting Malachi Constant's entrance to the Rumfoord estate
in Sirens of Titan, and of course Constant's subsequent problems with mental health, stability, and identity. A Trout
novel, picked up at random by Eliot, again introduces the
Tralfamadorians and the end. Not the end of the world, but
the death of "the Milky Way." That's the way it goes when
chrono-synclastic infundibulation sets in.

Cat's Cradle (published in 1963) is about a scientist who
read "nothing," was fascinated by processes, asked "What
is sin?"—and found a way to end the world: Ice-Nine. Perhaps inspired by Frost's nine-line poem on the subject,

Vonnegut shows one way that the unthinking, dispassionate curiosity of positivist science could end the world in the twentieth century, just incidentally, while employed in the service of technological war. Frost's poem suggests the treacherous hatred of Dante's ninth circle; it is in polar opposition to the heat of desire. In Vonnegut's world all emotion is dead, and the key word might be indifference. Disinterested science, dead to moral responsibility and indifferent to the implications of the processes it develops, perpetrates monumental, indeed, the ultimate, fraud.

In *Pentagon of Power* (the title ingeniously fuses the symbol for twentieth-century power with the traditional symbol for the dark metaphysics of magic), Lewis Mumford suggests that for the Faustian mind of this century there is a new categorical imperative: "If it can be done, it must be done." This same theme crops up in Erich Fromm's surprising *Anatomy of Human Destructiveness*. So it is with Vonnegut's scientist, Hoenikker, who is chillingly unlike Dr. Oppenheimer in whose image he appears to have been conceived. Whereas Dr. Oppenheimer reportedly sought refuge in the Bhagavad-Gita on the awesome morning in Yucca Flat, Dr. Hoenikker "plays" cat's cradle with his terrified son on the day that Hiroshima is blasted.

Hoenikker is an archetypal positivist. His simple faith is that he recovers "truth" by experimentation; that the more truth science reveals, the wealthier and better the world will be. Outwardly mild-mannered and inoffensive, Hoenikker relates the pyramidal stacks of cannon balls on courthouse lawns to the molecular models that form the matrix of his own enterprises. He smelled, his son recalls, "like the mouth of Hell." To his immediate supervisor, Hoenikker was a force of nature, but he himself observes with scientific superiority that though nature was competent to create Ice-One, it was for man to create Ice-Nine. Hoenikker is unconcerned with morals. Vonnegut places the obvious rejoinder in the mouth of a nonscientific observer: "How innocent is the man who made the bomb?" Having created both fire and ice sufficient to effect the world's end, Hoenikker is content merely to let fate decide which it will be. Vonnegut brings to bay the public morality of the twentieth century; here he evokes the sharp memory of Dr. Oppenheimer, charged by his country with the task of unlocking the atom's eschatological secret, then rebuked and censured for shrinking from the consequences of exploiting his awful vision.

The story line of *Cat's Cradle* is relatively simple, incorporating themes by now de rigueur in Vonnegut's Gothic fiction: lost manuscripts, apocryphal histories, protean characters, an unidentified narrator, a dominant strain of war, and a foretaste of the end of the world. The narrator looks for Hoenikker's children, seeking information for his own book now in progress. With his dog, Hoenikker is the first to taste the fruits of Ice-Nine, leaving a legacy sufficient to enable the world to follow in his frosty steps. Hoenikker evokes the memory of Rumfoord and his dog, Kazak. Rumfoord also sought to improve things, and thought he knew best. Hoenikker's children are Angela, the angular and unlovely clarinetist, Newton, the gnomish painter, and Frank, whose profession is architecture, encompassing both science and art in a questionable relationship. The search leads to Ilium, New York, and then to San Lorenzo. Directing the affairs of San Lorenzo's beloved dictator, Papa, Frank brings about disaster. Papa outlawed religion, that it may flourish and give the people hope in their misery. Felled by Big C., Papa opts out with Ice-Nine in a small personal suicide that is unfortunately complicated by a predestined and therefore necessary "accident."

Mr. Vonnegut's obsessive reflections on the predestinarian nature of the universe permeate this book, too. The narrator notes that events occur "as they are supposed to happen." A prelude to the arresting "bugs in amber" metaphor of *Slaughterhouse-Five* occurs in *Cat's Cradle* when Angela produces a family picture, images "trapped in plexiglas." Some of Vonnegut's devices, however, are almost unforgivable: the narrator is saved from death because he steps stage left to vomit the large part of his rich meal—an albatross shot from the very battlements of Castle San Lorenzo; preparing to play her clarinet, Angela's fingers "twittered idly over the noiseless keys"; on the day of the first atomic detonation, when a colleague remarks that science has now known sin, Dr. Hoenikker replies, "What is sin?"; in San Lorenzo, virtually the only capital offense involves playing footsie, literally; and, asked if people still die on the antique barbed device of execution that is one of the country's chief attractions, a native responds, "It's inevitably fatal."

The cat's cradle is a clever device, totally used up as symbol. Anthropologists have noted that the game is almost universal among peoples of the world, linking the most aboriginal to the most sophisticated of modern cultures. As everybody knows, the game is played with a loop of string which, when transferred from the fingers of one player to those of another, assumes a different configuration. It is obviously different things to different people.

Like the duly famous Cheshire cat, this image fades until only the faintest suggestion is left. Hoenikker's dwarf-son, Newt, introduces it, citing the day of Hiroshima, when his father leered through the tangled web of a cat's cradle; that was the day his father smelled like the "mouth of Hell." For Hoenikker, a man who read nothing and was amused by the antics of matter in motion, a cat's cradle provided the sole means of diversion. Here, science is the chameleon figure, progressively less comprehensible to the laymen since the great innovators of the seventeenth century completed their investigations, infinite in its alterations, and ultimately destructive. The cradle next materializes in the domain of San Lorenzo's Albert Schweitzer analogue, Julian Castle. Newt paints a picture allegedly fraught with the enigmatic possibilities of Conrad's blindfolded lady in *Heart of Darkness*. Vonnegut's narrator leaps to the attack, only to be preempted by Newt, who, for all his lack of stature, manages to trample all doubts underfoot, murmuring coyly, "It's a Cat's Cradle." Now, art is the cat's cradle. But soon the tale of Angela's sad marital adventure materializes. Assuring the narrator of her woeful condition, Newt holds up his hands, stringless, but appropriately positioned: "See the cat? See the cradle?" And so, life is the cat's cradle. Finally, the conversation swings, as it sometimes must, to religion—and Newt simply says, without fanfare, "See the cat? See the cradle?"

To conclude the discourse on the obligations and failure of art, the narrator turns, muttering a line from Keats's "Ode on a Grecian Urn," remembering Angela's suicide by clarinet and Ice-Nine as he views the frozen Caribbean: art to artifact, the world remains, testifying to the failure of both God and man.

The good-humored broad-band eclecticism that marks Vonnegut's novels is in its most vigorous form in *Cat's Cradle*. A page opened at random discloses paraphrases of Dickens and Shakespeare, drawn through the writer's mind to the lines of the story by irresistible impulse. But there is consistency present in all discussions of "fix't fate" and free will. Free will cannot exist in the dead mechanical world of Vonnegut's perverse deity, who looks on unmoved as man moves through the unavoidable maze of his existence like a "piggy-wig" en route to slaughter, performing each act "as it was supposed to happen." The pseudo-religion and philosophy of Bokonon are unremarkable.

Science and war, of course, are the agents of malevolent destiny. Hoenikker's research for the marines produces Ice-Nine, and the predestined path of one plane of the San Lorenzan Air Force precipitates the final disaster. The twin offspring of technology and the idea of progress ride triumphant, for "science is the strongest thing there is." But, as a colleague of Hoenikker's ruefully remarks, "People [are] still superstitious instead of scientific."

Slaughterhouse-Five (published in 1969) is a blend of science fiction and the traditional novel, created in a variant of Vonnegut's random-intentional style. It is a story of time. In "Four Quartets," T. S. Eliot writes: "Time present and time past / Are perhaps both present in time future, / And time future contained in time past." So it is in Vonnegut's most successful novel, his most audacious effort at handling a novelist's most formidable bugaboo. In *Catch-22*, the piecemeal revelation of Snowden's death provides some sense of straight-line continuity; this gradual unfolding binds the book together. *Slaughterhouse-Five* is unified, however slightly, by the slender thread that is Billy Pilgrim's destined path. But he is "unstuck," sliding unpredictably along the axis of the fourth dimension. This is ironical. There are numerous other ironies, many based on themes and characters introduced in previous books. The result is occasionally tedious preciosity.

The authorial gimmick of discussing the difficulty of a feat while he performs it is not new to Vonnegut. Having feinted in this direction in *Mother Night* and *Cat's Cradle*, here he devotes the entire first chapter to the conception, history, and execution of *Slaughterhouse-Five*—by now a miracle of compression, according to the authorial voice of chapter 1. But as is always the case, author and narrator cannot be assumed identical. So the game begins. D. H. Lawrence's warning is always good advice: even the soberest and most objective of men, when he sets up to write of himself, exercises certain ineluctable editorial constraints and a deep bias, though perhaps unconscious that he does so. All of Vonnegut's prefatory explanation is in fact contained in chapter 1 of a work of fiction.

It is mildly surprising that an author whose thematic foundation has consistently involved war should be so concerned with writing a overtly identified antiwar book. Indeed, few who write of war intend to glorify it. Straightforward narrative is probably the best medium for placing war in its proper light. Thomas Boyd's depiction of World War I in *Through the Wheat* remains a classic example of that truth. But Vonnegut will write humorously of Dresden's death; the narrator is a new Democritus, as rendered by Robert Burton in *Anatomy of Melancholy*. When despair is too deep for tears, only laughter can prevail against it. Regrettably though, there is in *Slaughterhouse-Five* considerable evidence of the defect James Russell Lowell thought he saw in Burton's work, "A mire ankle-deep of deliberate confusion."

The twenty-odd shifts in time throughout *Slaughterhouse-Five* are confusing. The confusion stems not only from proliferated allusions, but from inconsistencies among the internal references in *Slaughterhouse-Five* and from some metamorphic alterations to persons and events summoned forth from earlier parts of the Vonnegut canon.

These phenomena are perhaps caused by a literary manifestation of the Fitzgerald deformation. Billy's birth occurred in 1922, but seldom does his announced age match the straightline arithmetic calculation. Billy is, according to the author, unstuck in time. He also moves freely in space. This is acceptable, though, as taught by Spengler, to whom space is a function of time. To the Tralfamadorians, as to Spengler and to Milton's God in *Paradise Lost*, time defines space, which then becomes a form of duration, thenceforward always present. Billy's expanding radius, from amniotic sea to pangalactic space travel, marks the truly "involuntary and unqualified realization of depth" that "marks the frontier between child and . . . Man," according to Spengler.[1]

The womb images so noticeable in Vonnegut appear now in clusters, like the ideas that delight the Tralfamadorians in their 4-D novels. Billy flashes back variously from prenatal warmth to a near-death which he found not unpleasant, in the bottom of the YMCA pool. His blanket in the hospital, the boxcar that almost becomes his tomb, the cool depths of the Carlsbad Caverns, and the bubble of Earth in the hostile cyanide of Tralfamadore—all are protective cubby-holes for Billy. On the rim of the Grand Canyon pre-teen Billy experiences fear. He is still light-years from the voyage to Tralfamadore. And it is the protective grotto under Schlachthof-Funf that "saves" Billy for his unavoidable rendezvous with Lazzaro's "lazer" gun in Chicago.

Vonnegut's prose attempts a robot-like equivalent to the potential T. S. Eliot expresses in the lines quoted earlier. Henri Bergson sees the relationship between time and space as the interaction of two media, one homogeneous (space) the other heterogeneous (time). In *Time and Free Will*, he speaks of duration as a continuous process in which the past "gnaws" through the present into the future, and, once occurring, is always present. "Pure duration," Bergson insists, occurs when the ego "lets itself live." These moments of pure duration are "internal and heterogeneous to one another." Because time is heterogeneous and infinitely protean, it will not yield to any approaches by "science." Further, these bits of ultimate hu-

---

1. Oswald Spengler, *Decline of the West*, trans. C. F. Atkinson (New York, 1939), p. 173.

man experience are unlike Stephen's Germanic version in the "Proteus" episode of *Ulysses*, neither "nacheinander" nor "nebeneinander." Not one-after-another, or one-beside-the-other, the moments of true duration in time are interpenetrating, like "notes from a tune" melting in the air, "elements which pass over into one another."[2]

Billy's slipping and sliding through time sounds Bergsonian, but the image of "bugs in amber" is repeated throughout. Perhaps it is more appropriate to this technological context. It is more like Spengler: once generated in time, space remains, hardened, and—there. When Tralfamadorians look at stars they see spaghetti-like strands of light; when they look at man they see the protean being of the Sphinx's riddle. This is the long body of time. Once launched on his peregrinations, Billy soon learns part of his life by heart: all of it is always there.

Having interpreted the myth of Er in *God Bless You, Mr. Rosewater*, Vonnegut now addresses another central Platonic idea: the allegory of the cave. Whereas Plato's prisoner is constrained merely to look at pale secondary shadows of reality, the Tralfamadorian version of the human condition represents a victim cruelly fastened by steel to a rail-bound carriage. His head in a spherical device that allows no movement, the victim sees only a virtually dimensionless speck of light. He does see some of the actual, rather than shadows of imitation, but the safety of the cave is gone. Man hurtles through the infinite not even aware of motion. And the path is fixed.

Like Gulliver to the Houyhnhnms, Billy expounds on the unspeakable viciousness of his fellows on Earth. And just as he learns of war's literal universality, of the inevitable end, Billy is whisked back in time to the instant that he begets on vast Valencia a sterling Green Beret. The culpable space-exploring Tralfamadorian pilot always has and always will press the fatal starter button, igniting the Milky Way, "If it can be done, it must be done."

The characters from Vonnegut's past novels are flat here, with none of the rounded qualities the earlier books provided.

2. Henri Bergson, *Time and Free Will*, trans. F. L. Pogson (New York, 1959), pp. 77–79, 100, 226–40.

But so it is when the "fundibulum" of one life randomly intersects those of others. Eliot still admires Kilgore Trout hugely, still despairs of his terrible prose. But here Eliot is merely an alcoholic former captain, quivering with guilt. Howard Campbell is the pure heavy, an American traitor recruiting for the Free America Corps. Bernard V. O'Hare is the narrator's boon companion, with none of the maniacal obsessions noted in *Mother Night*. Indeed, to read *Slaughterhouse-Five* without having read the preceding works is to perpetuate on an individual basis the sad state, metaphorically represented by "bugs in amber," that is the human lot in Vonnegut's universe. For it is true that all the other books illuminate *Slaughterhouse-Five*, even as it offers commentary back on them.

Player Piano documents the rise and fall of a revolution against technology in upstate New York. Technology's great moment o'erleaps the boundaries of space-time in the final, inter-galactic cataclysm, as the Tralfamadorians of *Slaughterhouse-Five* recount, unemotionally, the end of the Milky Way. The books in between tell of war between Earth and Mars, World War II (the chronological center of *Slaughterhouse-Five*), a minor revolt in the South American latitudes, and the end of the world, through Ice-Nine. The man who created Ice-Nine, as part of a research and development contract with the U.S. Marines, also presided over development of the bomb. But the end of Earth in *Cat's Cradle* still evokes Frost's "Fire and Ice," which points to the lowest circle of Dante's hell, the ice of the fraudulent. Cold, culpable Reason, with its hand maiden Progress lead to unexpected eschatological excitement. And it is fitting, too, that the end of the Milky Way should be the result of a slight Tralfamadorian oversight. Nothing personal, just something that happens—a predestined "accident."

In the entire sequence, only Eliot Rosewater is really human. He is irrational, concerned about people who fail. Temporarily "mad," he returns to reality just in time to hear the bird's helpful "Poo-tee-weet?" It is fully illuminating as T. S. Eliot's bird in another garden. Eliot is the only member of the Vonnegut universe to feel true guilt. It acts on him like a fortunate fall, precipitating the illness through which he must pass to regain his former health. Vonnegut's pessimism about human nature and free will is overwhelmingly evident throughout all his novels.

So it goes. The advent of irresistible progress brings with it the end of guilt, and the absolute extinction of hope. The same notes that provide the backdrop for Eliot's triumphant reversal of Mushari's plot against him conclude the action of *Slaughterhouse-Five*. But, going in circles, Billy Pilgrim moves always toward the cross-hairs of the waiting laser gun, on rails though "unstuck" in time. Perhaps it is the end of *Breakfast of Champions*, otherwise an undistinguished work, that resolves the chord awakened by the Eliot's earlier birds. Philboyd Studge offers the apple to his creation, Trout. For all the ranting about robots and bad juices attributable to a bumbling God who has since lost interest in His creation, the apple suggests Adam and the greater good precipitated by the advent of sin. If man loses his understanding of sin, there is no feeling of responsibility, and he becomes less than human. Like "Poo-tee-weet?" it cannot be reduced exactly to rational terms.

The works preceding *Breakfast of Champions* lie well within the parameters defining the "war novel" as examined in this study. In Vonnegut's universe there is no free will, and war is an inevitable by-product of the intercourse among nations. Given the human propensity for intraspecific killing, joined with the genie from reason's bottle—technological progress—the end is categorically predetermined, as in Milton's "De Doctrina Christiana." The possibility of choice exists, but mankind made it by following Galileo into the Faustian promised land. Vonnegut's work is a unique fusion of science fiction, secular despair, man's losing battle against technology, and a cyclical vision of the end, even for Indianapolis. And war provides the central theme for it all.

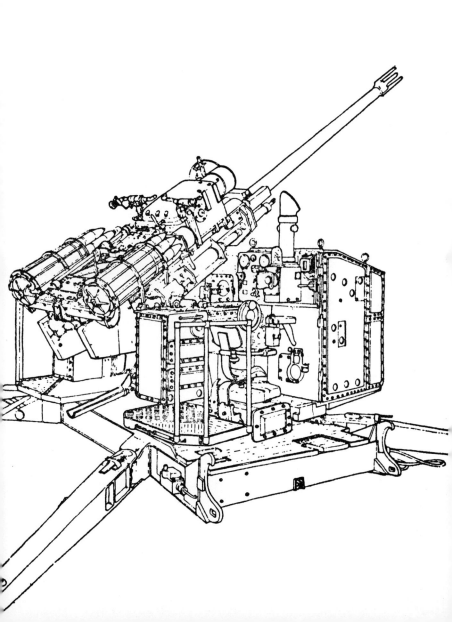

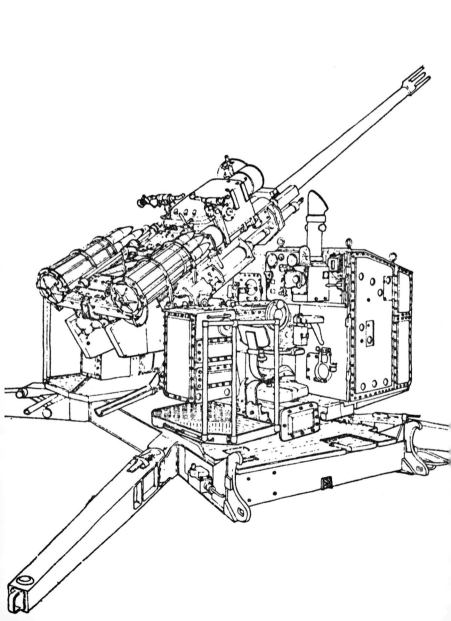

7.

CONCLUSION

This study has developed two primary ideas: first, that the war novel has come of age as a means of literary expression; second, that qualities intrinsic to the atmosphere of war are becoming increasingly applicable to the ambiance of modern technological society. No single viewpoint can provide a complete perspective for the war novel. Having evolved from the essentially subjective works of the First World War, the genre accommodates a wide range of individual reactions to a collective national experience, encompassing memorialization, reportage, analysis, critical commentary, outrage, and expressions of the absurd. Though ideas and emotion dominate the genre's mode of presentation, both style and structure are important keys to interpretation. The experience of war brooks no distinctions, generously embracing all divisions of the social scale. Accordingly, the sociological and psychological implications of the war novel are indicators of our national mood and intellectual climate, as is any other literary genre when referred to the situation within which it is created.

"The War Novel as *Bildungsroman*" is the mode most often resorted to by authors of war novels. The virtually overlapping wars since December 1941 have made military experience one of the most common in any story of a young American man's development and initiation into the affairs of the world.

The wide range of philosophical tone between Hackermeyer (of *The Beardless Warriors*) and D.J. (of *Why Are We in Vietnam?*) indicates divergent approaches to the same goal: determining the truth about war's position in human affairs. The protagonists of these contemporary novels are more aware of the larger issues than are their literary predecessors. Subjected to patterns of experience that parallel the adventures of

the Grail heroes and that conform sequentially to the novel
of education, these protagonists seek the deeper truth of human responsibility. Matheson's book places Hackermeyer in
a situation that is almost inevitable in the twentieth century.
The tone of *The Beardless Warriors* echoes that of Hemingway in his foreword to *Men at War*. Drawing on Clausewitz,
Hemingway described war as a normal aspect of the human
condition, a "part of the intercourse of the human race," more
like "business competition" than any other communal social
activity.[1] A modern-dress *Iliad*, Myrer's *The Big War* depicts
three possible reactions to the challenge. Only the uncom-
mitted Jay O'Neill survives. He manifests Sartre's existential
spirit, living from moment to moment, according to no plan.
Like Hemingway's "good soldier," he lives neither in the past
nor for the future, but "in the very second of the Present
minute."

With *From Here to Eternity*, *Catch-22*, and *Why Are
We in Vietnam?*, style and perspective become as important
as structure. Jones creates "Kid Galahad Prewitt" a romantic
rebel-hero of mythic proportions. By argumenting the articu-
lation of Prewitt's deepest thoughts, Jones dramatizes the
predicament of an individual trying to adjust to the changing
social environment. Formed by religion and family, Prewitt
struggles against an omnipotent bureaucratic organization,
embodied in the U.S. Army. In one instance Jones describes
his hero in terms of a chemical catalyst, an apt comparison.
He is absolutely unchanging throughout his experience. Stub-
bornly clinging to his precepts, Prewitt battles through the
archetypal adventures that culminate in his dying vision. He
realizes that to be human is to be forced into an endless series
of "decidings," which stretch on into the future before him.

The tragic vision terminates with Prewitt's death. Yossarian's education leads him to "desert" both the army and
modern society to accept his responsibilities as a human being.
Later, D.J. grimly awaits the next reel on the tape of his life.
Between the absurdity of *Catch-22* and the demonic black
humor of *Why Are We in Vietnam?* a breakdown has oc-

1. Ernest Hemingway, *Men at War* (New York, 1955), pp. 1–2.
2. Ibid., pp. xxvii.

curred. D.J. has much in common with "timeless" hero of
Kurt Vonnegut's *Slaughterhouse-Five*, who has the additional
advantage of access to the fourth dimension. Knowing with
certainty that men in time are like bugs trapped in amber,"
Billy Pilgrim is able to relax and resign himself to the "structure" of the moment at hand, knowing that all moments are
perpetually available.[3]

The novels collected under "The Literature of Command"
display the highest literary quality as a group. As previously
noted the subject has attracted experienced first-rate novelists
to one of the most easily identifiable trends. The predomi-
nance of military figures on the national and international
scene has not gone unnoticed. The writers of contemporary
war novels consistently set in opposition or in uneasy balance
a military leader and figures representing political power and
the influence of the press.

In presenting their arguments the authors use dramatic
structures and techniques of delivery, supporting Aristotle's
contentions about drama as a forum for the delineation of
human affairs. As expressed by these novelists, the single
most alarming trait in military leaders is their appetite for
power. Using the closed form of classical drama, the authors
imply a collective belief in the rational explanation of events
that typifies the drama of Aeschylus and Sophocles. The fact
that there are more relatively good war novels about flag-rank
officers than about any other military grade may be attributable to the American obsession with achievement or to the
beliefs that prompted Aristotle's inductive conclusions about
the ideal dramatic protagonist.

The literature of command is also an adaption of the
novel of manners, here devoted to studying the type of man
who succeeds under strenuous conditions. As in other American stories of success, the hero surrenders family, friends, and
personal happiness for the conquest of stars. The authors are
almost unanimous in one respect: weakness does not succeed.
On the other hand, men in whom the simple will to power
is sufficiently great to carry them to high command are poten-

3. Kurt Vonnegut, Jr., *Slaughterhouse-Five* (New York, 1969), p.
72.

tially dangerous. Two images of a commander emerge, represented best by Melville Goodwin and Mailer's General Cummings. In *Once an Eagle*, Myrer draws the types together in the characters of Sam Damon and Courtney Massengale. The novelists also generally conclude that some sort of benevolent unconscious genius animates the ideal military commander: a man of high rank who thinks excessively is dangerous.

Guard of Honor is the most successful of this group of war novels. In addition to its unity of time, place, and action, Cozzens's novel possesses the vital quality of credibility in plot development. Despite the superimposition of Colonel Ross as the divine arbiter of mortal differences, *Guard of Honor* provides a sense of perspective that is absent from *The Naked and the Dead* and *Once an Eagle*. Mailer sounds a call to arms, and Myrer runs the potential of a controlled experiment to the limit.

Finally, the novels of command reveal a theme more apparent in the works on sexuality and violence, but nonetheless important here: the fragmented psyche, first signaled in the war novel by the protagonists of John Dos Passos's *Three Soldiers*. In each novel the commander faces alternatives of action, or is tempted by antagonists who suggest courses of action other than the one he knows is right. His own darker urges may be represented by a loyal subordinate who executes the necessary, but crude or unacceptable, corollaries to the commander's actions. Especially in *Harm's Way*, *Command Decision*, *Guard of Honor*, *Show Me a Hero*, and *The Crusaders*, the hero is confronted by individuals who represent the darker potential of the human spirit.

In "Sexuality and Violence in the War Novel," an individual's reaction to the crises of war transcends all other considerations. This group of novels is nearer the center of contemporary American fiction than are the other groupings of the war novel, exhibiting the romantic protest against the machine age and its attendant dehumanization of the men who serve it. War exacerbates already difficult conditions, driving men to the breaking point.

The three main areas of examination were homosexuality,

the direct relationship between war's violence and human sexuality, and sexual response to the machines of war. In general, the writers concur that a sexually potent man will be an effective fighter. Incommunicative men are pictured as prime candidates for homosexuality, which develops from, or is accompanied by, an inability to relate satisfactorily to other people. Those unable to communicate except through violence or in other socially unacceptable ways, find sublimative release or, in the case of Buzz Marrow and Lieutenant Freeman of *The End of It*, direct sexual release in the duties war requires of them. Whether it grows from an individual's frustrating incapacity to adjust "normally" to life or is simply the mark of a well-adjusted mature man, sexuality is a consistent indicator of fighting potential in the novelists' versions of men at war.

These novels exhibit most clearly the "split psyche" and the human impact of "progress," both by-products of the collision between naked human nature and the omnipotent technology of the machine age at war with itself. Sire's Chico and Captain Brandon, Buzz Marrow and copilot Boman of *The War Lover*, the sexually competent characters of *The Thin Red Line*, and the self-destructive protagonists of the novels of homosexuality—all are primary examples of the interaction of "normal" adjustment and grotesque sexual distortion that typify this literature.

The thesis advanced by Leo Marx in *The Machine in the Garden* is supported throughout the entire body of war literature, but most particularly in the novels of sexuality and violence and in the work of Kurt Vonnegut. The general romantic resistance to the machine age, from Carlyle and Emerson forward, finds plentiful support in these pages. The body of allusion includes Whitman, Melville, and D. H. Lawrence, along with the theories of Freud, Erich Kahler, and Jung. The basic primal substructure of the American psyche delineated in these novels is an extrapolation of the savage heritage of violence, pillage, and rape revealed by William Carlos Williams's provocative appraisal of the American heritage, *In the American Grain*. On the whole, the judgments of Mailer's General Cummings and of Brigadier San Slater of *From Here to*

Eternity are resoundingly affirmed: the man of the machine age is perpetually apprehensive. Subordination to the machine solves some problems of human responsibility, but it raises questions of human integrity that can become too complex for resolution.

"The Psychology of Combat" develops issues implicit in many of the preceding novels but central to these works which focus on the predicament of combat to the virtual exclusion of all other elements. In general, these studies of combat are relatively recent; they include all of the selected works on Korea and Vietnam. Combat guilt and motivation are the central points of consideration, as protagonists grapple with the realities of their actions, whether personally killing the enemy or leading the men who do.

Numerous divergent theories appear. Edward Loomis's *End of a War* displays a protagonist who painstakingly rationalizes his way to the decision made by Agamemnon at Aulis: to do his public duty and endure the private consequences. Killing is a crime in the absolute, and no motive can expiate the act in advance. But in the novels of Korea, the enemy is no longer a group of hated individuals, he is merely another aspect of a generally hostile environment. There are no speeches of exhortation, no calls to arms against the atrocities of a bestial enemy as is typical in many World War II novels. Both *One Very Hot Day* and *M* demonstrate profound discontent with war, regardless of the motive or the circumstances. Another view of combat asserts that the natural fighter may be a peacetime misfit, an inherently pathological character outside the special arena of war. Still another insists that the best fighter is a well-adjusted man defending his rights or way of life.

The major point of crisis is killing another human being. Army historian Brig. Gen. S. L. A. Marshall reports findings that agree with Sigmund Freud's pronouncement in *Reflections on War and Death*, that killing is an absolute transgression of innate individual human taboos, and it must be acknowledged as such and somehow expiated.[4] Based on thou-

---

4. Sigmund Freud, *Reflections on War and Death*, trans. and ed. A. A. Brill and A. B. Kuttner (New York, 1918), pp. 62, 70.

sands of interviews and after-action reports from World War II, General Marshall concluded that normally only about one soldier in six will fire consistently against the enemy, regardless of the provocation, and he revealed that in studies of combat fatigue in World War II, "fear of killing rather than the fear of being killed, was the most common cause of battle failure in the individual, and [that] the fear of failure ran a strong second."[5] General Marshall also noted that there appeared to be a certain degree of correlation between superlative performance in battle and consistent inability to "soldier" in a peacetime situation. The relationship cannot, however, be reversed. Nor is there any indication, Marshall writes, that a good garrison soldier will falter in a fight.[6]

Several novels display conclusions that substantially parallel those of Freud and Marshall, specifically Glen Sire's *The Deathmakers*, Jones's *The Thin Red Line*, Ernest Frankel's *Band of Brothers*, and Tom Chamales's *Never So Few*. Killing a fellow human, as Doll realizes, involves a monstrously complex network of decision and consequence. The advent of "professionalism"—hailed by Samuel P. Huntington in *The Soldier and the State* as a characteristic of the Korean War, and confirmed by Americans during the Vietnam War—may have the deeper significance of alienation from human responsibilities, as the details of My-Lai clearly indicate. From Matheson's Private Hackermeyer to Sack's Demirgian, there has been a consistent tendency to accept war as one part of the whole human problem. Caught up by the collective will of his society, the soldier does his duty and then returns to his previous life. Or can he? Soldiers like Hackermeyer and Captain Beaupre of *One Very Hot Day* lend support to this notion, but figures such as Mailer's case-hardened Sgt. Croft, Chico of *The Deathmakers*, Danforth and Ringa of *Never So Few*, and the other "darker" aspects of the heroic performance in war literature, are all vestiges of the belief that to kill, a man must go against basic human nature or violate learned imperatives that are absolutely vital to the growth of the hu-

5. S. L. A. Marshall, *Men Against Fire* (Washington, D.C., 1947), pp. 50, 78.
6. Ibid., pp. 57–63.

man community. In either case, a degree of social malignancy develops.

Aside from Prewitt, religious guilt enters the contemporary American war novel only tangentially. Guilt arises from failure in battle and, among the works focusing on sexuality and violence, out of various departures from accepted sexual codes of behavior. Closely allied to the problem of guilt is the question of motivation, which novelists have collectively fixed some place between the extremes of Freud's stated limits: the rational belief that "certain abstract common ideals" exist for which the individual is willing to give his life, and the unconscious, fanatical inability of the psyche to accept the idea of personal death. Combat motivation in the war novels stems most often from the immediate circle of "buddies" with whom a man labors in combat—the members of his squad, fire-team, or vehicle crew.

The range of works included in this study shows that the modern war novel employs virtually every variant of style and structure. Moreover, it advances the image of the hero as victim, well within the current of contemporary literature. Prewitt, Yossarian, Sam Damon, General Logan of *Show Me a Hero*, most of the protagonists in the novels of sexuality and violence, Leggett, Con Reynolds, Beaupre, and even Demirgian—all are victimized by the circumstances that overwhelm them and determine their actions.

Carl Jung, who describes himself as an empiricist, declared in a 1946 radio broadcast, "Man's warlike instincts are ineradicable, and therefore a state of complete peace is unthinkable."[7] Jung calls democracy a "chronic state of mitigated civil war," explaining that in Switzerland the continuous sublimation of internal friction and aggressions through democratic argumentation, dissent, and laissez-faire factional collisions keep that republic nominally peaceful, at least externally. Elsewhere, Jung implies, where such a happy situation does not prevail, warfare is inevitable.

As technology reduces the buffer of time and space about the states of the world and science erodes the residual con-

7. Carl Jung, quoted by William F. Irmscher in *Man and Warfare* (Boston, 1964), pp. 122–27.

straints of previous ages, Erich Kahler's pronouncements concerning the vast collective that is world society are more widely applicable. Society is becoming an existential entity, self-created, living in an open-ended process toward no definite goal; life is a "happening." Just as modern drama displays the fact of this condition, so the modern war novel reflects the tensions and uncertainties that assail the inhabitants of that collective. Uncertainties prevail at every turn. Without a goal, any individual or group of individuals will become increasingly involved and obsessed with present action. Action becomes a sufficient end in itself. And more and more, that present action involves warfare. A society that is best characterized in war literature is not a sound one by the rationally conceived theoretical standards of civilization. Whether war is the cause or one of the effects of the central condition, it has become a natural metaphor for the plight of mankind in the twentieth century. No one has ever proved that man is, in fact, rational.

Among the novels examined in this study, *From Here to Eternity* is the best, the most likely to persevere as significant literature. Jones is not concerned with meticulous research, nor are his presentations of ideas particularly consistent or lucid, but he is a perceptive psychologist, particularly in detailing the actions of the Romantic rebel, writing of what he probably knows best. Just as the complex consequences of the plot in *Guard of Honor* grow credibly from the interaction of human relationships, so Prewitt exhibits consistently believable humanity in his stubborn drive to death. Like the hero of Greek tragedy, possessing that quality of humanity cited by Faulkner in his Nobel Prize acceptance speech, Prewitt embodies a mimetic representation of heroic human nature, not simply enduring but prevailing, and preserving intact to the end, his vision of himself.

Cozzens's *Guard of Honor*, Mailer's *The Naked and the Dead*, and Anton Myrer's *Once an Eagle* constitute the "best of the rest," with one exception. (Intriguing novels like Thomas Goethals's *Chains of Command*, Mitchell Goodman's *The End of It*, Edward Loomis's *End of a War*, Tom Chamales's *Never So Few*, and Harry Brown's *A Walk in the Sun* all mark the appearance of promising talent.) The exception is *Catch-22*, a novel in a class by itself. No other war story comes close to Heller's masterpiece. Funny in the way Aristophanes must have been, Heller shows that humor is the final refuge for sanity, reason's most effective weapon against omnipotent irrationality. No other American war novel so captures the spirit of our age. *Catch-22* depicts the horror of technology's quintessential inhumanity, while clearly marking the effect of both "branches" of the absurd. John Sack's *M* is clearly indebted to *Catch-22*, and *Why Are We in Vietnam?* and Vonnegut's *Slaughterhouse-Five* are firm indications of the same trend.

Black humor is absurd, an indication of existential pressures. It is the heart of GI humor, and as the predicament of the human race becomes increasingly desperate, society is appropriately more receptive to it and capable of a fuller appreciation. And, authors are more likely to be producing black humor.

This brings us to Kurt Vonnegut. Each of his books reflects a clever, facile mind; busy, busy, busy synthesizing. Individually, the novels are amusing, pointedly pessimistic, and totally unhappy about technology. Together, they create a coherent statement, the pattern of which requires every novel, a very midden-heap of trinkets, trash, and treasure. In *Sirens of Titan*, several thousand Martians, in reality kidnapped Earthlings, lobotomized and programmed, make a suicidal attack on Earth. In self-defense, the Earth renders the Moon uninhabitable for "ten million years," and does just about the same with retaliatory strikes on poor, vacant Mars. In *Mother Night*, Howard Campbell's government makes him a most effective double agent during World War II, but apparently all those who know about it die, leaving him at the mercy of the vengeful Israelis, who classify him with Eichmann. When the possibility of a reprieve suddenly surfaces only hours before his scheduled death, Campbell refuses it. Campbell sees death as his due for crimes against himself—for having allowed his soul to be bought for the service of war. In *God Bless You, Mr. Rosewater*, Eliot Rosewater spends his adult life trying to make amends for having killed some German firemen during World War II, when he shot the wrong kind of uniforms. The denizens of *Cat's Cradle's* San Lorenzo all avail themselves of Ice-Nine's miraculous powers, though most do it unwittingly. Science compensates for the failure of art by making the Earth an artifact. And Billy Pilgrim cycles through eternity, his entire existence centered on the death of Dresden by firebombing. In the end of the beginning, the citizens of *Player Piano's* Illium, New York, neo-Ghost Shirts and all, showed their supreme futility by busily setting about to rebuild the machines that they destroyed in their fight against technology.

It all comes down to Kilgore Trout, who is no more significant in the scheme of things than Paul Proteus's electri-fried cat or poor Kazak, the dog, or a piece of scrap metal. The cat got in the way of machines and was killed. Kazak belonged to Rumfoord in one book and was "chrono-synclastically infundibulated" with him. In *Breakfast of Champions* Kazak makes a heroic attempt to get at the creator, only to be defeated by a fence. Thus preserved, the maker of novelist Trout proceds to hand him the apple, beginning the highly predictable cycle all over. As Vonnegut so often has written: "As it was supposed to happen." But the apple suggests choice.

Vonnegut has played with the image of blue-white, azure feet—the feet of persecuted and/or murderously slain innocents—throughout his work, especially among the population of *Slaughterhouse-Five*. Wading through a stream polluted by plastic made by a government munitions contractor for bombs, Trout's feet, already "azure" and "artistic," become beautifully "nacreous," a pearly, perfect image of suffering and sacrifice. Earlier, Trout had deceitfully convinced Dwayne Hoover that he had free will. Naturally, Hoover went berserk. He also waded into the pearly water, but with shoes on, a lesser example than the failed intellectual Trout. As he was meant to do, Trout meets his maker and receives the fatal apple of apparent freedom, on behalf of everybody.

But Earth and all its agonies throughout eons of time had only the purpose of providing that four-inch piece of scrap for Salo's space ship so that he can continue his pointless appointed duty of carrying "Greetings" to . . . ? Like man making wars and doing the other things required by technology, Salo was "used," "wasted." Whether controlled by radio or programmed by bad juices, people don't stand a chance against "progerse." As Shakespeare wrote in a prepositivist age: "As flies to wanton boys are we to the gods, / They kill us for their sport."[8]

8. William Shakespeare, *King Lear*, act 4, sc. 1, lines 38–39.

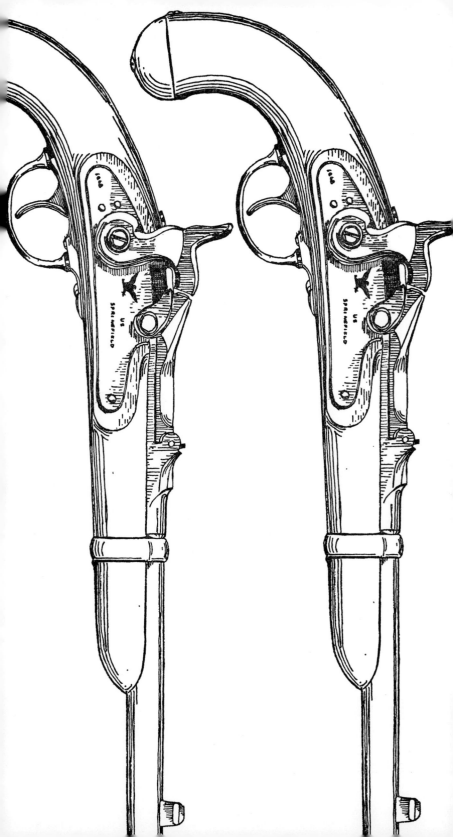

BIBLIOGRAPHY

Primary Sources

Anders, Curt. *The Price of Courage*. New York: Sagamore Press, 1957.

Anderson, Thomas. *Your Own Beloved Sons*. New York: Random House, 1956.

Atwell, Lester. *Private*. New York: Simon and Schuster, 1958.

Barr, George. *Epitaph for an Enemy*. New York: Harper's Magazine Press, 1959.

Bassett, James. *Harm's Way*. New York: World, 1962.

Bellow, Saul. *The Dangling Man*. New York: Vanguard Press, 1960.

Billany, Dan. *The Trap*. London: Faber and Faber, 1950.

Blacker, Irwin R. *Search and Destroy*. New York: Random House, 1966.

Bourjaily, Vance N. *The End of My Life*. New York: Dial Press, 1947.

Boyd, Thomas. *Through the Wheat*. New York: Charles Scribner's Sons, 1927.

Boyington, Gregory. *Tonya*. Indianapolis: Bobbs-Merrill, 1960.

Bonham, Frank. *The Burma Rifles*. New York: Thomas Y. Crowell Co., 1960.

Brelis, Dean. *The Mission*. New York: Random House, 1958.

Brinkley, William. *Don't Go Near the Water*. New York: Random House, 1956.

Brown, Eugene. *The Locust Fire*. New York: Doubleday & Co., 1946.

Brown, Harry. *A Walk in the Sun*. New York: Alfred A. Knopf, 1967.

Brown, Joe David. *Kings Go Forth*. New York: William Morrow and Co., 1956.

Burdick, Eugene, and Harvey Wheeler. *Fail Safe*. New York: McGraw-Hill, 1962.

Burns, John Horn. *The Gallery*. Garden City, N.Y.: Sun Dial Press, 1948.

Calmer, Ned. *The Strange Land*. New York: Charles Scribner's Sons, 1950.

Chamales, Tom T. *Never So Few*. New York: Charles Scribner's Sons, 1957.

Chamberlain, William. *Combat Stories of World War II and Korea*. New York: John Day Co., 1962.

——. *More Combat Stories of World War II and Korea*. New York: John Day Co., 1964.

Chaze, Elliott. *The Stainless Steel Kimono*. New York: Simon and Schuster, 1947.

Clagett, John. *The Slot*. New York: Crown, 1958.

Clark, R. W. *Ride the White Tiger*. Boston: Little, Brown and Co., 1959.

Cobb, Humphrey. *Paths of Glory*. New York: Viking Press, 1935.

Cobb, John. *The Gesture*. New York: Viking Press, 1948.

Cochrell, Boyd. *The Barren Beaches of Hell*. New York: Henry Holt & Co., 1959.

Coppel, Alfred. *The Gate of Hell*. New York: Harcourt, Brace & World, 1967.

Cozzens, James G. *Guard of Honor*. New York: Harcourt, Brace & Co., 1948.

Crane, Stephen. *The Red Badge of Courage*. New York: W. W. Norton & Co., 1962.

Crawford, William. *Give Me Tomorrow*. New York: Bantam Books, 1966.

——. *The Killing Zone*. New York: Harper's Magazine Press, 1970.

Crockett, Lucy H. *The Magnificent Bastards*. New York: Farrar, Straus, and Young, 1954.

Crowley, Robert T. *Not Soldiers All*. Garden City, N.Y.: Doubleday & Co., 1967.

Cummings, E. E. *The Enormous Room*. New York: Random House, 1934.

Davis, Paxton. *Two Soldiers*. New York: Simon and Schuster, 1956.

Dibner, Martin. *The Admiral*. New York: Doubleday & Co., 1968.

Dodson, Kenneth. *Away All Boats*. Boston: Little, Brown and Co., 1954.

Dos Passos, John. *Three Soldiers*. New York: A. S. Barnes & Co., 1932.

Downs, Hunton. *The Compassionate Tiger*. New York: Popular Library, 1961.

Falstein, Louis. *The Face of a Hero*. New York: Harcourt, Brace & Co., 1950.

Faulkner, William. *A Fable*. New York: Random House, 1950.

———. *Soldier's Pay*. New York: Liveright, 1926.

Fenton, Charles, ed. *The Best Short Stories of World War II*. New York: Viking Press, 1957.

Fersen, Nicholas. *Corridor of Honor*. Indianapolis: Bobbs-Merrill, 1958.

Fields, Arthur C. *World without Heroes*. New York: McGraw-Hill, 1950.

Flood, Charles B. *More Lives than One*. Boston: Houghton Mifflin Co., 1967.

Forbes, Gordon. *Goodbye to Some*. New York: W. W. Norton & Co., 1961.

Ford, Ford Madox. *Parade's End*. New York: Alfred A. Knopf, 1950.

Fuller, Robert G. *Danger: Marines at Work*. New York: Random House, 1959.

Frank, Pat. *Forbidden Area*. New York: J. B. Lippincott Co., 1956.

———. *Hold Back the Night*. New York: J. B. Lippincott Co., 1952.

Frankel, Ernest. *Band of Brothers*. New York: Macmillan Co., 1958.

Gage, William. *The Cruel Coast*. New York: New American Library, 1966.

Garfield, Brian. *The Last Bridge*. New York: David McKay Co., 1966.

Garrett, James. *And Save Them for Pallbearers*. New York: Bantam Books, 1958.

Garth, David. *The Watch on the Bridge*. New York: G. P. Putnam's Sons, 1959.

Giovannitti, Len. *The Prisoners of Combine D*. New York: Henry Holt and Co., 1957.

Goethals, Thomas. *Chains of Command*. New York: Random House, 1955.

Goodman, Mitchell. *The End of It*. New York: Horizon Press, 1961.

Grass, Günter. *The Tin Drum*. Translated by Ralph Mannheim. New York: Crest Paperbooks, 1961.

Graves, Robert. *Goodbye to All That*. New York: Jonathan Cope and Harrison Smith, 1930.

Gwaltney, Francis I. *The Day the Century Ended.* New York: Rinehart and Co., 1955.

Haines, William W. *Command Decision.* New York: Little, Brown and Co., 1947.

Halberstam, David. *One Very Hot Day.* Boston: Houghton Mifflin Co., 1967.

Hardy, William. *The Time of Killing.* New York: Dodd, Mead & Co., 1962.

——. *The Wolf Pack.* New York: Cornwall Press, 1960.

Harris, A. M. *The Tall Man.* New York: Farrar, Straus and Cudahy, 1958.

Hawkes, John. *The Cannibal.* New York: New Directions, 1962.

Hayes, Alfred. *All Thy Conquests.* New York: Howell, Sonskin, 1946.

——. *The Girl on the Via Flaminia.* New York: Harper and Brothers, 1949.

Heller, Joseph. *Catch-22.* New York: Simon and Schuster, 1961.

Hemingway, Ernest. *Across the River and into the Trees.* New York: Charles Scribner's Sons, 1950.

——. *A Farewell to Arms.* New York: Charles Scribner's Sons, 1929.

——. *For Whom the Bell Tolls.* New York: Charles Scribner's Sons, 1940.

——, ed. *Men at War.* New York: Bramhall House, 1955.

——. *The Short Stories of Ernest Hemingway.* New York: Charles Scribner's Sons, 1953.

Herber, William. *Tomorrow to Live.* New York: Coward McCann, 1957.

Hersey, John. *A Bell for Adano.* New York: Alfred A. Knopf, 1944.

——. *Into the Valley.* Garden City, N.Y.: Sun Dial Press, 1944.

——. *The Wall.* New York: Alfred A. Knopf, 1950.

——. *The War Lover.* New York: Alfred A. Knopf, 1959.

Heym, Stefan. *The Crusaders.* Boston: Little, Brown and Co., 1948.

Hollands, D. J. *Able Company.* Boston: Houghton Mifflin Co., 1956.

Hunt, Howard. *Limit of Darkness.* New York: Random House, 1944.

Hyman, Mac. *No Time for Sergeants.* New York: Random House, 1954.

Jonas, Carl. *Beachhead on the Wind.* Boston: Little, Brown and Co., 1945.

Jones, James. *From Here to Eternity.* New York: Charles Scribner's Sons, 1951.

———. *The Pistol.* New York: Charles Scribner's Sons, 1958.

———. *The Thin Red Line.* New York: Charles Scribner's Sons, 1962.

Kadish, M. R. *Point of Honor.* New York: Random House, 1951.

Keefe, Frederick L. *The Investigating Officer.* New York: Delacorte Press, 1966.

Klass, Joe. *Maybe I'm Dead.* New York: Victor Gollancz, 1955.

Knebel, Fletcher, and Charles Bailey II. *Seven Days in May.* New York: Harper and Row, 1962.

Krueger, Carl. *Wings of the Tiger.* New York: Frederick Fell, 1966.

Larteguy, Jean. *The Centurions.* New York: E. P. Dutton, 1962.

Lawrence, T. E. *The Seven Pillars of Wisdom.* New York: Dell, 1962.

Leveridge, Ralph. *Walk on the Water.* New York: Farrar, Straus and Young, 1951.

Levin, Dan. *Mask of Glory.* New York: McGraw-Hill, 1949.

Linakis, Steven. *In the Spring the War Ended.* New York: G. P. Putnam's Sons, 1965.

Loomis, Edward. *End of a War.* New York: Ballantine Books, 1958.

MacCuish, David. *Do Not Go Gentle.* Garden City, N.Y.: Doubleday and Co., 1946.

Mailer, Norman. *The Naked and the Dead.* New York: Random House, 1948.

———. *Why Are We in Vietnam?* New York: G. P. Putnam's Sons, 1967.

Manning, Frederick. *Her Privates We.* New York: G. P. Putnam's Sons, 1930.

Marquand, John P. *Melville Goodwin, USA.* Boston: Little, Brown and Co., 1951.

Mason, F. Van Wyck, ed. *American Men at War.* Boston: Little, Brown and Co., 1964.

Matheson, Richard. *The Beardless Warriors*. Boston: Little, Brown & Co., 1960.

McDonald, Charles B. *Company Commander*. New York: Ballantine Books, 1968.

Michener, James. *The Bridges at Toko-Ri*. New York: Random House, 1953.

———. *Sayonara*. New York: Random House, 1954.

Moore, Gene D. *The Killing at Ngo Tho*. New York: W. W. Norton & Co., 1967.

Moore, Robin. *The Country Team*. New York: Crown, 1967.

———. *The Green Berets*. New York: Avon Books, 1965.

Mulvihill, William. *Fire Mission*. New York: Ballantine Books, 1957.

Moss, Sidney, and Samuel Moss. *And Thy Men Shall Fail*. Chicago: Ziff-Davis, 1948.

Murphy, Dennis. *The Sergeant*. New York: Viking Press, 1958.

Myrer, Anton. *Once an Eagle*. New York: Holt, Rinehart and Winston, 1968.

———. *The Big War*. New York: Appleton-Century-Crofts, 1957.

Nathanson, E. M. *The Dirty Dozen*. New York: Dell, 1960.

New, Doyle A. *One Was a Marine*. New York: Greenwich Book Publishers, 1956.

O'Rourke, Frank. *"E" Company*. New York: Simon and Schuster, 1956.

Pashko, Stanley. *Ross Duncan at Bataan*. New York: Julian Messner, 1950.

Plagemann, Bentz. *The Steel Cocoon*. New York: Viking Press, 1958.

Powell, Anthony. *The Valley of Bones*. London: William Heinemann, 1964.

Powell, Richard. *The Soldier*. New York: Charles Scribner's Sons, 1960.

Pratt, Rex K. *You Tell My Son*. New York: Random House, 1958.

Remarque, Eric Maria. *All Quiet on the Western Front*. Boston: Little, Brown and Co., 1929.

Reynolds, Quentin. *The Man Who Wouldn't Talk*. New York: Random House, 1953.

Rigby, Ray. *The Hill*. New York: John Day Co., 1965.

Ross, Glenn. *The Last Campaign*. New York: Harper and Brothers, 1962.

Ross, James E. *The Dead Are Mine*. New York: David McKay Co., 1963.

Russ, Martin. *The Last Parallel*. New York: Rinehart & Co., 1957.

Sack, John. *From Here to Shimbashi*. New York: Harper and Brothers, 1955.

————. *M*. New York: New American Library, 1967.

Sanderson, James. *Boy with a Gun*. New York: Henry Holt & Co., 1958.

Scannell, F. P. *In the Line of Duty*. New York: Harper and Brothers, 1946.

Shapiro, Lionel S. *6th of June*. Garden City, N.Y.: Doubleday and Co., 1955.

Shaplen, Robert. *A Corner of the World*. New York: Alfred A. Knopf, 1949.

————. *A Forest of Tigers*. New York: Alfred A. Knopf, 1945.

Shaw, Irwin. *The Young Lions*. New York: Random House, 1948.

Shulman, Max. *Rally Round the Flag, Boys*. Garden City, N.Y.: Doubleday and Co., 1957.

Singer, Howard. *Wake Me when It's Over*. New York: G. P. Putnam's Sons, 1959.

Sire, Glen. *The Deathmakers*. New York: Simon and Schuster, 1960.

Snyder, Louis L., ed. *Masterpieces of War Reporting*. New York: Julian Messner, 1962.

Styron, William. *The Long March*. New York: New American Library, 1968.

Sutton, Jefferson. *The Missile Lords*. New York: G. P. Putnam's Sons, 1963.

Taylor, Thomas. *A-18*. New York: Crown, 1967.

Thorin, Duane. *A Ride to Panmunjom*. Chicago: Henry Regnery Co., 1956.

Unruh, Fritz Von. *The End Is Not Yet*. New York: Storm, 1947.

Uris, Leon. *Armageddon*. Garden City, N. Y.: Doubleday and Co., 1964.

————. *Battle Cry*. New York: G. P. Putnam's Sons, 1953.

————. *Exodus.* Garden City, N. Y.: Doubleday and Co., 1958.

————. *Mila 18.* New York: Doubleday and Co., 1961.

————. *Topaz.* New York: McGraw-Hill, 1967.

Vonnegut, Kurt, Jr. *Breakfast of Champions.* New York: Delacorte Press, 1973.

————. *Cat's Cradle.* New York: Dell, 1963.

————. *God Bless You, Mr. Rosewater.* New York: Dell, 1965.

————. *Mother Night.* New York: Avon Books, 1961.

————. *Player Piano.* New York: Avon Books, 1952.

————. *The Sirens of Titan.* New York: Dell, 1959.

————. *Slaughterhouse-Five.* New York: Delacorte Press, 1969.

Voorhees, Melvin. *Show Me a Hero.* New York: Simon & Schuster, 1954.

West, Morris L. *The Devil's Advocate.* New York: William Morrow Co., 1961.

Westcott, Glenway. *Apartment in Athens.* New York: Harper and Brothers, 1945.

Westheimer, David. *Von Ryan's Express.* Garden City, N.Y.: Doubleday and Co., 1964.

Whitcomb, E. D. *Escape from Corregidor.* Chicago: Henry Regnery Co., 1958.

White, Theodore, *The Mountain Road.* New York: William Sloane Associates, 1958.

Williams, Wirt. *The Enemy.* Boston: Houghton Mifflin Co., 1951.

Wouk, Herman. *The Caine Mutiny.* Garden City, N. Y.: Doubleday and Co., 1951.

SECONDARY SOURCES

Books

Abrams, M. H. *The Mirror and the Lamp.* New York: W. W. Norton & Co., 1953.

Acheson, Dean. *Present at the Creation.* New York: W. W. Norton & Co., 1969.

Allen, Walter. *The Modern Novel.* New York: E. P. Dutton, 1964.

Aldridge, John W. *After the Lost Generation.* New York: McGraw-Hill, 1951.

————. *A Time to Murder and Create.* New York: David McKay Co., 1966.

Anderson, Quentin, and Joseph Mazzeo, eds. *The Proper Study.* New York: St. Martin's Press, 1962.

Anderson, Sherwood. *Winesburg, Ohio.* New York: Viking Press, 1966.

Ardrey, Robert. *African Genesis.* New York: Dell, 1969.

Baker, Carlos. *Ernest Hemingway: A Life Story.* New York: Charles Scribner's Sons, 1969.

————. *Hemingway: The Writer as Artist.* Princeton, N.J.: Princeton University Press, 1956.

Barrett, William. *A Time of Need.* New York: Harper & Row, 1972.

Bergonzi, Bernard. *Heroes' Twilight.* New York: Coward-McCann, 1966.

Bergson, Henri. *Time and Free Will.* Translated by F. L. Pogson. New York: Macmillan Co., 1959.

Bodkin, Maud. *Archetypal Patterns in Poetry.* London: Oxford University Press, 1965.

Breisach, Ernst. *Introduction to Modern Existentialism.* New York: Grove Press, 1962.

Bruce, Charles T. *Major Literary Concepts of the Soldier in Certain War Novels.* Lubbock, Texas: Texas Technological College, 1960.

Burgum, Edwin. *The Novel and the World's Dilemma.* New York: Russell and Russell, 1963.

Camus, Albert. *The Fall.* Translated by Justin O'Brien. New York: Vintage Books, 1956.

————. *Lyrical and Critical Essays.* Translated by Ellen C. Kennedy. New York: Alfred A. Knopf, 1968.

————. *The Myth of Sisyphus.* Translated by Justin O'Brien. New York: Hamilton, 1955.

————. *The Plague.* Translated by Stuart Gilbert. New York: Random House, 1948.

————. *The Stranger.* Translated by Stuart Gilbert. New York: Alfred A. Knopf, 1958.

Chase, Richard. *The American Novel and Its Traditions.* New York: Doubleday Anchor Books, 1957.

Cooper, James F. *The Leatherstocking Saga.* Edited by Allan Nevins. New York: Random House, 1966.

Cowley, Malcolm, ed. *After the Genteel Tradition.* Carbondale, Ill.: Southern Illinois University Press, 1964.

————. *The Literary Situation*. New York: Viking Press, 1954.

Daiches, David. *Critical Approaches to Literature*. New York: W. W. Norton & Co., 1956.

Eberhart, Richard, and Selden Rodman, eds. *War and the Poet*. New York: Deven-Adair Co., 1945.

Eisinger, Chester E. *Fiction of the Forties*. Chicago: University of Chicago Press, 1963.

Eliade, Mircea. *Myth and Reality*. Translated by Willard R. Trask. New York: Harper Torch Books, 1963.

Eliot, T. S. *The Complete Poems and Plays*. New York: Harcourt, Brace & World, 1962.

Ellman, Richard, and Charles Feidelson, eds. *The Modern Tradition*. New York: Oxford University Press, 1965.

Ellison, Ralph. *The Invisible Man*. New York: New American Library, 1952.

Eltinge, Leroy. *Psychology of War*. Fort Leavenworth, Kan.: Army Service Schools Press, 1917.

Emerson, Ralph W. *Selections from Ralph Waldo Emerson*. Edited by Stephen Whicher. Boston: Houghton Mifflin Co., 1960.

Esposito, V. J., and T. D. Stamps, eds. *A Military History of World War I*, with atlas. West Point, New York: United States Military Academy Adjutant General Printing Office, 1950.

————. *A Military History of World War II*, with atlas. West Point, New York: United States Military Academy Adjutant General Printing Office, 1953.

Esslin, Martin. *Theatre of the Absurd*. New York: Doubleday Anchor Books, 1961.

Euripides. *Ten Plays*. Translated by Moses Hades and John McLean. New York: Bantam Books, 1960.

Fehrenback, T. R. *This Kind of War*. New York: Macmillan Co., 1963.

Fiedler, Leslie. *Love and Death in the American Novel*. New York: Stein and Day, 1967.

Finkelstein, S. *Existentialism and Alienation in American Literature*. New York: International Publishers, n.d.

Forster, E. M. *Aspects of the Novel*. New York: Harcourt, Brace and World, 1954.

Frazer, Sir Gordon James. *The New Golden Bough*. Edited by

T. H. Gaster. Garden City, N. Y.: Doubleday Anchor Books, 1961.

Freud, Sigmund. *Beyond the Pleasure Principle*. Translated by James Strachey, with an introduction by Gregory Zilboorg. New York: Bantam Books, 1967.

―――. *Civilization and Its Discontents*. Translated and edited by James Strachey. New York: W. W. Norton & Co., 1962.

―――. *The Ego and the Id*. Translated and edited by James Strachey. New York: W. W. Norton & Co., 1961.

―――. *Reflections on War and Death*. Translated and edited by A. A. Brill and A. B. Kuttner. New York: Moffatt, Yard and Co., 1918.

―――. *Totem and Taboo*. Translated by James Strachey. New York: W. W. Norton & Co., 1950.

Frohock, W. M. *The Novel of Violence in America*. Boston: Beacon Press, 1957.

Fromm, Erich. *The Anatomy of Human Destructiveness*. New York: Holt, Rinehart and Winston, 1973.

Frye, Northrup. *Anatomy of Criticism*. New York: Atheneum, 1969.

Fuller, Edmund M. *Man in Modern Fiction*. New York: Random House, 1958.

Geismar, Maxwell. *American Moderns*. New York: Hill & Wang, 1958.

Gide, André. *Corydon*. New York: Noonday Press, 1967.

Goethe, Johann Wolfgang von. *Faust*. Translated by Charles E. Passage. New York: Bobbs-Merrill, 1965.

Goerlitz, Walter. *History of the German General Staff*. Translated by Brian Battershaw. New York: Frederick A. Praeger, 1957.

Gossett, Louis Y. *Violence in Recent Southern Fiction*. Durham, N.C.: Duke University Press, 1966.

Griffin, Gwyn. *An Operational Necessity*. New York: New American Library, 1967.

Hamilton, Edith. *The Greek Way*. New York: W. W. Norton & Co., 1964.

Hassan, Ihab. *Radical Innocence*. New York: Harper Colophon Books, 1966.

Harper, Howard M. *Desperate Faith*. Chapel Hill: University of North Carolina Press, 1967.

Hatcher, Harlan. *Creating the Modern American Novel*. New York: Russell and Russell, 1965.

Heinemann, F. H., ed. *Existentialism and the Modern Predicament*. New York: Harper Torch Books, 1958.

Hesse, Hermann. *Magister Ludi*. Translated by Richard and Clara Winston. New York: Bantam Books, 1972.

Hicken, Victor. *The American Fighting Men*. New York: Macmillan Co., 1969.

Hoffman, Frederick J., and Olga W. Vickery. *William Faulkner: Three Decades of Criticism*. New York: Harcourt, Brace & World, 1960.

Homer. *The Iliad*. Translated by Richmond Lattimore. Chicago: University of Chicago Press, 1962.

Huntington, Samuel P. *The Soldier and the State*. New York: Vintage Books, 1967.

Irmscher, William F. *Man and Warfare*. Boston: Little, Brown and Co., 1964.

Jung, C. G. *Psychological Reflections*. Selected and edited by Jolande Jacobi. New York: Harper & Row, 1961.

Kahler, Erich. *Man the Measure*. New York: World, 1967.

———. *The Tower and the Abyss*. New York: Viking Press, 1967.

Kant, Immanuel. *The Philosophy of Kant*. Translated and edited by Carl J. Friedrich. New York: Random House, 1949.

Kazin, Alfred. *On Native Grounds*. New York: Anchor Books, 1956.

Kerouac, Jack. *On the Road*. New York: Viking Press, 1958.

Kesey, Ken. *One Flew Over the Cuckoo's Nest*. New York: Signet Books, 1962.

Klein, Marcus, ed. *The American Novel Since World War II*. New York: Fawcett, 1969.

Koestler, Authur. *Darkness at Noon*. Translated by Daphne Hardy. New York: New American Library, 1961.

Krutch, Joseph Wood. *The Modern Temper*. New York: Harcourt, Brace & World, 1956.

Lawrence, D. H. *Studies in Classic American Literature*. New York: Viking Press, 1966.

Litz, Walton A. *Modern American Fiction*. New York: Oxford University Press, 1963.

Mailer, Norman. *Advertisements for Myself*. New York: G. P. Putnam's Sons, 1959.

————. *An American Dream.* New York: Dial Press, 1965.

————. *Armies of the Night.* New York: New American Library, 1968.

————. *Cannibals and Christians.* New York: Dial Press, 1966.

————. *The Presidential Papers.* New York: G. P. Putnam's Sons, 1963.

Mann, Thomas. *The Magic Mountain.* Translated by H. T. Lowe-Porter. New York: Alfred A. Knopf, 1964.

Marshall, S. L. A. *Battle at Best.* New York: William Morrow & Co., 1963.

————. *Men Against Fire.* Washington, D.C.: Infantry Journal, 1947.

————. *Pork Chop Hill.* New York: William Morrow & Co., 1953.

Marx, Leo. *The Machine in the Garden.* New York: Oxford University Press, 1968.

Mazzeo, Joseph A. *Renaissance and Revolution.* New York: Pantheon Books, 1965.

Melville, Herman. *Moby Dick.* New York: Random House, 1950.

————. *White Jacket.* New York: Grove Press, 1956.

Mizener, Arthur. *The Sense of Life in the Modern Novel.* Boston: Houghton Mifflin Co., 1964.

Moore, Harry T. *Contemporary American Novelists.* Carbondale, Ill.: Southern Illinois University Press, 1966.

Morrison, Samuel Eliot. *The Oxford History of the American People.* New York: Oxford University Press, 1965.

Mumford, Lewis. *The Pentagon of Power.* New York: Harcourt Brace Jovanovich, 1970.

Peden, William. *The American Short Story.* Boston: Houghton Mifflin Co., 1964.

Plato. *Five Great Dialogues.* Translated by Benjamin Jowett. Edited with an introduction by Louise Ropes Loomis. New York: Walter J. Black, 1942.

Salinger, J. D. *The Catcher in the Rye.* New York: Bantam Books, 1969.

Sanders, David. *John Hersey.* New York: Twayne, 1967.

Sartre, Jean-Paul. *Existentialism and Human Emotions.* Translated by Bernard Frechtman. New York: Wisdom Library, 1957.

————. *Literature and Existentialism.* Translated by Bernard Frechtman. New York: Citadel Press, 1962.

————. *What Is Literature?* Translated by Bernard Frechtman. New York: Harper Colophon Books, 1965

Scholes, Robert. *The Fabulators.* New York: Oxford University Press, 1967.

Sophocles. *The Theban Plays.* Translated by E. F. Watling. Baltimore: Penguin Books, 1964.

Spinoza, Baruch de. *The Philosophy of Spinoza.* Translated and edited by Joseph Ratner. New York: Random House, 1954.

Steele, Matthew Forney. *American Campaigns,* with atlas. Washington, D. C.: Combat Forces Press, 1951.

Swift, Jonathan. *Gulliver's Travels and Other Writings.* Edited by Ricardo Quintana. New York: Random House, 1958.

Trilling, Lionel. "Art and Neurosis," in *The Liberal Imagination,* New York: Viking Press, 1950, pp. 160–80.

————. "Freud and Literature," in *The Liberal Imagination,* New York: Viking Press, 1950, pp. 3–30.

————. "Freud: Within and Beyond Culture," in *Beyond Culture,* New York: Viking Press, 1965, pp. 89–118.

————. "On the Teaching of Modern Literature," in *Beyond Culture,* New York: Viking Press, 1965, pp. 3–30.

United States Military Academy, Department of Military Art and Engineering. *Summaries of Selected Military Campaigns.* West Point, N. Y.: United States Military Academy, 1953.

Volpe, Edmund L. *A Reader's Guide to William Faulkner.* New York: Noonday Press, 1964.

Von Kraft-Ebing, Richard. *Psychopathia Sexualis.* Translated and introduced by F. S. Klaf. New York: Stein and Day, 1968.

Wagenknecht, Edward C. *The Cavalcade of the American Novel.* New York: Holt, Rinehart and Winston, 1952.

Waldmeier, Joseph J. *Recent American Fiction.* Boston: Houghton Mifflin Co., 1963.

Weber, Max. *The Protestant Ethic and the Spirit of Capitalism.* New York: Charles Scribner's Sons, 1958.

West, Nathanael. *The Complete Works of Nathanael West.* New York: Farrar, Straus & Giroux, 1966.

Weston, Jessie L. *From Ritual to Romance*. Garden City, N.Y.: Doubleday & Co., 1957.

———. *The Quest of the Holy Grail*. New York: Haskell House, 1965.

Whitman, Walt. *Complete Poetry and Selected Prose*. Edited by James E. Miller, Jr. Boston: Houghton Mifflin Co., 1959.

Williams, William Carlos. *In the American Grain*. New York: New Directions, 1925.

Wilson, Edmund. *Patriotic Gore*. New York: Oxford University Press, 1962.

———, ed. *The Shock of Recognition*. New York: Random House, 1955.

———. *The Wound and the Bow*. New York: Oxford University Press, 1965.

Witham, Tasker. *The Adolescent in the American Novel*. New York: Frederick Unger, 1964.

Wrenn, John W. *John Dos Passos*. New York: Twayne, 1961.

Wright, Nathalia, *American Novelists in Italy*. Philadelphia: University of Pennsylvania Press, 1965.

———. *Ernest Hemingway: A Reconsideration*. University Park: Pennsylvania State University Press, 1966.

PERIODICALS

Baldwin, James. "The Black Boy Looks at the White Boy: Norman Mailer." *Esquire* 55, no. 5: 102–6.

Bersoni, Leo. "The Interpretation of Dreams." *Partisan Review* 32 (1965): 603–8.

Blotner, Joseph. "Faulkner's 'A Fable.'" *New York Times Book Review*, May 25, 1969, p. 2.

Brady, Susan. "Laughing All the Way to the Truth." *New York Times Magazine*, October 14, 1968, p. 42.

Brewer, Joseph E. "The Anti-Hero in Contemporary Literature." *Iowa English Bulletin: Yearbook* 12:55–60.

Buckeye, Robert. "The Anatomy of the Psychic Novel." *Critique: Studies in Modern Fiction* 9, no. 2:33–45.

Cook, Bruce A. "Norman Mailer: The Temptation to Power." *Renascence* 14:206.

DeMott, Benjamin. "An Unprofessional Eye: Docket No. 15883." *American Scholar* 30 (Spring 1961): 232–37.

Dennison, Constance. "The American Romance-Parody: A Study of Purdy's *Malcolm* and Heller's *Catch-22*." *Emporia State Research Studies* 14, no. 2(1965): 42.

Diesntfrey, Harris. "The Fiction of Norman Mailer." *On Contemporary Literature* 14: 422–36.

———. "The Novels of Vance Bourjaily." *Commentary* 31 (April 1961): 360–63.

Doskow, Minna. "The Night Journey in *Catch-22*." *Twentieth-Century Literature* 12: 186–93.

Eisinger, Chester E. "The American War Novel: An Affirmative Flame." *Pacific Spectator* 9 (Summer 1955): 272–87.

Frederick, John T. "Fiction of the Second World War." *College English* 17 (January 1956):197–204.

Glicksberg, Charles I. "Norman Mailer: The Angry Young Novelist in America." *Wisconsin Studies in Contemporary Literature* 1 (Winter 1960): 25–34.

———. "Sex in Contemporary Literature." *Colorado Quarterly* 9 (Winter 1961): 277–87.

Goldstone, Herbert. "The Novels of Norman Mailer." *English Journal* 45 (March 1956): 113–21.

Gordon, Caroline, and Jeanne Richardson. "Flies in Their Eyes? A Note on Joseph Heller's *Catch-22*." *Southern Review* 3: 96–105.

Greenfield, Josh. "22 Was Funnier than 14." *New York Times Book Review*, March 13, 1968, p. 1.

Hassan, Ihab. "The Novel of Outrage: Post-War American Fiction." *American Scholar* 34: 239–53.

Hoffman, Frederick. "Norman Mailer and the Revolt of the Ego: Some Observations on Recent American Literature." *Wisconsin Studies in Contemporary American Literature* 1 (Fall 1960): 5–12.

Hovey, Richard B. "A Farewell to Arms: Hemingway's Liebestod II." *University Review* 33: 163–68.

Hux, Samuel Holland. "American Myth and Existential Vision: The Indigenous Existentialism of Mailer, et al." *Dissertation Abstracts* 26: 5437.

Kazin, Alfred. "The Trouble He's Seen." *The New York Times Book Review* (*Armies of the Night*), May 5, 1968, p. 1.

Krim, Seymour. "A Hungry Mental Lion." *Evergreen Review* 55 (January-February 1960): 178–85.

Lehan, Richard, and Jerry Patch. "*Catch-22*: The Making of a Novel." *Minnesota Review* 7: 238–44.

Linick, Anthony. "A History of the American Literature Avant Garde Since World War II," *Dissertation Abstracts* 25: 7226.

Mailer, Norman. "Miami Beach and Chicago." *Harper's Magazine*, November 1968, pp. 41–130.

———. "Modes and Mutations: Quick Comments on the Modern American Novel." *Commentary* 41, no. 3: 37–40.

———. "On the Steps of the Pentagon." *Harper's Magazine*, March 1968, pp. 47–142.

Maloff, Saul. "*Armies of the Night.*" *Newsweek*, May 6, 1968, pp. 107–8.

Newman, Paul B. "Mailer: The Jew as Existentialist." *North American Review* 2, no. 3 (1965): 48–55.

Pritchard, William H. "Norman Mailer's Extravagences." *Minnesota Review* 8: 562.

Ritter, Jesse P. "Fearful Comedy: The Fiction of Joseph Heller, Günter Grass, and the Social Surrealist Genre." *Dissertation Abstracts* 28: 1447A.

Rexroth, Kenneth. "*Parade's End:* F. M. Ford's Anti-War Novel." *Saturday Review* 51 (March 16, 1968): 44.

Rosenthal, M. L. "Alienation of Sensibility and Modernity." *Arts and Sciences*, Spring 1964, pp. 19–25.

Schrader, George A. "Norman Mailer and the Despair of Defiance." *Yale Review* 51 (Winter 1962): 267–80.

Schlesinger, Arthur. "USA/USSR: The End of the Age of Super-powers." *Harper's Magazine*, March 1969, pp. 41–49.

Sheed, Wilfrid. "Miami and the Siege of Chicago." *New York Times Book Review*, December 8, 1968, p. 3.

Shenker, Israel. "Did Heller Bomb on Broadway?" *New York Times*, December 29, 1968, p. D1.

Sokolov, Raymond A. "Flying High with Mailer." *Newsweek*, December 9, 1968, pp. 84–88.

Solomon, Jan. "The Structure of Joseph Heller's *Catch-22.*" *Critique: Studies in Modern Fiction* 9, no. 2: 46–57.

Solotaroff, Robert. "Down Mailer's Way." *Chicago Review* 19, no. 3: 11–25.

Sheehan, Neil. "The 99 Days of Captain Arnheiter." *New York Times Magazine*, August 11, 1968, p. 7.

Steiner, George. "Naked But Not Dead." *Encounter* 17 (December 1961):67–70.

Toback, James. "Norman Mailer Today." *Commentary* 64, no. 4: 68–76.

Trilling, Diana. "Norman Mailer." *Encounter* 19 (November 1962): 45–56.

Wood, Margery. "Norman Mailer and N. Sarraute: A Comparison of Existential Novels." *Minnesota Review* 6: 67–72.

INDEX

chines, 95, 105–6; symbolic use in war novel, 5–6

Machine in the Garden, The, 15, 53, 60–61, 145, 148, 158, 229

Mailer, Norman, 6, 43, 44, 96, 122, 161; *An American Dream*, 154; antecedents of, 53–54; *Cannibals and Christians*, 44–45, 171–72; father-son relationships, 57, 62, 63, 64, 95, 115, 144, 152–56, 160, 161, 225, 226, 234; initiation, 56, 57–59; *The Naked and the Dead*, 6, 12, 26, 43, 68, 69, 72, 79, 87–96, 109, 110, 144, 157, 172, 182, 183, 228, 231, 233; role of guns, 55–56; *Why Are We in Vietnam?*, 7, 9, 14, 19, 110, 144, 157, 172, 182, 183, 228, 231, 233

Manhattan Transfer, 89

Mann, Thomas, 10, 20, 21, 45, 61, 65; *The Magic Mountain*, 10, 12, 20, 22, 45, 61

Marshall, Brig. Gen. S.L.A., 230–31

Mason, F. van Wyck, 1

Melville, Herman, 15, 128; *Moby Dick*, 128, 129, 179; *White Jacket*, 128

Melville Goodwin, USA, 68, 71, 84, 85, 86, 110

Miller, Henry, 53, 57

Milton, John, 82, 222

Mumford, Lewis, 214

Myrer, Anton, 3, 6, 7; *The Big War*, 6, 7, 19, 20, 21, 23, 27–31, 44, 62, 63, 64, 167, 226; Kant, 104, 109, 115, 139, 156–57, 199–200, 228, 233; *Once an Eagle*, 13, 14, 69, 71, 72, 99–105; structure, 101–4; types of commander, 100

N

Nemerov, Howard, 20

Never So Few, 3, 15, 164, 178–82, 231

Nietzsche, Friedrich, 15, 91

O

Oedipus, 34

One Flew Over the Cuckoo's Nest, 65, 138

One Very Hot Day, 15, 164, 190–94, 197, 230, 231

Oppenheimer, Dr. Robert, 214–15

P

Paths of Glory, 9, 10–11, 67

Patton, General George S., 71, 72

Plato, 15, 212, 220

Predestination, 35, 41

Price of Courage, The, 184

Progress, 53, 161

Protestant Ethic and the Spirit of Capitalism, The, 145

Psyche: 6, 115, 136–37, 228

R

Red Badge of Courage, The, 5, 9, 10, 12, 19, 22, 23, 144, 166

Rousseau, J. J., 198–99

S

Santayana, George, 48

Sartre, Jean-Paul, 16, 31, 32, 177, 185, 200

Schlesinger, Arthur, 72–73

Sergeant, The, 114, 120, 123–28, 161

Seven Days in May, 99

Seven Pillars of Wisdom, The, 116–17

Sexuality: and aggression (Freud), 155–56; distorted response, 113–57, passim, 228–29; and violence in the war novel, 13–14, 115–16

Show Me A Hero, 68, 69, 72, 84, 85, 86, 109, 185, 228

Soldier and the State, The, 178, 231

Spengler, Oswald, 219

Spinoza, Baruch de, 15, 36, 39–40

Steel Cocoon, The, 114, 120, 128–32, 161

Swift, Jonathan, 46, 48, 222

T

Technology: in combat, 165; as element of the absurd, 195, 199, 203–22 passim, 229, 232–33; in first modern war novel, 5; im-

Library of Congress Cataloging in Publication Data

Jones, Peter G   1929–
    War and the novelist.

    Bibliography: p.
    Includes index.
    1. American fiction—20th century—History and
criticism. 2. War in literature. I. Title.
PS379.J6   813'.5'409   76–23268
ISBN 0–8262–0211–X

Illustrations on pp. i, and xi–xiv from Kenneth Macksey and John
H. Batchelor, *Tank: A History of the Armoured Fighting Vehicle*, ©
1971, reproduced by permission of Ballantine Books, Inc.

Illustrations on pp. ii, 17, and 18 from Carl D. Corse, Jr., *Introduction to Shipboard Weapons*, © 1975, reproduced by permission of
Naval Institute Press.

Illustrations on pp. iv, v, 201, and 202 from *Jane's All the World's
Aircraft*, ed. W. R. Taylor, © 1963, reproduced by permission of B. P. C.
Publishing Limited, London.

Illustrations on p. vi from "Mask Protective Field M17," Department of the Army *Technical Manual* TM 3–4240–202–15 (1966), cour-
tesy of the U. S. Army.

Illustration on p. 66 from *Jane's Fighting Ships*, ed. Raymond V. B.
Blackman, © 1960, reproduced by permission of the B. P. C. Publishing
Limited, London.

Illustrations on pp. 111 and 112 from W. H. B. Smith and Joseph
E. Smith, *Small Arms of the World: A Basic Manual of Military Small
Arms*, © 1962, reproduced by permission of The Stackpole Company.

Illustration on p. 162 from John Batchelor and Ian Hogg, *Artillery*,
© 1972, reproduced by permission of Charles Scribner's Sons.

Illustrations on pp. 223 and 224 from *Guns: An Illustrated History
of Artillery*, ed. Joseph Jobe, © 1971, reproduced by permission of
Crescent Books.

Illustration on p. 237 from James E. Hicks, *U. S. Firearms 1776–
1956: Notes on U. S. Ordnance, Vol. I.* © 1957 reproduced by permission of James E. Hicks & Sons.